# Elizabeth

## Rainbow Dancer

Elizabeth Luft Desrochers

ISBN: 979-8-89406-372-0

# Contents

# Dedication

I dedicate this book to **my husband Al**; for his unconditional Love, guidance and support which allowed me to follow my guidance without limitations.

To all of my students, clients and teachers with deepest gratitude… The magnitude of my gratitude is beyond anything that could be expressed here in words.

You are all the wind beneath my wings.

# Acknowledgments

I would like to thank the following…

**My Husband Al** for his continuous Love and support throughout our lives.

**My son Marco** for his never-ending Love, support and amazing wisdom.

**My cousin Danny Angelone** for keeping me grounded on Earth with his wise words of wisdom.

**Judy Lavine** for her wisdom, teaching me to listen when God's talking.

**Mary Hardy** for her wisdom, friendship and Sisterhood of the Emerald Fire.

**Dr. Norma Milanovich** for her friendship, advice and wisdom to dream higher than the stars.

**Ilka Lomonaco** for her friendship and steadfast facts, keeping me on tract to always seek truth.

**Marie Rebello**, my soul sister always leaves me with belly aches from laughing too hard!

**Claudia Allore**, my soul Sister for our deep heart-to-heart conversations about topics, no one else would understand.

**Connie Jacavone** for her friendship, wisdom and keeping me healthy with her eggs & garden.

**All of my Brothers and Sisters in law**, I couldn't have asked for a better or more supportive and loving family, I am truly blessed to be in this amazing family of Desrochers', Thank you all!

**The American Society of Dowsers** ~ for opening my eyes to always verify truth.

**All of my adopted, biological and extended family** ~ God surely blessed me with all of your Love and support.

To all of my **Clients & Students**, (my Soul Group) I know we have been through many lifetimes together; you all inspire me daily and I am eternally grateful, you are truly the Wind beneath my wings.

**My New Sister Lucia** for her Love, Support & Wisdom from the Elders.

**My twin from another mother, Noreen Charpentier Dussault**, You truly amaze me; thank you for the fun!

# About the Author

Elizabeth grew up in a small town in Rhode Island, USA. By age six, with too many questions, she was always fighting for the underdog. She was ahead of her time, always interested in things outside the norm. Her soul was captivated by spirituality and never took "no" for an answer. As a natural healer, she knew she could always renegotiate with God.

Elizabeth became the first female Certified Welder, Welding Inspector and Senior Field Engineer for Narragansett Electric, hired in 1978. She loved the comradery and helping with her remedies. Following her deepest intuition, she became a Doctor of Divinity, Author, Spiritual Healer, Reiki Master Teacher, Certified in Clinical Hypnosis, NLP, and an expert in QHHT ~ Quantum Healing Hypnosis Therapy.

Elizabeth is also a specialist with Essential oils, a speaker and a lifetime member of the American Society of Dowsers. As a teacher of healers, she is a gifted visionary with a unique ability to activate wellness and joy with each client.

You can find Elizabeth at:

www.ancientwiz.com and www.QHHT-Elizabeth.com

**Elizabeth, in the words of her Husband:** My wife of 43 years continues to amaze me with her endless mission to help other people.

Elizabeth has over 26 years building her skills to broaden her experiences and education. Elizabeth has done it all, from working as a professional welder, field engineer and due to life changing experiences, her current position as a Spiritual Healer and author of three books.

Her work has earned praises from Dr. Norma Milanovich, Mary Hardy, Judy Lavine, Don Martin Pinedo Acuna and Dolores Cannon to name a few. Elizabeth's compassion has helped me experience the options we have to help change, improve and broaden our lives. After you read her books, you can learn from her commitment to serve others. She will help show you how to expand your horizons and experience opportunities to improve your life, and even better, someone else's.

Elizabeth, you have been a beacon of Love, a provider of compassion, a promoter of kindness. Thank you for enhancing my life and the countless people whose lives you touched. Love Al

# Author's Note

Now that I am over Fifty years old, I have so much to tell. Finding my place in this world was never an easy task. When I was a child, I was adopted. I wondered if I would ever fit in. The task of finding myself has been quite a journey. I have finally learned to follow my own intuition and walk to the beat of my own drum. As I grew up, I thought that intuition should be taught to us in elementary school so life wouldn't be so difficult. Then we could have more fun and avoid the pitfalls of life. Now, I realize that if it wasn't for stumbling around in 'Life's Lessons,' we'd never gain the wisdom needed for our Soul to grow to the next level.

These are my stories, with comments as life went on when my perspective changed as I realized I worked for God.

Although some of the names have been changed, the stories are all true. The journey took me from being adopted at four days old to the 'Material Girl' princess and from being the first Female Certified Welder at the Electric Powerplant to becoming a Shaman, a Spiritual Medicine Woman, traveling the world, teaching the Ancient ways of healing with Divine Guidance from God. It has been and continues to be an amazing journey.

When I first began studying with the Shamans, my very first teacher told me, "Your reality will change; you will soon find out that what you thought was real isn't, and what you thought wasn't real is." That was a statement I would soon find out to be true. My way of living life in the fast lane would not be tolerated in this Spiritual world. Yet, ultimately, I found myself living a life that is truly Heaven on Earth and better than I could have ever imagined.

Know that no matter where life takes you, it is all for your Soul's growth, for your Highest Good, and all part of the Divine plan. Know that you actually signed up for all of this before you were born. Yes, all of it

Thank you for reading, and I hope you enjoy it.

*Elizabeth*

*The italicized words in this book are the additions to my story as life went on. Originally, I began writing this book when I was Fifty years old. It couldn't be published because there were always more chapters to write. As life continued, I traveled, teaching and gaining more wisdom; each issue of my past came into focus with more clarity and why I had to experience things exactly as they happened. God carefully orchestrated the sequence of events to unfold exactly as they did to get me where I am today.*

*Some of the stories are raw and vulgar, as it was back in the day. I certainly would not consciously participate in that now, yet I can see that God certainly had a sense of humor as he raised my consciousness from birth in a 3D life to higher states.*

*The past sixteen years, life happened so quickly that I didn't have time to write. Now that I'm Sixty-six, it looks like this book may be volume one of two or three… so much to tell. I guess I've got to get on with it! Here goes & I hope you like it!*

*Grab an oil, open the bottle, give it a good sniff, and ahhhh, life is good. Of course, make sure it is a Young Living Essential Oil, 100% therapeutic grade, non-GMO, PURE! You will see that smelling a Young Living Essential oil will click the amygdala gland forward, and the neurons in your brain will fire in the proper sequence as God designed.*

*We fully support all of God's medicine because he designed it perfectly for us!*

# **Adopted**

February 26, 1957—They're giving away a baby; do you want one? Yes, it's true. Dr. Adenisio just delivered a baby girl, and the mother can't keep her; she told her family she had a tumor… and just gave birth to me. What? They don't want me? Oh My! How on Earth can this be? Just nine months ago, I was a Soul up in Heaven when God asked if I wanted to come back to Earth for another mission. A mission that, when accomplished, would make my Soul jump to the next level. Of course, I said, "YES!"

Now, here I am, and nobody wants me? I was supposed to come to Earth to be born into a loving family who would nurture me and help me grow. They would support me in my mission and let me learn all of life's lessons. Something MUST be wrong. Surely this can't be! There must be a way I can go back and talk to God. Something is definitely wrong.

I remember coming down the birth canal. I remember the journey from that 'perfect place' and the brightest White Light you could ever see… sliding into the darkest valley and out onto a metal table with doctors and nurses all ooh-ing and ahh-ing over me and my big brown eyes. They swept me away from my mother, Teresa, quickly. What? Wasn't I supposed to bond with my new mom? Where is she going? Where are they taking me? Why are we separated? I can hear Dr. Adenisio say, "I can't take her home; my wife will kill me; I already have five kids!"

*What on Earth is going on?* I thought.

Dr. Adenisio called Dora, Dolly's mother. Dolly called her friend Jennie, "Do you want a baby girl???" "Dolly, don't joke around. That's not funny," Jennie replied. When she realized Dolly was serious…

"Yes, Yes, YES!" Jennie yelled with delight. (Yes, things are starting to look better).

It will be easier now. Jennie and John are so happy to take me home. Look at all the cars. Oh my God, there are at least ten cars filled with people who have eagerly anticipated my arrival. Who knew there would be a parade of family & friends to celebrate my homecoming? I think I'll like it here.

I am only four days old, but I can see and hear many things. I have that complete knowledge of where I came from before birth. I know what my mission is here on Earth. It will be a long journey with many lessons. I will accomplish many feats. I am unique, yet one with God. I am to be a healer and a teacher to help many people. I am responsible for twelve thousand people to plant seeds in their hearts. I must get them to think beyond the box, their belief systems that limit their soul's growth. I'm ready. This will be a good life.

Yes, it is good. I am treated like a princess. Jennie & John's friends and family couldn't wait to meet me! I don't even have to cry for food; just a coo will do, and I'm fed the most delicious meal. Jennie tends to my every need. I'm not even wet for two minutes, and she changes me. Wow, this is really going to be nice. Life is good. I am only one week old.

The month after my birth, we had a big party. Mom and Dad took me to church for something called a Baptism. Uncle Sal and Dolly are my Godparents. That big church was the closest thing to where I came from. It is so beautiful. I recognized many of the families I had in Heaven, standing right here and even some made of stone. What is this stone likeness of Jesus? I understand they call it a statue. I don't really understand why. Can't these humans see what I see? Blessed Mother Mary was right there next to Uncle Dan at the Church. Why didn't he talk with her? Why *can't* he see her? People seem to pay more attention to the statues. I just don't understand all of it yet. I know, in time, it should make sense. My brothers and sisters up in Heaven told me it might be like this after I was born. They even told me I might forget Heaven. God, I can't *even* imagine that.

Three years before I was born, Jennie fell down the stairs. She was pregnant with a baby boy & he died. The injuries left her incapable of bearing any more children. Jennie was a very sick woman *(Aunty Irene & I once calculated twenty-three operations in a ten-year period).* At twenty-three years old, she was admitted to a hospital in upstate New York when a Catholic priest came to give her death rites. He introduced her to an Indian Saint, **Kateri Tekakwitha**; he said she would grant miracles. Jennie survived this sickness, and she continued to pray to this Saint every day. Doctors said she made medical history; in those days, people died from Trichinosis (pork poison), and she lived.

It was customary for people to send money for Novenas, special relics, or prayer cards of their favorite saint. Jennie told everyone about the miracle of Kateri. One morning, the mailman arrived and handed Mom a package with a prayer card and a little package of dirt from Kateri's grave. Jennie was so excited and said her prayers would forever be granted with this dirt. At this very same time that Kateri's dirt came in the mail was the very moment in time that she received a phone call to adopt me. Jennie is MOM now. Kateri and I were connected from day one.

Mom told everyone I was born in a mushroom basket and delivered to her by the Indians (Kateri). I know Kateri is my Guardian Angel. Kateri said she'd help me and I should pray to her when I need to. She is telling me now that things will be okay. She is a good friend. Thank God she is with me. I certainly wouldn't want to do this journey to Earth alone. She explains everything to me, telling me I've been adopted. This means that one woman gives birth to you, she is called your biological mother, and then another woman takes you home and raises you; she is now your mom. Okay. I can understand that now I have a biological mom, Teresa, and a MOM-mom, Jennie. That's clear, but where did Teresa go? Who is my bio-dad? Kateri tells me, "That is not important at this time. Focus on your new Mom and Dad, Jennie & John. They love you very much."

# Dad

John Hans Von Luft is now my dad. As the story goes, he was born in 1901 and came to the USA when he was ten years old, from Germany, with a dime in his pocket. When he arrived at Ellis Island, and they asked for his middle name, he said he didn't have one. They insisted so much he said "HANS"! Little did they know Hans in German means John.

He was five-foot-four inches tall, debonair, sophisticated and German. It has been said he was "a man of infinite class, who would fill a five-star restaurant or a stool in the local watering hole with the same dignified presence." Many said he was so good-hearted that he was always giving things away: money, cars, and just about anything he thought they could use. Through hard work and dedication, he made a good living as a toolmaker. He had a successful business, "Luft, Tool and Die Works", in Providence, Rhode Island, which made tools for the jewellery industry. He often brought bums (as my mom called them), as well as family and friends, home to eat. He was well-dressed, fun, loving and kind. They were always throwing parties in the 'rumpus room' for everyone. One time, as a joke, Uncle Sal and Aunty Elsie put signs outside on the road pointing to where the party was. Mom said the house was loaded with people she didn't know. They had lots of friends and tons of fun. Dad owned a sixty-foot Yacht and even employed a captain to drive it. It must have been a blast because the family continued to reminisce about these stories every time they got together.

During the 1938 Hurricane, Dad lost it all. (There are still markings on the sides of buildings in the city showing how high the floods came.) In those days, no one had insurance. This was when he began to drink heavily, and things started to go downhill. Mom would water down the alcohol. She was only trying to help. By 1959, Dad was still trying to rebuild the business but still drinking. He would often travel to Colorado and the southwest area on Business. Mom said it was good for his Asthma.

In April 1959, Dad died. I was two years old. The Police said he committed suicide. Mom refused to believe this. She insisted there was a bunch of bananas *(in those days, they used green tape to hold the bundle together)* on the counter; the green tape was broken, and one was missing. Dad did NOT like bananas. And there was the issue of the bullets. There was one in his head and one in the wall. He could not have fixed himself with his hands under the sheets that way; someone *had* to do it. And there were scribbles on the top of the dresser, as if someone wrote a note and pushed hard through the paper with the pen. It was illegible but definitely scribbled into the wood; the marks are still there to this day.

Dad was buried before Mom even thought to demand an autopsy to find out if he actually ate that banana. Everyone was shocked. Mom was given tranquillizers and could hardly function. She couldn't go back to that house. She was devastated. There was NO insurance money for Dad's death because it was ruled a suicide. Her life had changed instantly.

Mom had an eighth-grade education because her mother died when she was fifteen years old. Her father worked three jobs to support his seven children; the twins were only four years old. Mom and my Aunt Theresa quit school to raise the family.

With no income and no education, when Dad died, we moved to the second floor of Uncle Dan and Aunty Theresa's house. That is when Mom began to look for work. At least we had a home in the comfort and safety of Uncle Dan and Aunty Theresa. They had two children, Danny and Maria. Danny was only nine months younger than I was, and immediately we became best friends.

Maria was four years older than us. When Mom wasn't watching, she'd pinch me. Let me re-phrase that: Mom was always watching, and she would often catch Maria pinching me. I know Mom never took an eye off me. She would say to me, "You're all I got". Danny and I spent hours upon hours in the sandbox that Uncle Dan built for us. Danny had the best Tonka trucks that kept me amused all day.

I was raised with Mom's Italian brothers and sisters. All seven of them, their spouses and children, were our family. We were very close. My cousins were closer to me than other people's real brothers and sisters. We had lots of Italian ways, right down to the little slang words that are still with me today, like "hand me the *mopina*," referring to a dish towel, and pass the *skola macarone*—referring to the spaghetti strainer.

Uncle Dan had a way of making me feel special. He used to tell me, "You were chosen. We *had* to take Danny and Maria; we had no choice, but you, you were chosen, you were picked, we wanted you!" I knew I was special.

Mom sheltered me so much that I was 25 years old and married before I was told about Dad's suicide. Mom always tried to protect me. She painted life as a rose garden, and I truly believed it was so. I believed everyone and everything was good, and no one would ever hurt me. Maria, on the other hand, experienced life before me and told me the cold, hard facts about Dad's suicide. Needless to say, I was very upset. I always thought my dad died of a heart attack.

# Safe at Uncle Dan's

Mom began working for Uncle Dan. He had a car business. As a child, I can remember Uncle Dan selling one car at a time. He would buy it at the auction, clean it, fix it up, and sell it to make money. Mom did the bookkeeping for him. She became really good at it.

*Years later, when she was sick, he'd bring her the books in the hospital to work on, and I would get so angry, thinking he wanted her to work. I didn't realize how much they needed each other, and it was because she insisted she was such a big part of that business. She felt she owed him her life for helping us when we needed it.*

When mom was working, I'd spend most of the time with Grandpa. The rest of the time was spent at Aunty Theresa and Uncle Dan's beach house. The beach was my favorite. You could walk out their back door, down twelve stairs, and be right into Narragansett Bay, which was part of the Atlantic Ocean. Every summer I'd stay with Aunty Theresa, Maria and Danny at the beach.

Waking up at the beach had a certain feel to it. The windows were always open. Before you opened your eyes, you could smell the crisp, fresh, salty air. Then you'd hear the waves crashing on the wall at high tide and the cawing of the seagulls flying overhead. Breakfast was a bowl of cereal and toast. Sometimes, on special occasions, Aunty would make eggs, bacon, sausage, and home fries. Once in a while, we could feast on our favorite donuts! We always had to help clean up before we were allowed to go out to play. Play consisted of hanging around at the water's edge, talking, and sharing our innermost thoughts. Danny and I dreamed big; we talked about everything and never fought like some of our cousins.

We wore shorts, mostly "Jean" shorts cut from an old pair of dungarees and a tank top. Barefoot all the time, of course. *To this day, I prefer bare feet, even in winter!*

Cool mornings turning into the sun baking you from the outside first, then in. *Not like Arizona, where the sun seems to warm you from the inside first.* We never wore sunscreen. Aunty told us to go slow at the first sign of the sun. Now I understand what she meant. Don't run outside from winter white skin and bake in the sun for hours… you're surely to burn! At the beginning of the season, we had to go out in the sun for ten minutes at a time, then in… then out… gradually our skin tanned, and we only burned when we tried to rush the process! When we did it gradually, we had the most bronze skin tans that lasted all summer long and no freckles!

*Now I realize it's sunscreen that causes cancer, never God's sun! I'm so grateful we can bathe in the beauty of the Sun and know the truth!*

The beach neighborhood was actually a peninsula of land called Potowomet. It stretched out into Narragansett Bay (locals called this Greenwich Bay, which is a smaller part of Narragansett Bay) with one end we called "the Point." That was the part of land that literally stretched into a point of rocks going directly into the water.

The wind was always wild at the Point.

There was only one market near that strip of land. Maggie's. It was the smallest store I'd ever seen, but it did have all your essentials.

Danny and I were best friends. We rarely got into trouble, but one time, playing in the front yard, we threw sand at a passing car. Oh My! Never did we think the "man in the car" would chase us and ring the doorbell to complain about what we'd done. I was six years old. We were grounded and had to spend the rest of the day in the bunk bed room looking out the window at our friends Ryan and Ken, who were still out playing.

*Later on in life, I could see how that discipline worked to our benefit. To this day, I still hear gossip that Ryan is still in trouble. He grew up to be a real bad boy, known in town as a "shady character". Our parents used to say, "His parents let him get away with murder."*

*Many years later, I was out with friends who introduced me to another group of their friends. One thing led to another as a man stated, "Oh, do you know Ryan so and so?" As he proceeded to say how Ryan had screwed him out of a lot of money. It was a deal gone bad! This man wanted to kill him for it. I was totally embarrassed for even acknowledging that I knew him. All I could think was: 'Here I am at 27 years old, and he is still doing that?' His parents were so nice; how could this be?*

Aunty Theresa and Uncle Dan had their main house back in Johnston. That's where they lived most of the time. They called that the city house. One thing I remember was Aunty always fussing about that special dress she wanted to wear, and it was at the city house! She was mad because she'd have to drive all the way back there to get it.

Literally it was thirty-five minutes away!

One Saturday morning, back at his city house, Danny and I were watching 'Alice Through the Looking Glass' on TV while eating a bowl of Jell-O… Sitting on the new bar stools, Danny swung me around, pushing my feet, where I spun around so quickly, we couldn't stop giggling… Next thing I knew, we were taking turns flipping the Jell-O out of the bowl on a spoon, like a slingshot, while spinning around. We were nine years old. That was the biggest *baddest* thing we ever did as children. *I remember Aunty Theresa saying they still found Jell-O in the baseboard when they were cleaning to sell that house years later!*

Maria, being so much older, had her own friends and rarely hung out with Danny and me. One scene that plays over and over in my mind when I think of my childhood is a time when Maria was fifteen, and she dated a nineteen-year-old boy on the sneak. I can still see the scene as if it is playing on a movie screen. Danny and I were standing in the living room. I saw Uncle Dan WHACK Maria with a backhand... It seemed as though she flew three feet off the floor across the dining room, which was about ten feet long! I'll never forget it. I can still see her with her back up against the dining room wall, crying on the floor, in her school uniform. How on Earth did he know Ronny was picking her up at the bus stop? Uncle Dan's word was Gospel. You didn't question it. He demanded respect. She was too young to be dating. Maria challenged his every word, and her teenage years were miserable for it. Danny and I just watched from the sidelines and often did our best to stay out of the way. I knew I never, *ever* wanted to piss off Uncle Dan.

Uncle Dan always had a big boat and a skiff. He always said, "A boat is a hole in the water that you throw money into," and then he'd grunt. The skiff was a little boat with a tiny motor that was tied to something that looked like a clothesline. We'd reel it into shore when we needed it and reeled it back out in deeper water so the motor never touched bottom. The skiff was used to get us out to the big boat. The big boat was tied to a mooring out in front of the house in deeper water. Before Danny was old enough to drive it, we'd use the skiff, or in low tide, we'd swim out to the big boat and sit there for hours, pretending he was driving. Singing to the latest tunes on the radio, we thought we were so cool.

Aunty Theresa would put the floodlights on if we had to come back inshore. If we didn't see the lights, we could stay out there until sundown. (*There were no cell phones back then*). It was the life! We never spent time inside unless we were in trouble and grounded. Our fingers would get wrinkled, and our lips would turn blue before we were scolded to come out of the water!

Every year, there was an excess of something in the water. One year, it was jellyfish. We were so carefree. I can remember scooping them up with our hands and throwing them at each other. We never knew they could be poisonous. Another year, there would be an enormous amount of horseshoe crabs; one of the neighbor's teenage sons speared them with a pitchfork. That was the first I saw of their blue blood. I remember crying when I saw him killing the horseshoe crabs, and I was only nine years old. Another year, there would be countless amounts of sea shells. Life at the beach was always fascinating.

# Rules

Mom did the best she could do to raise me. She was very strict and demanded respect. I swear she had hands bigger than any man I know! She would think nothing of swinging a backhand across my face if I said the word "shit." *The last time that happened, I was thirty-five years old. My nine-year-old Son was shocked.* I swear my mother could hit me with a shoe from a hundred feet! And to think she never tried out for the Yankees! (That statement was our family joke for decades).

Everyone grew up with discipline/ a light spanking was all that was needed in those days. It kept you in line. You wouldn't even *think* of answering back! You usually got the *LOOK* to know you were doing something wrong. If it was really bad, you'd find her making a face as she bit her index finger with the rest of her fingers waving at you; it's an Italian thing. I wish I could put a video here so you could see it. Don't get me wrong. I deserved every spanking I got. After growing up, I could see how she was right. There is a fine line between physical abuse and spanking. Physical abuse is wrong! However, a spanking, that's different. Kids need to know who the boss is. There is a huge loss of respect from my generation to the kids of today. Young ones today have no respect. They answer back in ways that we'd get the crap beat out of us if we spoke like that to our parents. Most children were taught right from wrong back then. There were consequences when you did something wrong. It didn't take physical abuse to straighten you out; you learned after one whack. *What has happened to our society? Children don't know right from wrong, and there is a huge lack of respect for authority & elders.*

*When my son played soccer at five years old, my husband & I became coaches (actually, it was more like babysitting). The Athletic Department told us there were to be NO losers. Everyone was a winner. They stated that it was the politically correct way of doing things so each child would feel they were special. What on Earth are they doing? This has changed the way our children learn to thrive in society. Children no longer know how to prevail. Many kids today can't hold jobs because they think the boss owes it to be "nice" to them. They don't know how to 'strive for perfection'. I see this with some of the new kid's right out of college; they're filled with attitudes and barely get the job done. Instead of strengthening their core spirit, they are emotionally weak, expecting the world to tip-toe around their feelings.*

*This was the beginning of my wondering who makes these ridiculous rules…*

*Taking prayer out of schools?—There should be prayers OF ALL RELIGIONS in schools. Not just Catholic… but EVERY RELIGION.*

*No nativity scenes in public places?—EVERY RELIGION SHOULD BE EXPRESSED AND RESPECTED… EVERY ONE that has a benefit to Mother Earth and all her inhabitants.*

*What! No Christmas trees at the Doctor's office? …Because they didn't want to OFFEND anyone?—NO, NO, NO; they have it all wrong! This is America! The land where there is a blend of all languages, all races, and all religions—WE SHOULD ACKNOWLEDGE AND RESPECT ALL OF THEM—all of their flags, all religions, respect all customs and practices that benefit all of Earth and all of humanity!*

*What a beautiful place this would be!*

# Cumadda's, Cumbada's & Friends

Now that I look back on this stage of my life, I realize how much the support of my mom's family, extended family, and friends helped me through my whole life.

Aunty Anna and Uncle Joe, Aunty Marie, and Uncle Louie, and the entire Marchetti family were no blood relation. They were mom's best friends we called aunty and uncle out of 'respect.' After every dance recital, they would shower me with flowers and gifts. I felt like a real princess. Even Mom's first and second cousins we called Aunty and Uncle. "Thicker than blood," they were so close to me and Mom. It was as if they all cradled us in their love cocoon. Aunty Irene was Mom's sister; she never married and was always there for me. She would say to my mom, "Las'a'la'e," *slang* Italian "lasciala stare," meaning 'leave her be.' Mom was always yelling at me about something, especially when I was in my teens. She was trying to make me perfect so I would have a better life, but we clashed like oil and water.

In those days, the only TV programs for kids were the Saturday morning cartoons. Any other time, Mom would take me to visit her friends who had kids. It's what you did back then. You played with other kids your age. You played outside until dark, or it rained. One week, we'd visit my mom's friend Grace. She had five daughters. They taught me to eat peanut butter on toast. They always wanted me to teach them ballet. I'd dance and show them the steps I'd learned. I couldn't understand their desire for me to show them because, to me, I really didn't think I was good at all.

Boy, could they play the piano! I wished I could do that! They were all so beautiful. I wished I could be as pretty as they were.

One of the toddlers was so funny with her limited vocabulary; she'd scream "boogers"! That word would make me giggle uncontrollably. Still, to this day, I still think of that little child and giggle when I hear the word booger.

I remember her adorable little face, big green eyes, Platinum blonde hair with her finger up to her second knuckle in her nose, saying "boo-ger, BOOG-ER!" Isn't it funny when some things just stick in your head from the past? It can totally change your mood. It's like hearing a song on the radio that can bring you right back to a specific place or time in your life that will make you smile.

Another week, we'd visit my mom's cousin Frankie. He was married to Shirley, and they had six kids. They all had chores and couldn't watch TV or play outside until homework and chores were done. This was a real family, the way it was supposed to be, with real brothers and sisters who all got along. "Aunty Shirley" was really good to me. I could talk to her about anything. There were times I would walk there from school and confide in her about things mom did to upset me. Aunty Shirley had the biggest heart and was so calm and serene. She could comfort me in five minutes. Gary was one of her children. He also became a protector of mine in school. I think his assignment in life was to help me through elementary school. Gary and Danny were both my protectors. One time at recess, Gary beat up one of the big kids who used to steal my Fritos.

Did their mom love them more than mine loved me? I don't think so. At Christmas, I had a room full of presents. I got presents for every holiday: Valentine's Day, St. Patrick's Day, Easter, April Fool's Day, Memorial Day, and 4th of July. There was one day each month for celebration that my mom would wake me up in bed with presents. She was so good at it. It was always exactly what I wanted. I would think, "How did she know?" *Later on, I figured it out; whenever we were shopping, she would make a note if I said "I like" this or that. She'd buy it for me when I wasn't looking!*

I certainly got MORE presents than Danny or Gary or any of my cousins or friends. I really was SPECIAL. I began to think My Mom Loved me MORE *because* I WAS ADOPTED… YES, she did! She gave me more! This was the beginning of my 'MATERIAL GIRL' era. It was the way you showed Love. Wasn't it? I was a Princess (as long as I maintained good behavior). She would strip me of any presents as fast as I got them if I disobeyed. Although she was good to me, she demanded perfection. If I played with my dolls, I had to put them back in their place when I was done. Everything had a place, and everything must be in its place. Even my closet was immaculate, almost to the point where it was even color-coordinated. At least until some of my cousins came to visit, then surely something was broken.

# Ju-Ju

Once in a great while, Mom would drive over the bridge to East Providence to see Aunty Elsie and Uncle Mike. They had two kids, Michael and Michele. At five years old, Michael came home and said, "Mommy, can I have a monkey?" Aunty Elsie said, "Michael, no one is going to give you a monkey." Michael insisted, "But Mommy, the man said I can have the monkey." Aunty replied, "Michael, if the man is going to *GIVE* you a monkey, and you do *NOT* have to pay anything for it, yes, Michael, you can have a monkey." So, the next day, here comes Michael walking home with a paper bag with a monkey in it. His name was JuJu; he was a squirrel monkey. Aunty bought a cage for this little creature, and it lived in their kitchen.

One Sunday, Mom and I made the great adventure to drive 'all the way over the bridge to East Providence' to see Aunty Elsie. I say this because in Rhode Island, to drive anywhere more than ten minutes is like going across the country. You'd think it was the bridge to Portugal. We call this the "RI mentality".

I remember standing in Aunty Elsie's kitchen, meeting JuJu for the first time. Then I watched this little monkey grab his pee-pee and jerk it around really fast. I was only seven years old. Michael & Michele were giggling. I didn't know what he was doing. I'd *never* seen anything like that before. I was just about to ask when Mom grabbed my arm and scooted me out of that house so fast; I didn't know what happened. "Get in the Car!" She commanded. I was looking for an explanation, and Mom would only say over and over again, "he's *filthy* dirty, stay away from him"!

Obviously, JuJu had a really bad habit of pleasuring himself. ... *CONTINUOUSLY.* Well, I don't know what ever happened to JuJu, but it was a real long time before we ever visited Aunty Elsie again.

# Angelina

Angelina was a few years older than me and lived next door. She began to teach me how to pray to get answers. She spoke of "Listening to God" on a daily basis, meditating, and how to "get what you want." She talked of Angels and how to talk with them, "just like us"; she'd explain. They weren't far away; they were close and our friends. She showed me how to talk with God and call upon him when I needed. She said I could even make my future the way I wanted. She had me sit with her every sunrise & have the sun's rays pour into my forehead. She called this area of my forehead my third eye. She said I should feed it like this while praying every morning. As the first rays of the sun came over the horizon, the very first seven minutes of the rising sun, staring right at it (squint if you must, but later on, you will be able to watch it directly in the center). That is where the knowledge of all that is lies. When we pour it into our third eye, it will open the door and allow us to follow the path of enlightenment. At home, I continued this ritual and saw how it worked. Then, it scared me because I saw how a situation can turn badly. I was nine years old.

One afternoon in elementary school, I got very angry at a classmate who was making fun of my frizzy hair. Just as my anger went *poof* like a cloud up in the air, the girl doubled over in pain. Oh my God, did I do that? I thought it was my fault and it scared me so much! I stopped meditating. Back to the old-fashioned prayer I went, the way Mom, the priest, and the nuns at catechism taught me, praying for forgiveness over and over again. "*God, please forgive me,*" I prayed.

# It Was Wrong!

Being raised Italian, we always kissed on the cheek when we greeted or said goodbye to family and friends. I called everyone aunty and uncle even though most of these people were my mother's cousins. Some were godmothers or godfathers, called in slang Italian 'cumadda' or 'cum-bada. Others were just her friends. Mom insisted on this type of 'greeting' because she said: "it was respect."

I was 11 years old when my mother's cousin, Greg, was babysitting me. My mom and Greg's wife went to the hospital to see a friend's new baby. Greg really liked this greeting stuff, and after we were alone, he decided to chase me around the house to get more. He was so scary! He molested me. I didn't know what to do, but I was smart enough to know this was wrong! I was in such a panic and in such shock that my spirit flew out of my body. I could see myself as if I was on the ceiling looking down at my own body. I let him think I had to go to the bathroom, and I ran to the upstairs phone to call my mother.

*To this day, I look back on that incident and still can't remember where the intelligence came from for me to even find the hospital phone number to call Mom because I was so young. This was obviously my first out-of-body experience. God was surely with me.*

Mom did rush to pick me up. When we got home that night, I told her everything. She quickly hushed me and told me *not* to say a word to anyone. As time went on, I later realized what happened and how WRONG it was. I hated my mother for **not** *doing* something about it. This is when our relationship changed. I knew my mother was wrong. I used to dream of fighting him. I could even see myself grabbing him by the hair and swinging him up and down, smashing him on the ground like a rag-doll over and over in my dreams. I saw this in cartoons one morning; Popeye had that strength! I then would pray to my Indian Saint Kateri, and she would comfort me as I cried myself to sleep.

By the time I was fifteen years old, I had my own personality and rules. No one could lie to me again; I had a strong will and would not be duped again. One summer day, the whole family was at Aunty Theresa's beach house for a cookout. We all had a habit of rinsing off in our bathing suits on the side of the house after we came in from swimming. This was to get the salt off from swimming in the ocean. *(I now realize it was probably because the Providence River ran into the bay, and the water treatment plant used to overflow every time it rained).* Greg snuck over to me and made a comment to give him a kiss. I kicked him so hard in the balls he went down on his knees. I didn't care who saw this; I really flipped out! I was extremely upset and ran inside to tell Uncle Dan. I told him everything. I held nothing back! His head got so red, and his eyes got extremely big! I don't even want to think of what Uncle Dan did about it. I can't imagine how, but I trusted he took care of it! Uncle Dan would never let anyone hurt me. He was my tower of strength.

I stumbled through my teenage years clumsily, even though my mom took me to all kinds of dance classes. I was just too top-heavy to stand up straight. Ballet, Tap, Jazz; Mom always helped out at the recitals. I hated them. She would dress me up and convince me to do a good job before I was sent out to perform in front of an auditorium full of people. I tried very hard to dance, but I wasn't very good at it. I would try *so* hard. In class, we had to practice in front of a mirror. I would watch all the other girls and think, 'They are so pretty.' They danced so gracefully and were so good at it. I'd pray that I could do that. Then I'd watch myself and became more self-conscious. My head just could not get my body to do those graceful moves no matter what I did. My feet were already a size seven by the time I was ten years old. The rest of me just hadn't grown into them yet. Ugh, the awkward years of puberty!

I grew very tall very quickly; in 5th grade, I was already 5'3" tall. I was awfully skinny with big feet, and they called me a hockey stick with hair. I was called "Frizzy Lizzy" until I found a cream rinse. By 8th grade, I was still *very* naïve, sheltered & still playing with Barbie dolls.

# Grandpa

I was Grandpa's favorite. I'm sure it was because he was also adopted. He was literally left on a doorstep in Italy. A child in a basket with his family name tag on his ankle he was found and raised by the Carnevale family. Apparently, back in Italy, his mother got pregnant with a man from a Royal family. Uncle Sal investigated this family in the early '70s, and they wanted NOTHING to do with us. They thought we'd want some of the *Royal* money. Uncle Sal thought, like the rest of us, we don't need your "Stinkin' money"! Or as Aunty Irene said, "Sis, on you pister, you're not so muckin futch." Aunty Irene never swore, making this phrase funnier every time she said it.

When Mom had to work, I would stay at Grandpa's house. My best friend was Maria. She lived right at the back of Grandpa. Only the hedges separated the two houses. We'd play for hours pretending with little kittles and horses; we had a very good life. We'd rock in the hammock, read the Readers' Digest to each other, and talk for hours on end. It was nice. It was comfortable. It was a more extended family. I remember playing in the yard with Maria and her older Sister Paula. Paula was the funny one. We were always playing, laughing, and having fun. One time, I remember playing a game where you'd get dragged by your feet. Sure enough, I ended up getting dragged right through dog poop. I was covered in it from head to toe. I had to wear an outfit of Aunty Irene's tied with a string to hold it up for the rest of the day.

Maria's grandmother was Nonni; she and grandpa spent hours sitting on the big swing in the yard talking Italian. Maria's aunt was also my Aunty Ida. She and Aunty Irene were best friends, so in reality, this was another family that was MY family also. I considered

Maria's sisters, Pamela, Patricia, and Paula, my sisters, and when I was eleven years old, their brother Michael was born. This little baby was my brother too! I was so lucky to have so much love and so many people around me who were MY true family.

This was truly the meaning of the phrase *"it takes a village"* to raise a child.

Maria and I did everything together. Every day, at 11:00 am, we were sent to Frankie's store to buy a loaf of bread. For sure, Grandpa knew what time Crugnale's Bakery would deliver it because it was still warm. Walking back up the hill to Grandpa's, I couldn't resist. I'd break the end of the bread and start eating it! Some of the time, there would only be half of a loaf left by the time we got back to the house. Grandpa would just laugh and, in his Italian accent, scold me with a smile, saying, "Now whadda we gonna do for suppa?" "What's Yidd-aine gonna eat-a??"

He always called Aunty Irene "Yidd-aine." Surly that was more Italian slang.

I was everything to Grandpa. Mom would yell at me, and Grandpa would go to bat for me every time. He was a strong man, and his word meant everything. He had the respect of the entire community. At 84 years old, he still walked five miles a day, visiting friends along the way. After I started driving, Mom would send me looking for him, and I'd find him walking way up Cherry Hill Road near Atwood Ave! People came from all over to see him and grab a taste of his tomatoes, cherries, pears, or grapes right off the vine. His grapevine extended the entire length of the driveway, and Aunty Irene used to park her car under it. His garden was the entire length of the house.

When I was a teen, Grandpa was not feeling well. I volunteered to help him with the garden. He had a fifty-five-gallon drum of a mixture he called in his accent, "Ah suppatha." This mixture was just the perfect mixture of part horse manure, part cow manure, and a little chicken manure, and then filled to the top with water. This was the a-soup-pa-tha (soup/manure) for the vegetables. You had to dip the ladle into the mixture, stir it up, and ever so gently pour a little bit around the tomato plants, making sure not to touch the stalk, or it would burn the plant. Of course, I was still clumsy. I dipped the ladle into the mixture, and it splashed on my face. I thought Grandpa was going to split a gut laughing. He was holding his side and laughed right out loud. Oh my, what a site I was. Aunty Irene wouldn't let me in the house. She handed me a robe and said, hose off before you come in!

As I got older, I became more "brazen". When I was fifteen, my mom was in the hospital, and I was staying at Grandpa's. I went next door to Gail's house. She was two years older than me. One day, boys drove up in a car and parked in front of her house. I was leaning into the car talking with them, and Grandpa came over, grabbed my ponytail, and dragged me all the way back to the house. I was so embarrassed! To him, that was unacceptable. You were a "pu'tana" or "slut" if you did things like that. Boys were supposed to come into the house, meet the parents, and sit in the parlor to talk with the family. That was courting!

# K. Drive

Uncle Dan decided that it was time for his family to move. He sold the two-family house that we were living in to Ed and Roberta. They were nice to Mom and me. They had two little babies and when I got older, they let me baby sit. We got very close, and even Roberta's mother taught me how to sew. I can remember feeling so bad for Roberta because every time we entered the hallway, it would stink really bad. Mom would say it was "Roberta's cooking; she's a newlywed and is still learning." Every day, it had a new smell. I used to hold my breath as I ran up the stairs from school. Eventually, I figured it must have been broccoli or cabbage. One day after school, Roberta came upstairs and said, "Jennie, we've decided we need the whole house. You have thirty days to move". Mom was crying so hard. Our lives were about to change again.

*I had no idea at the time what really happened.*

*Many years later, I was driving home from work when I stopped to see Roberta. I was in my 30's. We had a nice conversation, and she told me why we were asked to leave. Even though they told us, they wanted the house for themselves. It really was because of my mother. Mom drove Roberta crazy. She even ended up in the hospital because of it. I could see that my mother was a control freak and how she really could get under your skin. I guess she needed a psychiatrist back in 1959 when "dad died," but they didn't do that back then. It was taboo.*

When Mom told Uncle Dan we had to move, he took action. He did everything he could to help mom find a house for us. Once again, it was 1972, and God took care of us. At a time when the going rate for houses was over Fifty-Thousand dollars, Uncle Dan found us a raised ranch for twenty-four thousand dollars. It was a mess. Apparently, it was rented for low-income housing. There were holes and writing on the walls, a smell that you couldn't even identify, and not even one blade of grass in the yard. The house was filthy and dirty. So, at fifteen years old, I found work at a Mister Donut to help Mom pay the mortgage. One day at a time, Mom and I would rake the yard and fix things. Then, little by little, we began to plant grass, trees, and flowers. It took over a year to get that house looking presentable. When I transferred to the local high school, I heard kids calling it "whore's plat." Later in life, I'd hear mom talking about when we first moved in. She saw neighbors running from house to house in their underwear.

Our house was the first of the "rented ones" that got sold. It was six months before the "whores" were thrown out of all the rented houses, and all the neighborhood houses were bought by nice families. Mom made friends with all of the new neighbors. On a hot summer night, she'd make iced coffee, and everyone would gather at the front steps to share stories and snacks. It became a real tight community on this little dead-end street.

When we moved into that house, there was a platform in the basement. It was approx. 12ft by 12ft wide and 6ft high. The realtor said the previous occupants had children who tap danced. We thought nothing of it because, at this time, I finally could dance with finesse and was practicing daily. For years, my mother would listen to the neighbors saying, "One of these houses has a huge rock in it." My mom would wonder what on earth they were talking about. She thought they were nuts.

Finally, we had a home of our own, just me and Mom. I always wanted a dog, and when we were renting, it was impossible. As soon as we bought this house, Danny and I went to the local dog pound. He bought me a puppy for a five-dollar donation. "Dandy," a little Mutt was a pathetic-looking pooch with wiry hair. No matter how much cream rinse I would use in his bath, it always stuck straight up.

When I graduated High School, I bought Damion, an Afghan hound who even the vet said: "Something is mentally wrong with him because there's not an animal alive that will pee and poo in his own water bowl." Yes, Damion would literally back his ass up to his water bucket and poop in it. He was quite unique and stood thirty-nine inches tall on all four legs. He was beautiful with no brains! Standing on his two hind legs, he was taller than me!

Back then, our dogs were always confined to a leash or the pen because the town had a "leash law." One day, I thought he got loose, so I ran to catch him. I was crying, "Damion! Come back!" I followed him through the woods for hours, jumping through streams and over logs and rocks. He would just look at me from fifty feet away like I was crazy and keep running. I continue crying and chasing him! Finally, after I couldn't keep up anymore and lost sight of him, I went home exhausted. My mother was frantic, "where were you?" she yelled. When I explained what happened, she said, "You idiot, Damion is in the cellar." *Who the hell was I chasing?*

Easter morning, all of mom's brothers and sisters, including Uncle Vic and his family from Connecticut, were at our house for dinner. (Mom always had a knack for putting together an Italian seven-course meal out of nothing.) This time was Easter Holiday, so she had prepared this dinner for weeks. The whole family was seated at the table. Mom was in the kitchen putting together the last details. She was barking out orders, and I was taking the prepared food to the table when, in the blink of an eye, Damion took the Ham right off the kitchen counter! It happened so quickly that I think he swallowed it whole! We were all right there, watching and frozen with disbelief. I reached down and tried to get it out of his mouth. In a split second, it was gone!

*Now, as I think about it, even if I did get that ham back, would anyone have eaten it?*

# Al

I met my soul mate when I was fifteen years old. We must have piled eight kids in Bill's Camaro to get to the beach that day. Cars were scarce. Something happened, and Bill had to leave. I needed a ride home, and I was talking to Al. We just met a few hours earlier, and I knew it was true love at first sight. I asked him for a ride. I never felt this way before. Back then, you never asked a stranger for a ride. I took a big chance.

There was no doubt in my mind that he was for me, standing there on the boardwalk at Scarborough Beach. His tanned bronze skin, sandy brown hair blowing in the wind, a navy-blue bandana tied around his neck, he was wearing cut-off jean shorts. This is a sight I will never forget. He was literally beautiful. It was 1972. He was with his friend Mike, who said, "We have no back seat in the car, so we only have room for one of you." I repeated that to Maria, and she reluctantly agreed to find a ride somewhere else. (There must be truth to "Love at first sight" because I was NOT letting him out of my sight). They were not kidding. The car was a clunker with no back seat. I climbed in the front between the two of them.

On the ride home, we talked about where I lived, and Al explained how much he wanted to get his family out of Providence. I couldn't resist the opportunity. When Mike dropped us off, I took Al to see the house across the street. I knew how to get in because my mom was helping a man sell the house.

Within a month, Al's family moved in. I thought it was going to be perfect; God brought him to me, and this was the way it was supposed to be. I had no doubt. This is what little girls dream about finding the love of their life. The wedding, the bridesmaids, the flowers, the friends, then marriage and children, this is what was supposed to happen. Little did I know how much I would cry because he had so many girl-friends'. Day after day, I'd see them come to pick him up to take him out on dates. My Mom hated him for making me cry. I was still only fifteen.

Every Saturday, Mom had a hair dresser appointment at eleven o'clock. Promptly at eleven am, Al would ring my doorbell and ask, "Got any meatballs?" Of course, I would let him in & heat them up. I was delighted at the sight of him. I loved to listen to him speak. I loved to be near him. When he would leave, & Mom came home, she would whack me across the face with a backhand because I had a boy in the house when she was not home. I'd be grounded for another month. For years, I couldn't understand how she knew.

*Come to find out, years later, I was talking with a neighbor, and she told me mom counted the meatballs!*

# The Teenage Years

In the new high school, I was *not* miss-popular anymore. This new high school began in grade nine, and I had completed my ninth grade in my old Junior high school. By the time I came to this new town, I had entered the high school in grade ten. All the "clicks" had already been formed. The Majorettes, the Cheerleaders, the Jocks, the Brains, and the (few) potheads. I didn't fit in with any of them.

*During high school 1972-1975, there were only 2 potheads that I knew of; maybe the rest of them hid it so well that it really wasn't a thing back then.*

Most of the time, I hung out with my cousin Danny and our friends. We always had fun. When I turned sixteen, Aunty Irene gave me her 1964 Chevrolet Impala. It was originally maroon, but by the time I got it, after years of her parking it under the grapevine. It looked like it was tie-dyed in maroon and bleach-stained grape. We would pile as many kids in the car as we could and go joyriding. Gas was really cheap back then.

One time, we went to the gravel pit. I thought I was "Duke of hazard" and could fly as we drove off a huge pile of dirt. Of course, we had to get towed out. It's amazing no one got hurt. I was game for anything and loved to make people laugh.

There was a beautiful running brook in the back of our house. Depending on the rain, it would widen and flow rapidly. It was really wonderful. Across the brook was a horse that was owned by Stevie, a "bad boy," a diesel mechanic who worked at the corner gas station. Mom disliked him because he quit school. He named his horse 'Taco' after the captain of the Police. He was about ten years older than me. Mom said I was not to go near him, but he was really nice to me and let me stay with the horse as long as I wanted. I couldn't resist. I loved animals. All kinds! I would always sneak over there.

That horse was wild with everyone but me. *Taco* used to talk to me. *He* would listen to me, and nay. I knew he understood me. I could look in his eyes and stroke his neck for hours. I knew he just wanted to run free. I used to pretend he was mine. Mom always knew when I would go there because most of the time, I'd fall in the brook and come home wet. Yes, I was still clumsy. She would punish me every time I went there, but it was *so* worth it!

At sixteen, I was driving. If it was five minutes after my curfew, I would be in trouble with Mom, and lord knows I didn't want another confrontation. I'd call home from the phone at the gas station down the street, telling Mom I was stuck. I'd pull out one of the wires in the car, and then at the bus stop in the morning, I'd tell Dougie, the mechanic at the gas station, which wire I pulled out. It kept me out of trouble and gave him extra work. I thought it was a great agreement.

Well, the old Chevy finally died. Uncle Dan found me a crème colored 65 Mustang with a black convertible top. Can you believe I drove it for a day and said, "I didn't like it"?

A few days later, he found me a 1967 Cougar for eight hundred dollars. Now, that car was my favorite! It needed some bodywork, and by now, Danny was learning. Uncle Dan owned the car dealership, and Danny and I went there every day after school. We did all the bodywork on that Cougar all by ourselves. Vinny, the body-man at Uncle Dan's shop, was really upset because we used his tools and left a mess, but we had lots of fun! We thought it came out beautiful. We installed the latest technology: an 8-track tape player! That music was so fine!

Just a few days after the car was finished, I was driving through the back roads with Dandy, singing along with Elton John, when a woman in a station wagon ran a stop sign. It all happened so quickly. My car wouldn't move; the engine was racing. Smoke and antifreeze were pouring out of the engine. No one ever told me that cars could blow up. A woman came quickly to shut off my car and tend to my wounds. My head was spinning as the ambulance driver took me away. I didn't know what happened to Dandy; I was in shock. Mom came to the hospital to pick me up and said a nice lady took Dandy home. Dandy and I were both fine. Thank God.

Mom started rebelling against me, getting my own personality. I guess every teenager goes through these times. Mom wasn't going through them without a fight. She got physical when I'd answer her back; it got really ugly. My life was changing so much. Mom was someone I could *not* talk to. It felt as if everything I did in her eyes was wrong, and I still hated her for betraying me at eleven years old. She would wake me up early Saturday mornings by snapping the shades on the windows up to let in the sun, screaming and yelling that I had to get up because there were chores to do. It would drive me nuts! My job was to clean the house. I dusted and vacuumed every weekend. I often thought about Teresa, my bio mom, and hated the fact that she gave me away.

One Saturday, I went to my first football game with my friend Amy. She had little pills and said, "Do you want to try one?" Everyone was taking them. If this was how to have more FUN… sure… I took the tiny little pill. At this point, and the fights with Mom, I hated my life. I knew there had to be something more to life. I was the only one of my friends with a car; seven of us piled in, and we went to the football game. I remember climbing up the bleachers and later trying to stand up. I couldn't feel my legs; I fell down the entire set of bleachers. The next morning, I woke up at noon time. Mom came in and dragged me out of bed by the hair. She was so strong. I'd swear she had the hands of a man! I spent the rest of the day in my room cleaning. No lock on the door because Mom forbade it! She came in hourly to remind me of how stupid I was by whacking me again as she continued yelling at me. Finally, after Mom left, I called Amy.

I asked, "What happened?" She said, "Wow, girl, haven't you ever done THC before? It's just a little horse tranquilizer. You couldn't handle it at all! We had to drive you home!" Damn, that tiny little pill did that! I'd never, ever touch *that* again!

Back to church, I'd go, crying my heart out in front of the Altar. God, why? This hurts so much. I don't want to fight with Mom. I want my mom to love me like she used to. I don't want to fight anymore. I knew life was supposed to be different, but I couldn't figure out how to change it. I felt as if I had no control and often thought of leaving Earth the way my father did; I wanted to get out of there so much! Somehow, Danny and our friends helped me survive. I prayed and prayed. Kateri, help me.

# Aliz

I knew for sure Al was the one for me, but something was wrong because he didn't. I also knew I couldn't just stand around and wait. I thought maybe I could be wrong, and Al was a lost cause, so I began dating. I got involved with "this boy," who gave me a pre-engagement ring. Although it didn't feel right, I thought he loved me and would be good to me. I didn't love him. He was really good to me and gave me lots of presents. Surely, he must have loved me. That is how you show affection, right?

Is this what you do to get a husband? Go with someone who loves *you*? Still in the illusion of what life was all about, we dated for a year, and then, one day, I realized I had to get out! I woke up one day and knew I needed to end this false relationship at once. I had to RUN from this. It was horrible for me to do this, knowing '*I didn't love him.*' I must be true to MYSELF! I was so scared, but I just knew I had to get OUT! Danny actually slept on the floor of my room that weekend because I was so terrified that the boy would hurt me because he was so upset.

A week later, Al came over, "I heard you're going to get married," he said,

"You can't do that, you're too young"! When I told him I had already broken it off, he smiled, and we began dating. On our first real date, Al took me to dinner. We had the most amazing conversation, and I knew it was true love. When we were leaving and got to the car, Al was unlocking my door. There was piss all over it, on the passenger door, and on the ground. I knew it was piss. (We had run into "that boy" at the restaurant.) Al was such a gentleman; he told me it was orange soda so I wouldn't be upset.

# Italy

I always wanted to travel. My first trip was to Italy when I was a Junior in High School. It was interesting to see such a different country. I had never been away from home, and this was quite a learning experience. I saw ancient history all over the country: the Coliseum, Ruins, Capri, and Pompeii with petrified people and pets from the volcano devastation. I'll never forget how sick I felt seeing the Catacombs in Naples; there were piles of skulls behind bars underground! To make this trip affordable, the school skimped on hotel accommodations. Our rooms were filthy and bug-ridden. I was so upset. I'd never seen cockroaches before! When I called Mom, she called her friends, Melinda and Libero in Italy, who came to rescue me. They had such an elegant home I thought it was a real palace. Still embedded in my mind to this day is the beautiful staircase with the marble floors. It was huge, breathtakingly beautiful, and clean! Thank God they were there; my extended family of friends again came to the rescue. Their son picked me up and brought me to Angelina's house. Oh my God, her home was so big. It was so breathtakingly beautiful; it looked like it came right out of an elegant movie.

This was my first recollection of collecting stones from *sacred places*. Before this, I gathered stones from all my favorite places. I couldn't leave anywhere without a stone in my pocket. I was always hiding them from Mom. She thought they belonged outside. I fought to keep them in my room. I swear they talk with me, and certain ones want to come home with me. *(God, I still love rocks, minerals, meteorites, and Stones)*.

# Venezuela

After graduating high School, I went on to become a graduate of the Sawyer School of Business. My graduating class went on a trip to Venezuela. It was an amazing country that I fell in love with. The people spoke Spanish; the language was so similar to Italian that I felt at home. The landscape was something I had never seen. It was like I had walked into a postcard. The waterfalls were breathtaking; I remember Angel Falls being the biggest in the world. The rainforest had plants just like I did at home, except they were absolutely humongous! The Sun, oh my God, the Sun bathed you in the warmth that felt totally amazing. It was a magnificent feeling. Venezuela is absolutely marvelous. This was my first introduction to 'energy.' The energy of this place touched my Soul. I felt alive in ways never before known. Something had been awakened that sparked my life. The 'energy' of the Holy Spirit was active in every cell of my body. I can still see the breakfast buffet in the hotel lobby. Melons, cantaloupes, pineapples, mangos, and so many fresh fruits of all colors it was magnificent! My first introduction to Mother Earth was here in this sacred place. The natives prayed over everything. Every piece of food before placing it into their mouth and every phone call they made was prayed over before dialing. They seemed to pray over everything to make it perfect even before they embarked on their journey into the jungle. Every time I think about Venezuela, my heart sings.

*For years, I wanted to go back, but Mom and Al would say, "You can't go there; they have military guerillas that will rape you!" Somehow, deep down, I knew it wasn't true, and they were loving people just like us. I still have that longing in my heart to return there. I know someday I will.*

# Steady

When Al and I went "steady," there was no one else but us. We were engrossed in the love I knew to be true, and it was wonderful. At this time, I was driving a 1977 Chevrolet Camaro; it was my first real car and my first real car loan. I also had my first real job. Al bought a 1978 Ford Bronco with huge "monster-mudder" tires. I loved that truck! We would take it 4'wheelin' at the sand dunes in Coventry. It was a lot of fun. I think I drove it more than he did. I even got a set of air horns for a Christmas present! I ripped many skirts climbing into that truck; it was so high up! It was at the time when the first real "Big Foot" monster truck was popular, and it was a *real* truck, not fiberglass, with fake headlights like they have nowadays. We would attend all the Monster truck shows at the civic center and watch from the front row because, of course, I always had to be upfront and involved—this time, I insisted against all Al's warnings, and within ten minutes of the "Big Foot" competition, we got covered with mud. Al was so mad, and I continued to laugh hysterically! There was literally mud hanging off my eyelashes!

We had loads of laughs and lots of fun.

My love for animals and their ability to communicate with me led me to study veterinary medicine. I was totally hooked on gaining knowledge. I was driven to know everything about everything and how it was made. I wasn't interested in mundane things at all. My thirst for knowledge could never be quenched, but chemistry was *not* my friend. I was having a difficult time at it when my cousin Maria called to say *"Digitronics"* was hiring. "You'd be perfect for the job, just come for an interview," she said. That was when I realized I could buy the animals I wanted if I accepted that job. So, I did; I became the secretary/stenographer for four international salesmen. Maria was definitely responsible for me getting this job. Is this her payback for pinching me when I was a kid? Now I think *that's* funny. I thank you, Maria. This was a great Job!

# Blizzard of '78

Driving on the way to work one day, the radio announcement between songs indicated we were getting a snowstorm. Weather predictions in New England can change from minute to minute, so most people disregard all "warnings." During this snowstorm in February of 1978, they called it a blizzard. It wasn't until later on to be known as the *"Blizzard of '78"*. The snow came down so fast that we had three feet of snow before noon.

Maria and I were still working at Digitronics. At lunchtime, I ran across the street to pick up my boots from the cobblers; we were really having a blizzard. You could hardly see your hand in front of your face. When I came back into the office, several managers noticed how covered I was with snow, and they called a meeting. At 1:00 pm, they released us to go home. Sure, right in the middle of it! Maria and I lived on the same street, so we left work and followed each other, driving down Rt. 295. There was so much snow it broke the front spoiler right off my 77 Camaro. As we drove up the exit ramp onto Route 44, a huge tractor-trailer tanker truck got stuck and slid across the ramp, blocking everyone else from passing! Maria ran out of her '77 Monte-Carlo and jumped into my car. We sat there with the heat on, talking about what to do, waiting for that huge tanker truck to move. Maria had on open-toe shoes, I had boots on! Good thing I picked up my other pair of boots at the cobbler at lunchtime, and Maria and I had the same size shoe! The snow was getting higher and higher, and that tanker truck wasn't moving.

People were now walking up the ramp past our cars, abandoning their cars behind us. We had been waiting over an hour. We realized if we didn't get out and walk, we'd never get home. She put on the extra pair of boots, and we began walking up the ramp. It seemed to take another hour to get to the main road, and this was only a short off-ramp from the highway. This was the worst blizzard I had ever seen. You could hardly keep your eyes open. Hail was pitting against our faces. Finally, we got to the top of the ramp on Route 44. A huge orange dump truck (sander) stopped with two men in it. The guy swung the door open and said, "Do you need a ride? We can only take one of you". I jumped in and grabbed Maria onto my lap! No way was I going in that truck alone! The driver said I can only take you to the bottom of George Waterman Road. "That's okay; it'll get us halfway there," I said. This was about a mile and a half down the road. They dropped us off at the corner. We ran into a car lot, which just happened to be still open. A classmate of mine worked there and let us use the phone. Maria called her boyfriend Peter, who picked us up in his 4-wheel Drive and got us home. By now, there was well over four feet of snow along the sides of the road. The snowplows couldn't keep up with keeping the roads clear; they were impassable. Only 4-wheel drive vehicles were able to drive anywhere.

As time went on, many roads were closed.

Television reported there were bans on driving. Police would not let you pass if you didn't have proof of an emergency; it was crazy.

When I got home, I called Al—of course, he was still at work. He was so dedicated. When he began climbing the corporate ladder to success, he put every raise in payback into the company stock. He was so committed to that company as if it was his own. Well, phone call after phone call, the snow kept coming down. I must have spoken to Al ten times that day, trying to convince him to leave and come home. Day turned into night. There were only a handful of employees left with him at work. They were snowed in for four days. When they ran out of food, they started eating from the candy machine; eventually, even that went empty!

From the upstairs windows, they could see kids from the projects next door breaking into cars in their parking lot, and there was nothing they could do about it. The snow was so high no one in his building could open any of the downstairs doors to exit the building. Al was in a suit and tie, with dress shoes on. I know he would have jumped out a window and walked home if he had proper clothing with him.

On the fourth day, two of Al's brothers and his cousin Richard walked with knapsacks of clothing and extra food for the people who were stuck there. Al changed and walked all the way back home with them. If you know anyone who was in Rhode Island in February of 1978, everyone has a story of "the blizzard of '78". Some people actually died because they stayed in their cars on the high-way, and snow covered their exhaust pipes. Some people were stranded for five days. Cars were left all over the roads, and highways looked like parking lots. All of Rhode Island and many parts of New England were affected by this.

There was no electricity, no heat; some were without water for a week! It was declared the worst storm in New England in centuries. The actual snowfall was fifty-five inches in some areas, which fell on top of the six inches that came the day before. When snow plows came, there was nowhere to put the snow. Mountains of snow lined the sidewalks. The snow piled up was over eight feet high at most intersections. You have to see the pictures of this storm to appreciate the devastation. To date, there are still stories on the internet about this blizzard. And this is one of the main reasons we'll never be without a 4-wheel drive, as long as we live in New England!

New England has a saying: "If you don't like the weather, wait a few minutes." There is even a book written about this storm, and details can be found on Wikipedia on the internet.

I think it was this event and the time away from each other that made Al & I have even more appreciation for our relationship. He finally declared his love for me. When he got home, we were inseparable.

# Jose'

Al always wanted a parrot and found one at the pet store in Providence.

He had been looking for a talking bird, and as always, he researched it thoroughly!

He decided that an "African grey" was the best talker. So here we are, standing in this pet store looking at an ugly grey bird just staring at us when this green bird, slightly larger with yellow on the back of his neck, starts talking. "Hello ~ how are YOUUUUUUUUUUUU?" We were stunned and couldn't stop laughing as this ball of green feathers entertained us. He went to the bottom of the cage, sticking his foot out, saying, "Shake my hand, what's your name? My name's Jose".

I looked at Al and Said, "Looks like it's obvious; this is the bird you want." We put a deposit on him with the promise to pay each month. During the Blizzard of '78, we got a phone call to "come get the bird." They had no heat, and said the animals were going to die. Annette's husband Joe had a 4-wheel drive at that time, so he drove Al with a bunch of blankets to pick up Jose`.

Jose` moved in with Al's family until we got married. He picked up a phrase for every person in the house. Raymond was about sixteen at the time and got the most phone calls, so every time the phone rang, Jose` would yell at the top of his lungs, "RAY-MOND! TEL-A-PHOOONE!!! Other times, he'd be screaming, "Hey Annette ~ Hey Annette! Chris-to-pher! Da de de do—de do." Everything after Christopher was just a song of notes and tones because Christopher was Al's little nephew, and Al's mom was always saying things like, "Christopher" don't throw sand. Christopher, don't go in the street. Christopher, come eat lunch. So, the parrot would only repeat things that were repetitive, like his name. Christopher. The rest sounded like someone practicing singing lessons with vowels, notes, and tones ~ all yelling at the top of his lungs, of course! Everything Jose` would say was in a "sing-song" type of speech. He'd sing a special song, "Hooo-O-say can you see?" to the tune of the Star—Spangled Banner.

He would also sing. "Can I walk to school? Can I walk to school, La de de—do—de do." He counted to ten and sometimes to twenty. He would sing another song, "Oh, GLOR-RI-AAA, Oh GLORIA." And he would actually tease you, too. He was a jokester and laughed and laughed. People used to say parrots only mimic; no way! This bird had his own unique personality. He talked! Al's little sister Jeanne did an interview with him as "lifestyles of the rich and famous" for a project she was doing in high school. We still have that VCR tape here somewhere.

When we moved to Pine Hill, Jose` was on the back porch, yelling when the doorbell rang. It was our neighbor across the street who came to say he didn't appreciate us making fun of his wife. Al & I just looked at each other, wondering what he was talking about, when we heard the bird yelling from the porch. "TONE-EEE TONE-EEEE!!!" Oh my God, the bird sounded exactly like Tony's wife when she'd called for their little son Tony!!! This bird was a hoot and always kept us laughing.

I was the only one who could handle him. He loved me and would bite anyone else who stuck a finger in the cage. One time, I was weeding the garden and ran into the house to go to the bathroom. I was the only one home and was going right back outside, so I neglected to lock the front door. While I was on the toilet, someone knocked, and Jose` yelled, "COME IN!" My brother-in-law started to open the front door just as I was screaming, "Wait a minute"!!!

One Christmas, Al's sister was standing next to the cage; Jose` backed his butt up and projectile pooped right on her white jacket.

Years later, Raymond came by to see Al; as he was standing in the kitchen talking to Jose, 'he remarked about how Jose' used to kiss him on the nose when he was a kid. He stuck his nose in the cage, and Jose` almost took a chunk out of it!

*What was he thinking?!*

*Jose` lived in our kitchen in a huge cage and came out daily to entertain us for forty years! When he passed, I put his video and picture on Facebook, and people commented, sending condolences from all over. I had no idea he touched so many lives in so many ways; everyone had something sweet to say about Jose`.*

# Electric Co.

Back at *"Digitronics,"* the receptionist was out on pregnancy leave. The company hired a "Kelly" girl to replace her. A "Kelly" girl comes from a temporary agency to fill in until the employee returns back to work. Her name was Jane. One day, she said, "Come, take a ride with me on lunch. I'm going to put in an application at the Electric Company; you should too". 'Sure, why not?' I thought, 'I've got a good job if I get it okay. If not, no great loss.'

When I realized what their starting pay was, I couldn't believe it. Within a day, we received a call and had to report for a "urine" test. Jane and I reported to a nurse's office early the next morning. There was a girl already sitting there named Lynn. She was going on and on about how "They should give you a funnel. How on earth am I going to pee in this little Dixie cup!" she said. Jane and I couldn't stop laughing! She was so funny! The three of us got hired. That was the first day of a long, fun friendship with Lynn & Jane.

Way back then, computers were rare. My cousin Maria worked on one at *"Digitronics."* It was so big it took up the whole back room. Here at the Electric Company, everything was still filed on paper. There were drawers and drawers of little index cards with customers' names, addresses, and billing information. They were filed by a twelve-digit account number by city and neighborhood. Wow. On our first day of work, we were standing on our feet for eight solid hours, filing customer information cards in all those little drawers.

Of course, with me being "the material girl princess" that I was, I worked in my six-inch spikes and little dressy dress. I could hardly walk by the time I went home. I remember Al rubbing my feet as we watched the nightly news. I was crying. "I don't think I'm going to make it in this job." He assured me the money was so good I would make it. Sure enough, this was the beginning of being swallowed up in the money trap. I was making $7 per hour when the minimum wage was $2.65 per hour. Of course, I could make it! Things quickly got better. I now had friends there. Lynn and I had a lot in common. We loved to laugh. Together, we progressed easily. We were in the Union. As someone got hired below you, you took tests and moved up to the next level. We molded ourselves to the job and fit in perfectly.

We progressed from file clerk to Customer Service. We often filled in when Joanne (the telephone operator) went on break. Lynn and I were a team. We had a lot of fun together. We had a knack for calming the customers down, so everyone was happy.

Back then, one complaint from a customer was when they had no power and saw a line truck at the local bar. They never thought the guys deserved a "lunch break" when they were out of power. Little did they know the best home-cooked meal was found at the local bars!

*Our linemen worked with ethics and integrity. Do you have any idea what linemen actually go through? Sure, they had a weather clause in their contract until there was a storm. (All weather clauses went out the window during an emergency.) They climb up a pole in the worst of the weather, hail, and snow pelting them in the face, with only rubber gloves to protect them from 7 to 12 thousand volts of electricity. In a storm, they were forced to work "18 & 6"—this contract clause meant they worked 18 hours non-stop and 6 hours off when there was a storm. What that really meant was that you were released to go home after 18 hours of work, then had to drive home, shower, eat dinner, see your family & hopefully grab a few hours of sleep before coming back on the job before the end of those 6 hours off the clock. And they did it all over again the next day and the next until all power was restored. There were times when this went on for weeks! These guys should be honored for the jobs they do & how they risk their lives just to put their power back on!*

*The company had a policy when some of these workers were injured and could not return to their normal jobs; they would find inside jobs for them. In the 70s, I worked next to some of the most amazing linemen who were retrogressed to Customer service because they had been electrocuted. I learned so much from these amazing men. They were living legends with hearts of gold and a surplus of wise words.*

# Mrs. D

Al was working in a company where he progressed rapidly, from truck driver to Salesman, to Sales Manager, and finally, Vice President. He was dedicated and proud of what he did. I was so proud of him, too. We had come such a long way. We were both making good money and preparing for our future together.

Mom and I; our battles continued. One day, she was yelling at me so much I had enough and tried to leave. She grabbed my shirt, trying to grab onto my hair to prevent me from leaving. It was so painful to stay there & take that. I finally broke free with half of my shirt in her hands. I ran out of the house to the backyard of Al's house to hide. I was sobbing uncontrollably, hiding next to the bulkhead in Al's backyard. His mom came out. My blouse was ripped, and I was red with bruises. Al's mom was so serene. She talked with me until I stopped crying. I was so embarrassed that she saw this. (We never spoke of this day—His mom was truly an angel.)

Christmas Eve 1978, Al was driving me to his relatives for a holiday party. Instead of taking a turn to the left, he headed right and continued off the road near the Baptist church. We drove up a huge mound of dirt. He got out of the car. (This was a place where we frequently went 4-wheelin). I thought, surely, he's lost his mind; we don't have time to play around! He came around to my side of the truck and got down on one knee! The truck was so high he had to finally stand up to hand me the ring box. I was so surprised! He was truly my knight in shining armor. He asked me to marry him. He even said he asked my mother's permission, and she said yes. I had no idea. I was shocked and stayed up all night staring at the ring. It was a dream come true; I was living the fairy tale.

We picked a date and booked the church and the hall. Danny & Diane got engaged that very same night and booked their wedding date five weeks before ours. I never thought it might be hard on our families. At that time, I didn't think of anyone but ME. I was a princess! Of course, Danny and I stood up for each other. We were all so close; I loved Diane (his wife-to-be), and we wouldn't have it any other way.

Two weeks after our engagement was printed in the paper, I got a phone call. It was a woman with a raspy voice. She said, "Hello, is Jennie there?" I said, "No, may I take a message?" The woman said, "I've got some information about her daughter's mother." I said, "Well, I'm her daughter. Tell me." The woman hung up. I told my mom when she got home. We never heard any more about that call. Mom insisted she didn't know who it was that gave birth to me. She promised that if she did, she would have told me. I called Uncle Sal. He always made me feel better. Well, it seemed as if no one knew about my biological mom, or at least they were still not talking.

Al & I got married on November 1, 1980, 'All Saints Day'. This wedding had to be so perfect I drove everyone nuts. I insisted Aunty Rose (my mother's friend) make my wedding gown, and we went with her to buy the material. My gown was to be satin with a lace overlay. The dress was halfway done when I changed my mind!

*Today, I look back and think if I was Aunty Rose, I would have shoved that dress up my ass!*

When the dress was finally done, Mom and I went there for a final fitting.

The top part of this dress was POINTY!

I CRIED and CRIED. *(This was way before Madonna's cone-shaped bustier was in style!)* I had to go for a photo shoot for the newspaper with a dress like that. I wasn't laughing! Finally, Aunty Rose worked miracles and fixed it perfectly. Every detail of this wedding was precisely planned. I left nothing undone, or so I thought.

When the Limousine came, it was picture-perfect. As we headed to the church, I looked out the back window of the limo to our house; I could see snowflakes and mom's beautiful purple rhododendrons in full bloom. This was truly picture-perfect, just as I'd planned.

Then, at the church, Uncle Joe and I were waiting to walk down the aisle. I heard the music I picked out. It was my song as the bridesmaids walked down the aisle. Then, as we entered and touched the white carpet, they started playing the *wedding march. THIS WAS NOT MY SONG!* I specifically wanted Billy Preston and Syreeta's song, "With you, I'm born again". They were supposed to play whatever they wanted when the girls were coming down the aisle. And then **MY SONG**, when Uncle Joe and I were walking down the aisle. I looked at Uncle Joe and said, "THAT'S NOT MY SONG!"

I was so mad! To me, it sounded like the "Addams Family" wedding song; I wanted to cry! Uncle Joe was so sweet, he just calmly said, "Okay, so, what do you want to do? Go home?" I said, "No, damn it ~ let's go"!

Wide-eyed and shocked, he kissed my cheek, and we walked down the aisle. Uncle Joe was a Saint. No wonder Mom used to call him "San Guiseppe" (St. Joseph).

The reception was beautiful. We began with a Champagne hour with fruit, cheese, appetizers, and the finest assortment of wines, etc. It was very elegant. But of course, I was a princess; nothing less than the best for the princess. Until I entered the reception area. When I was given my first glass of champagne, I ended up spilling it all over my wedding gown! At that point, I took my veil & shoes off and let my hair down. Mom chased me all over the hall, yelling, "Put that veil on! Where are your shoes? Chick (the photographer) is *still* taking pictures"! It didn't matter, we were all having fun! Aunty Elsie was celebrating her cancer being in remission, Uncle Sal was doing his impression of the 'Three Stooges' dancing circles on the floor, and one of Al's aunts danced so much she broke her foot!

It was a night to remember.

*Update: 25 years later. Marco gave us an invitation to our "25th wedding anniversary" with instructions to be formally dressed for a night out, and a limousine would pick us up at 5:00 pm. Marco duplicated our wedding exactly as it was 25 years ago.*

*We were brought to the place of our original wedding. As soon as we entered the foyer, I saw my cousin without his wife, Al's sister without her husband, and his cousin without her husband. It took a while to register that this was MY ORIGINAL WEDDING PARTY - and none of them were married in 1980. Marco had copied our wedding exactly, with every detail, even the feathered-flower centerpieces (yes, I had to have feathers shaped in the form of flowers because I saw feathered chrysanthemums at a flower show. Geesh! I sent Uncle Mike crazy when he was doing my flowers for the wedding!) Marco even made sure the special 3-layer cake was an exact duplicate. The biggest surprise was a huge ice sculpture of a giant heart with Al & Eliz in the center. Again, even 25 years later, people still talk about this party as being one of the best ever!*

While planning for the wedding, we were also building an apartment on the first floor of my mother's house. As construction took place, Al and his dad lifted *THAT* platform, the one we thought was for tap dancing. THERE WAS A BOULDER UNDER IT! The foundation of the house was poured—literally poured—around this huge rock!!! It was a riot! I ran upstairs to get Mom. You had to see her face when she saw that rock! We couldn't believe it! All these years, we thought the *neighbors* were nuts. *We* were the ones that had the big rock in *our* cellar! You had to see how hard Al and Richard worked to jackhammer the top of that boulder out! (I would always see big, fat, huge guys using jackhammers at work.) They are not heavy enough to hold the jackhammer down. It was brute force of determination and strength that they accomplished that feat.

Al and his father, who was a plasterer by trade, built our entire apartment. Al's Mother did all the woodworking and painting. Al's family was so talented. The only one we needed to call outside Al's family was my mother's cousin Sal, the plumber.

We worked hard, and everything was done to excellence. That little apartment was perfect. There were two bedrooms with the living room, dining room, and kitchen area all open. The bottom half of the outside walls of the house was part of the foundation (Cement). This made a perfect shelve that always seemed to keep the heat in winter and kept us cooler in summer. That space was always the perfect temperature without excess heat or A/C.

Al and I were building a life together. We worked hard. We played hard. We hung out with all our friends and cousins. We had big plans. We were saving to build a house.

We did everything ourselves. I was cooking, cleaning, sewing, and learning how to be the perfect wife. I even cut Al's hair.

This brings out what we call the "poor Al" stories. Yes, by now, I had the personality of "I Love Lucy." I'd try really hard but end up with the "oops" every so often! I never did get rid of that clumsy gene. One time, I cut Al's hair, and it made a "Z" on the side of his head because I forgot to put the attachment on the hair clippers. That night, he had insisted I give him a trim because he had an important meeting at work. After that "Z" mistake I made, he had to postpone that meeting for two weeks. That meeting was to tell one of his salesmen to "lose the ponytail or lose your job." That mistake saved that guy his job because Al certainly couldn't say *that* while looking like a Rap Star!

Another time, I was trimming Al's beard using scissors; I cut his earlobe. Damn, those suckers can bleed!

One other time, I thought I would surprise Al and cut the grass. I figured if I ran with the lawn mower, then I'd get exercise, too. So, I ran. As I came around the corner of the house, I took out the downspout of the gutter system. Oops, that little downspout was totally chewed up.

Here are some more of the funny stories of that time in our lives:

Our neighbor Roger liked his pot. We were sitting on the porch one day, watching Roger prepare for his Saturday ritual of cutting the grass. Donned in shorts, sneakers & headphones blasting his favorite tunes, we watched him push the mower ever so gently row upon row in the backyard. This went on for half an hour before Al finally stood up & motioned with his arms. "Hey, Roger. What are you doing?" Roger removed the headphones and yelled back "whhhhhhhhaaaaaaaattt?" Al yelled back, "Are you going to *START* the lawn mower?" Ah, and they say marijuana does *not* alter your thinking!!!

We had a neighbor, Billy. Many of the guys back then did all the projects themselves. Well, Billy decided he wanted to 'widen' the brook to make a little pond. This little brook ran through the back of all the yards on that side of the street. He was going to put fish in his little pond.

The next thing we knew, we could hear his wife yelling. Billy rented a back-hoe and flipped it over in the middle of his backyard. He finally did widen the stream and bought a bunch of big fish. Within a week, we had rain, which caused an overflow, and all his fish went downstream.

# Baby "D"

Summer of 1982, Al and I decided to start a family. Marco was planned in so much detail I can tell you the moment his soul went into my body. My body started doing things it never did before. I'd be sound asleep, and just before I woke up, my body would do this "trucker type of fart!" It was so loud my mom could hear it upstairs!

I knew *something* was going on; my body never, ever before had such eruptions! These loud enormous "truck-driver" farts would wake me up. I found it so funny I'd giggle for the whole morning. I was pregnant! It was a hoot to see Al tell the story of me sleeping like a princess then a huge fart would actually wake us up! *(Farts always made me giggle, they're just downright funny!)*

Christmas of 1982, I bought presents for my mom and everyone from BABY "D." That was Marco, the first nine months in my belly. My Mom, family and friends. Everyone who knew us was so excited and happy for us. It was the event of the year!

On my first prenatal examination, he said, "How long has it been since you've had this hemorrhoid?" I said, "What? I don't have a hemorrhoid!" His reply was, "Hmmm, any bigger, and you'd have to put a saddle on it!" What! That? Isn't that a lobe? The look on his face clearly indicated he did not know what I was saying. I repeated, you know, like an EAR-lobe? He burst out laughing. In my innocence, I explained more. I thought everyone had that. I have three; two on each of the bottom of my ears and one on my butt! In his laughter, I realized he was not kidding. Oh My! How embarrassing! This was my first introduction to "Charlie". Always ready to make a joke out of everything, friends cracked up laughing at my naming Charlie, my newfound friend! Our friends now had a "name" when someone was behaving like an A--hole, and they'd call them Charlie!

*As I got older, it was one of the most embarrassing moments in my life. "Charlie" had to be removed. It was my first surgery. It hurt so much, and I couldn't poo for days after surgery. Finally, I took a mirror to look and see what was going on down there. When I could see a strip of cloth, I gave it a little tug. It started unraveling! The doctor neglected to tell me they packed the hole!*

*Years later, the same doctor did laparoscopic surgery on my fibroid tumors. I remember waking up after surgery and screaming to Al, "They forgot something in me"! No one told me I would have metal staples sticking out of my stomach!!! Many years of pain continued after that, and another doctor operated to remove what looked like a paper clip. YES, that first doctor certainly did leave something in me. Dr. C. told me it was typically used as a clamp to stop bleeding, but they're supposed to remove it before they stitch you back up!*

I stopped all junk food and alcohol while I was pregnant; I drove everyone nuts. I read so much that I knew which week the baby's brain was forming. I would eat fish and the proper foods to nourish that portion of his body on that day and week! I was so afraid of being without food I'd stash it away everywhere. One day at work, still in the Customer Service Department, I left an egg salad sandwich on my desk—over the entire weekend! On Monday morning, the entire office reeked as if something died. I can still see that supervisor's face as I waddled in, nine months pregnant, to his office to get scolded. Every window was open & the smell lingered through the entire building all day.

I gained fifty-eight pounds. I was so uncomfortable; for me, it was a very long pregnancy. By the time I was nine months pregnant, I was totally done! In each of the three nights before I delivered, I went into five-minute contractions. Al stayed up with me every time and went to work exhausted in the morning. Each night, I had false contractions.

There's a lot of truth to "old wives' tales". One common one is to go for a ride to help make the baby come! So, on Saturday, Al took out his Harley Davidson, and I hopped on the back. He took me up and down the street. I can still see his mother and mine running out of the houses, yelling for me to get off that bike! I knew the vibrations would help BABY "D" come out! We were *so* ready! And it worked!

That night, I went into full-blown labor at 3 am. I knew it was real because of "spotting" the tiny spot of blood shown before the baby came. I kept trying to wake Al, but he just wouldn't get up. He kept saying, "Call me when it's real". Yes, this was real, and I couldn't wake him. Too many false alarms this past week!

Contractions never got closer than five minutes. At 9 am, we headed to the hospital. Al tried to help me climb into our '78 Bronco with monster tires. It wasn't easy; we had to move in between the contractions.

In the hospital emergency room, Al was helping me up onto the exam table. I got a severe contraction just as he was doing this. The next thing I knew, the table went flying onto another shelf holding all those little glass containers with cotton balls, gauze, tongue depressors, etc. Down on the floor, I went, with a huge crash and bang! Yep, here's "I Love Lucy," trying to have a baby. (The wheels were not locked on the exam table.) Doctors and Nurses came running from all directions.

We stayed there for a few hours; they were going to send me home. The Doctor wanted contractions to be closer than 5 minutes. NO way! I knew this was it! I refused to leave. Good thing we stayed. They placed a monitor on me and then realized I was right. I was almost fully dilated. I insisted on doing everything naturally without any drugs. But after the first set of contractions were so extremely intense, I literally grabbed the Doctor by the collar and screamed,

"*Gimme* something NOW!!!" He gave me an epidural, and it really slowed things down. Boy, was I sorry; Baby D was NOT coming out!

It was a long day, and Al had nothing to eat. I finally convinced him to get a bite to eat. The Doctor insisted on 'breaking my water' just as Al went to dinner! I prayed. Labor was so long that a nurse gave *me* a drink of orange juice and a piece of Danish. I took 2 bites. Later, I remembered in our pre-childbirth classes—saying, "DO NOT EAT when you go into labor." I should have listened; nineteen and a half hours of labor. Finally, here comes baby "D" down the birth canal, and my head is in a sheet, vomiting with dry heaves! Even though they had mirrors set up so we could see from every angle, I missed the entire birth.

I knew Baby D was a boy since my five-month sonogram. Al didn't want to know; he wanted to be surprised. I can still see Al's face when I delivered this 8-lb, 1 oz. Baby boy, *Marco*. Al had tears in his eyes and kept saying over and over again, "It's a boy, Elizabeth, he's a boy"! I confessed, "I've known for four months." My friend Lynn had all baby BOY things at her house so Al wouldn't see. The day after I delivered, Lynn came up to the hospital with boxes and boxes of little boy clothes and toys that I'd been hiding at her place. There were trucks and cars, toys, Harley Davidson shirts, boots, piggy banks, and hats because one of Al's favorite things was his Harley Davidson. Al was so proud that I had given him a son.

The first week was such an adjustment. Marco would eat and fall asleep eating, so he never got enough to keep him content. Within a half hour, he wanted to eat again. I was a walking zombie. I thought I'd never make it through, but by the third week, we were on a schedule, and life was grand all over again.

After Marco came into this world, no one could pry us apart. Marco and I had bonded. We did everything together. (Have boob will travel was my new motto). We went everywhere. Shopping, truck and tractor pulls, Flea markets, Martha's Vineyard. I couldn't understand why anyone would not nurse their baby. I watched other kids screaming while their mom would be heating up the bottle. Marco never had to wait; his food was always ready. Why wouldn't everyone do that?

After Al and I got married, Mom was proud of us. When Marco came into the world, it even got better. Mom was now called Gram, and she was a big part of our lives; we were a real family. Interestingly enough, Marco even had my grandfather's eyes. As soon as he was born, I thought, oh my God, it's Grandpa!

With the birth of Marco, my life completely changed. It blew my mind. I had no blood relatives, and now, I've created one. Marco was beautiful. The "Me" part of my life was definitely put on hold. Now it was all about Marco; I was obsessed!

*This is when I thought of my blood relatives. Who are they? Where did this coloring come from? Was my father blonde? Did he have blue eyes? I no longer hated my bio-mom, Teresa, who gave me away. I now had a respect for her. I thought, surely, she must have HAD to do it. I'll bet there was no other choice for her than to give me up. That really was the first time I thought, 'That poor woman'! How can anyone give up their flesh and blood? That baby is like a part of your Soul. It's amazing how much my opinion of her has changed since the birth of my own son. I really feel bad for her. I wondered what she went through. Imagine all those years wondering if your baby is okay. It must have been really hard for her. I got on my knees and prayed for her.*

*I wished I could be in a crowded room and have someone say to me, that's them over there. Just to see what my parents looked like and where Marco came from.*

With my mother living upstairs, I returned to work with the confidence that Marco would be in good hands. She loved him. Everything she did was for him. It was a comfort to know she could be with him when I went back to work. This was perfect. Mom loved to cook, so some nights, she'd even have supper for us. What a blessing.

Three months later, Danny's wife gave birth to a baby boy, Daniel. Their daughter Christina was already one year old. We spent a lot of time together. We had a lot of fun. Summertime, we'd spend playing in the yard in those kiddy pools. I have pictures of all of us trying to fit in, holding the babies in the pool! (I don't think that pool was four feet in diameter and eight inches high!) That picture is worth a thousand words; it's just too funny.

One Easter at my mother's house, I wanted Daniel to try artichokes. He was only two years old. Diane said, "He won't eat that." I refused to acknowledge this because I thought he was too small to have an opinion. I put the leaf to Daniel's lips, and he proceeded to projectile vomit right at me! Lesson learned? When dealing with a baby, LISTEN TO THE MOTHER!

Our apartment was small, so Al would go across the street to work out in the basement of his father's home. As he lay on the bench lifting weights over his head, he could see black & white legs walking by the little window. At 5:00 am, he rubbed his eyes, thinking he must be hallucinating. When it happened a second time, he went outside to look. Our neighborhood was infested with cows. Someone let the cows out from the slaughterhouse down the street. The name of that place was "Johnston Dressed Beef". By the time I came out with Marco in my arms, the neighbors were trying to hold back the cows. One was nibbling on the headlight of my car. Al's little brother Ray gave Jeanne (the baby of the family) a rope that was tied to a cow and told her to hold it. Jeanne was just a child herself; afraid to let go, the cow began to drag her across the front lawn. Finally, the men with white coats and large black boots came to round up the rest of the cows. Life was always a hoot.

*I knew then we should write these stories down, for you would never believe them to be true, yet they're so crazy, we don't even have the imagination to make them up. We have pictures!*

# Coke

There was so much to do; I worked eight hours a day, then went home to take care of the baby, cooking, sewing, laundry, cleaning, etc.… Trying to keep the house clean, do all the chores, and have time to have fun was tough! I used to think I was not Wonder Woman. How do people do this with two or three kids??? I was raised to do everything for my husband, everything. He works and comes home to eat, do chores, play with the baby, then sleep…

*I will never be the reason for anyone's demise; some things are not meant for anyone's ears. Let me just say trouble didn't begin with me; even though everyone thought it did, it didn't.*

*Trouble started, and my spirit was crushed.*

It became too much, and one day at work, the girl sitting in front of me turned around and said, "Honey, what's going on? You look like shit!" I said, "I was up with the baby all night." She said, "Honey, come with me. I know what you need!" Into the bathroom we went as she dragged me into the stall. She put these white powdered lines on the toilet tank and said, "Here, put this up your nose." I can still hear her Jamaican accent. I asked, "Are you sure I can't eat it? I'm Italian and will eat just about anything". It was appalling to think I had to put it up my nose. She insisted it would fix all my problems, and I was desperate.

Once I did, it was amazing. It felt so good. I WAS WONDER WOMAN! I could do everything and still have time for more! I was the perfect mother, the perfect wife, the perfect everything! I sewed a three-piece suit for Al in one weekend! I cleaned Al's motorcycle spokes with Q-tips! I made Marco the Care Bear costume for Halloween in one night, and my house was spotless. It was amazing.

I never slept. I used to think… *They should put this stuff in vitamins; the world would be such a happy place!*

Little by little, all I wanted was the white stuff; more and more… I kept justifying my actions by repeating, "Marco's with his dad". What a better place for him to be, to bond with his dad. I'd stay out, drinking, buying more Coke, and sharing with everyone. I thought they were all my friends. We laughed a lot. I had so many sources to buy it from that no one knew I had a problem. I'd get a little bit here and there. I would drive around the state singing Madonna songs— She was my hero. I *WAS* that material girl. I had the car, diamonds, furs… anything a girl could want—at my fingertips. Al was so busy working that he didn't notice. Then, more and more, I wanted more of the white stuff and less of being home. I would park my truck at the beach and watch the waves, counting them one by one for hours, snorting line after line all by myself.

Gradually, Al began to see there was a problem. We then went to a counselor. I showed up high. I was hooked. I couldn't stop. Al thought I had a boyfriend. When I finally said to Al, "It's not another man. It's Coke," he didn't believe it.

I stayed out later and later, more and more. One morning, I strolled in at 3 am. The baby's room was empty. Marco was gone. Al was gone, his closet was empty, and all their stuff was gone. They *moved* across the street to his mother's house. This was the worst day of my life. I was in shock. These things happen on TV, not to me. I didn't see what I had done. I was all alone and shocked into reality. We were in court within days. My head was spinning. Within a month, we were getting a divorce. I showed up in court alone. There was no one I could turn to. By now, all my friends, or who I thought were my friends, were gone; they wanted no part of this. Al got custody of Marco. He was one and a half years old.

My Mother had a neighbor take my dogs (Damion and Dandy) to be put to sleep. Al had our boxer Mack put to rest. I didn't even know what was happening; I was truly a mess. Even now, I look back on this time, so many bad things happened at once, a lot of it is a blur. I guess I still don't want to remember it because it hurts so much.

Mack was in the Pen in the backyard. It was totally enclosed, and there was a neighbor's pesky little dog who would circle the pen day after day, tantalizing my Mack. When Mack got out, that little dog paid the price. Mack went after him and grabbed him and shook him so much it broke his neck. This was really unfair. Marco was beginning to walk—Mack made a quick move to come near Marco. Al grabbed him, and that was the last time I saw Mack. It was so sad. I wonder if Mack would have truly hurt the baby. Even after all these years, to write this story still makes my heart ache.

By this time, there was so much gossip at work my supervisor began making a pass at me. He made life very difficult. He insisted I go with him to another office to "look up some files". On the way, he stopped off on a secluded road and tried to kiss me. It made me furious! I flipped out at him, telling him I'd call his wife! I didn't even care if I got fired.

My life was really messed up. Al was my best friend, and I couldn't go to him. I had gotten away from praying. There was no time. I was working so much and had so many chores to do I didn't have time to pray. During that time, I kept saying I didn't have TIME to pray. In reality, "I couldn't afford *NOT* to pray." I needed help now and started praying big time!

Kateri, help me!

The day Al moved out with Marco, I surrendered, got on my knees, and prayed my hardest, asking God to forgive me and asking Kateri to forgive me and help me. They were back in my life, and things began to turn around little by little.

# The Plant

One good thing about working at the Electric Co. was that you could bid for another job anywhere in the company. This meant you could put your name in for a job and work *anywhere* the company had an opening in all of New England. And you could also try the position for thirty days before committing to it.

I saw a job posted on the board for a "yardman" at the power plant. I thought for sure I could cut the grass and take care of the flowers; it'd be a nice change. I had quit drugs totally and bid out of customer service dept. So, I went to the Power Plant, to a new job, "Yardman," and began mending my Soul.

The Manchester Street Station was a gigantic brick building surrounded by a huge fence. As I drove into the entrance, I noticed a small guard shack. There was a man sitting on a chair with his feet stretched out on the desk. A small can of "some sort of drink" was in his hand with a paper towel wrapped around it (as if to conceal its name). He was watching TV and ignored my presence. I interrupted him by asking where Mr. Smith was. He grunted and said, "Go around the oil tanks and park next to the coal pile. You'll see the guys out back." The paper was ripped; it looked like a can of beer. I thought, 'This is insane; you've *got* to be kidding me!'

Driving around back, I could see a group of men bickering about a baseball game. I asked, "Where is Mr. Smith?" I was in dress pants and hi-heels. I was *obviously* not prepared for this environment. It was dirty beyond belief. Mr. Smith was a husky man with greasy grey hair, and his armpits were soaking wet. I hoped I would not have to work next to him; you could smell his stench from ten feet away.

He told me where to park and to meet him in his office. It was a tiny room inside a small garage. There were many pieces of wooden planks, sawdust, and cutting machines all around, so I assumed this was some sort of woodworking shop. The first thing he said was, "You must be Eliz; I don't know why you want to come to work down the plant, but if you insist, you'll have to change your clothes. The guys won't get any work done around here with you dressed like that." He told me my main job focus would be maintaining the grounds— tending to the flowers, cutting shrubs and trees, and picking up papers on the ground. I *needed* a change and accepted the job.

Donned in Jeans, sneakers, and a tee shirt, I reported to work at 7 am. Mr. Smith said, "Nice outfit," and handed me a garbage bag, a pair of gloves & a three-foot stick with a nail pointed out the bottom of it. I looked at it confused & he said, "Use it like this," as he poked it into a gum wrapper on the ground. I embraced the *'no mind'* job as relief from the office 'gossip' and headed round the corner.

Working every day, I got back to praying. I prayed to my Indian Saint Kateri Tekakwitha. My mother introduced me to her when I was born. Kateri had helped Mom when she was given last rites in a hospital in NY. Mom survived that pork poison incident and said I should always pray to her. As a child, I did, faithfully. Somehow, during the dance with cocaine, I forgot many things. Now, at this time of despair, I began praying again.

It was so painful to come home from work and see Marco playing outside (across the street at my in-laws) and not be able to go to him! I worked harder and harder and absorbed knowledge like a sponge. Within a few months, I put another bid slip in for a Mechanical repair helper. It was challenging, but I passed the necessary tests.

# I'm Back

Al was always there for me, no matter what. Even when he moved out of the house, he made sure to check on me daily. I thought we could never get back together because of all the damage we had done. We said so many painful words… we were both wounded beyond belief… I still loved him *so* much. I was scared. Could we ever be *us* again? We proceeded with caution.

During the time when Al and I were apart, he built a little ranch house for himself and Marco. Marco would drive his little toy "Big Foot" truck with one brick at a time to help Al build the house. When Marco talked about "building the house with Dad," it would rip my heart apart.

*It was difficult to think about that time of our lives apart; even though it was only nine months, it felt like an eternity. As I look back on my life, I can see how these events shifted my Soul to the next level. If all of this had not happened to me, I wouldn't be where I am today. I never thought I would ever say, "My divorce was the worst, yet the best thing that ever happened to me". If I didn't have trouble and had to leave all the gossip in customer service, I would have never bid out of there. I'd probably still be answering those phones at $8.00/hr. Instead of transferring to a plant job, being fulfilled, making the big bucks, and pushing myself to new heights!*

Al's house was almost done. We had reconciled to the point where I was staying there all the time. However, we were not ready for anyone else to know just yet. He'd hide my car in the garage so his brother Ray (who lived next door) wouldn't see it. One day, Ray asked, "How come you take Eliz's car out of the garage every morning?" That's when we decided not to hide anymore.

By now, Al and I strengthened our love and learned a new respect for one another. He does laundry, and I can change the oil in the car. Whoever gets home first starts making dinner. We are in love, and nothing will *ever* come between us again. We are truly equal and complement each other perfectly. We are better than ever.

# Uncle Joe

My Uncle Joe died. He and Aunty Anna were Mom's best friends. They used to come over and visit with her all the time. Mom would serve coffee and pastry, and we'd all talk and tell stories. On the night he died, it was his birthday. For some stupid reason, I didn't go to his house as we always did. On Birthdays, we used to bring a small present for good luck, and Aunty Anna would bake a cake and have coffee. Everyone would be there: his brothers and sisters, their spouses. It was a birthday ritual with all the Italian families we knew. I was really upset when my mom called to tell me he had died. As I lay in bed, I cried so hard, and for so long, I thought I would never stop.

It was then that I saw my first orb of light. It looked like spiraling energy, much like when you see the heat rising off the hot pavement on the roads in summer. It entered through my window, spinning about three feet from me, hovering there in the air, sending out a calmness, surrounding me with unconditional love and peace… I knew it was my Uncle Joe. I knew; he said it was alright and I need not cry anymore. Without words, I completely understood and knew he was okay. It was the first time I got to view the other side of the "veil" that people talk about, saying when you die, that "veil that separates us is very thin". Now, I knew what they were talking about, and I was NOT freaked out. I was very calm. I knew God was showing me something that I had known all along: Uncle Joe's Spirit. The part of him that moves on when the human body dies; I knew the Soul never died. I knew it.

# Dukie

Back at work, Jack's champion golden retriever got raped! Yep, the black lab held a gun to her head! That was the joke back then; we got one of the pups, and we called him Dukie. Well, he is not well trained. He has some quirks. For instance, he likes to be "up high". We'd often find him lying on top of the table when we'd come home… He was also a great escape artist. I was always afraid he'd get hit by a car, so we kept him in a huge dog pen (18 feet wide x 12 feet long x 6 feet high) with an 8-foot by 4-foot heated dog house while we worked.

Al and I often wondered how Dukie would escape. Once in a while, we would return home from work, and he would be running down the street. Finally, one evening, Al yelled from our room as I entered the house, "Eliz, hurry, you've got to see this!" Dukie literally climbed the fence, placing one paw over the other, then poof jumped over the side. I chased him all over town with a box of cookies, yelling, "Cookie Dukie'. It was the only way he'd come. Or so I thought. One day, I searched for hours, only to return to see him sitting in front of the garage with Al.

It took years for Al's family to warm up to me again. It also took time for my family to warm up to Al as well. I knew my body and brain took a vacation, and that wasn't me. It was as if someone took over and made me do the cocaine. I wanted to call everyone one day and say, "This is ME. I'm BACK!" But I couldn't. People just wouldn't understand. I had to work hard every day, focusing on Al & Marco and ignoring everyone else. In time, they would see for themselves that our love prevails, and they would begin to accept me again.

*Today's our 40th anniversary; every paragraph as I edit and write more on this is a merry-go-round of emotions. Originally, I wrote the entire book and stopped in 2006. At that time, I had everything in chronological order just as it happened, then life took off so quickly, and each time I'd edit… I'd add or make changes to clarify, hopefully, to make more sense. Like the powerplant stories, even though they span many years, I wanted the funny stories to be all in one chapter. Oh well—That's why we have the italics inserted like this… because here, from my perception at 63 years old, the story has so much more meaning and clarity that I want to add. Because now, from my Universal perception, so many of the stories of my life have been perfectly orchestrated in Divine Order, just as God wanted, to bring me exactly where I am now.*

*So, I continue to type as I talk, and I sincerely hope you're enjoying this.*

# Mechanical Repair Dept.

Once I started working at the Plant, it didn't take long for me to see familiar faces. Some of the guys that once worked in the offices were here. It was like a family reunion. Timmy elected to give me the grand tour of inside the plant. It was extremely noisy, with a mix of smells around every corner. There was a Machine shop for the mechanical repairmen, and the Electricians had their own workshop and even an instrumentation shop for another group of guys that maintained the 'instruments' that monitored the production of electricity. (These instruments looked much like the gauges in your car.) The place was complex and huge!

Around another corner was a large board of gauges, some that looked like clocks and timers; they called this the boiler room board. Opposite it was a desk with three shifts of men on duty 24/7 to *watch* the board. Apparently, someone had to watch this board all the time because if an alarm went off, they had to "do" something very quickly to prevent the boiler from blowing up! *Holy Shit,* I thought, this is really crazy!

Behind this desk, where the men sat, was the boiler. It stood eight stories high and was bigger than my whole house from front to back; it was the biggest thing I'd ever seen inside a building! It must have been 99 degrees sitting at that desk in front of the boiler. A huge flame extended out of the burners not ten feet from the desk. These burners streamed flames into the boiler to heat the water in the tubes (pipes) along the walls into steam which went by force of high pressure, to many larger pipes which turned the turbine on the other side of the wall, at 3600 RPM which in turn; turned the generator. That is basically how electricity is made with an oil-fired boiler and a steam turbine. It was amazing; totally amazing. I was utterly fascinated, and I wanted to know more.

There were many pieces of machinery which were much bigger than my car! The nuts and bolts on this machinery were bigger than my head, and the wrenches used to loosen them were so big they had to use a crane to pick them up! There was an overhead crane in the turbine hall, which drove east and west on the roof of this monstrosity of a building, and the crane *hook* had the capability of traveling north and south. This was the coolest contraption I'd ever seen.

*Little did I know one day, I would be operating that enormous crane all by myself. One day, I got stuck up there because it broke down & I had to climb out and walk the "rail" over to the 5th-floor doorway. This "Railing" was a 12-inch I-beam with a tiny handrail to hold on. Safety, you say? No such thing back then. You had common sense, and you held on. There were no safety harnesses back then!*

*On one of the jobs, I was the crane operator, and Ira was on the turbine floor with a crew disassembling the turbine for an overhaul (cleaning & maintenance). He was calling me to bring the hook over to him. There were no walkie-talkies back then… there was just yelling and hand signals from five floors below. Then Jack was yelling from the other end of the hall; he also needed the crane for his job. It was challenging to be in more than one place at a time, but we managed to prevail with good intuition.*

Originally, the men who worked there wanted a man to do the job. They thought I wouldn't hold my own and they might have to pick up the slack. I proved them wrong by working my butt off. I was in the best shape ever, stronger than an ox, and eventually earned their respect.

My first day as a Mechanic's helper was at South Street Station in Providence, RI. This was only a block away from Manchester Street, where I'd been working for the past few months. Two Mechanics were busting me and asked me sarcastically if I had ever seen the boiler inside. I was not going to show any fear here, and I said, "No, show me". This structure had an 18-inch foot access door. It was an opening to the inside of the boiler, which was 40 feet square, lined with one-and-a-half to two-inch boiler tubes. The tubes surrounded the inside walls of the boiler. They stood approximately 100 ft high. The smell of Sulfur was almost unbearable. I took a deep breath before I climbed in and followed them as they climbed up on the staging.

It was right after lunch. We were at the burner level, four stories up, and the staging machinery broke. It wouldn't go up or down! The three of us were stuck on it. The only connection to the outside world was a three-inch pipe through the burner, which we used to talk to the guys working on the other side! We were stuck in there for over three hours! Finally, they got the machine to kick in, but even then, only one side of the staging would go down. They fed us ropes so we could knot it and climb to the bottom. We were so high up the burner level was close to fifty feet off the ground! The real kicker here was the two guys had to pee so badly! Me? I was fine!

They didn't mess with me after that. I showed no fear the entire time. I just thought they were jerks for trying to scare me!

On my 2nd day at the plant, I was helping John move a piece of equipment across the floor on a dolly. The dolly took off, and I tried to stop it. It was over 500 lbs., and little me got my finger caught between it and the railing. Thus breaking my middle finger! That was a hoot because every time someone would yell, "Hey Eliz, what finger did you break?" I'd raise my hand with the huge bandage on my middle finger; it looked like I was flipping them the bird! Everyone seemed to get a kick out of that one, and they were always joking around.

# Welding

Dennis was the best welder at the plant. He introduced me to welding. He would let me go to the welding shop on lunch and breaks to practice. He connected me with his buddy Frank when he knew I was serious. Frank was a welding supervisor at Electric Boat, who taught classes at a West Bay Vocational. I enrolled in their night classes, and I loved it! *I went to Welding school from 6:00 pm to 10:00 pm—four nights a week for two and a half years.*

One of the jobs of the welder was to be a good 'cutter'. This job consisted of moving heavy 2500 psi oxygen and acetylene tanks, connecting the gauges, hoses, and torch, using a striker to ignite the flame, and finally turning the dials to make sure the flame was the proper mixture of gases to cut metal. The very first night of class, the gas popped. It made a noise that sounded like a small explosion. It was always unexpected and always startled me; it made me jump! Frank insisted I couldn't be seen jumping like at the plant. He was right. The guys would have a field day with that!

For the entire four hours of class that night, my task was to carry the twenty-foot strip of metal, secure it in place, move the oxygen and acetylene tank out of the cages to the jobsite, connect the gauges, connect the hoses, connect the torch, ignite the flame and adjust it to the appropriate bluish-purple flame and finally made the perfect cut, one inch of metal. Then, I had to disassemble the entire process all the way to locking them back in the cages as if we were going home for the night. And then, start all over again and cut one more inch. I did that twenty times that night, cutting one inch of metal at a time.

I was mentally exhausted in the first hour but determined to prove myself; I worked through it. By the end of the night, I had prevailed! I was soaking wet with sweat when Frank came over to me and said, "You're not afraid of it anymore, huh"? No, I wasn't! At the end of that night, I had made peace with the flame and could have it dancing in my hands.

When the job came up for bid, I put in a slip to apply for the 'Welders' job. The head supervisor called me in. His nickname was Doc Haley; He was about 6'4" tall—a huge, stern, professional, always in a bright white button-down shirt and tie and dark dress pants. He laughed at the idea of a woman welder but could not deny me the opportunity to test.

After eight hours of testing at the Brayton Point facility in Swansea, Massachusetts, SMAW Stick welding (what we called 2000 lb. pressurized boiler tubes) one-and-a-half-inch pipe on a 45-degree angle, all uphill welding… the pipe was sent to the testing facility for inspection. There were several inspections, including X-rays and Bend tests. Then, I waited for the results for a week. I can still see the scene right now as I type this. I was standing in the machine shop when my union representative, Joe, answered the phone. He called me over, saying, "Congratulations, Eliz, you passed the test!" I screamed for joy! *Thinking* I got the welding job.

Surely, I did, I passed THE TEST!

When I was called into Doc's office, he stated, "Well, you know, Eliz, the insurance company now has different rules. You must take a GTAW Heli-Arc (Tig welding) test." I couldn't believe it, so I said, "Bring it on". The following week, I was back at Brayton Point, Tig welding another eight hours. Several days later came the phone call; The Union Rep- congratulated me again: "Eliz! You passed the Heli-arc test! Congratulations"!

Surely this MUST mean I got the job, no? NO! I was back in Doc's office, only for him to explain that I needed to take a test in Stainless now! He said it was a new requirement from our insurance company.

Later, I was told… NONE of the other Providence welders had to go through *any* of these welding tests before, and now I must pass *three*! I questioned, "Are you serious?" He said, "Yes" you can go to Brayton Point tomorrow and take the Stainless test. I wondered if the "insurance company" statement was true. This obstacle gave me more determination to prove I could do it; I welcomed the challenge.

Well, after the 3$^{rd}$ Certification test, X-rays, visuals, and Bend tests… Doc said I certainly earned the right to have the Welding job. I wasn't going to tell you what I was thinking. Many people said I should have filed charges, but I wasn't like that. I just wanted to be given a chance. I was actually so proud that I proved myself more than all that came before me.

I was finally given the 'Welders' Job. With Certification number SC-158 issued to me, I was now accepted as one of the Welders. Elizabeth was now NEPSCO New England Power Service Company 2000 lb. pressurized boiler tube; SMAW Stick / GTAW Heli-arc & Stainless welding certified. It was a super fantastic feeling!

I worked day and night. There were only three Certified Welders in our company: two at Manchester Street Station and one at South Street Station. I was assigned to South Street, which made me the only welder in a machine shop of mechanics, riggers, pipe coverers, and machinists. In actuality, I was the first female welder in all of New England Electric System. Believe me, there was no recognition. You would think it was a milestone, but no, it was only the beginning of proving myself, which continued day after day for years.

Not everyone was pleased with my accomplishments. On a beautiful spring day, one of my jobs was to weld plates on the roof at South Street. The welding machine was in the basement. To connect the leads from the machine, I had to carry them up all ten flights of stairs because the elevator was again *out of service*. Those leads were 1/0 cable and over 100 feet long, weighing more than 75 lbs. each. I'd carry one at a time all by myself; at 5'3", I was so strong! This particular day, some jerk kept turning the heat up on my machine, so when I would begin to weld, it burnt a hole in the metal. I wasn't accomplishing anything but running up and down the stairs. Finally, Doc caught them! Rumor has it that he reamed them out a new ass for messing with me. It was a blessing that the head supervisor caught them. God always protected me. There's an old saying that if you give them enough rope, they will hang themselves. This metaphor was appropriate for many of the troublemakers at work. It was a merry-go-round watching them day after day, always the same ones in the crap.

The company made a women's locker room at South Street just for me. I can't even begin to tell you how much soap, shampoo, cream rinse, and lotion I went through to keep myself clean and soft. I'd scrub so much daily to remove debris and transform into a woman before emerging out of that plant. I was committed to staying feminine while doing a man's job!

One day, I was feeling pretty low; my nails were all broken, I had a burn on my face & I needed to do something to remind me I was a woman. I wore a silk teddy under my work clothes. I figured no one would ever know, but me & it would remind me to stay "Pretty" on the inside while working in such a dungeon. That's the day a piece of hot slag found its way down under my clothes. Believe me, the last material you want next to your skin is silk when 'somethin's a burnin'!!! The silk melted right onto my skin!

I tried everything to stay feminine—I think I started the fake nail craze because I was determined to be a pretty woman outside the plant. (Each Friday, I'd apply acrylic to lengthen my fingernails and rip them off on a Monday morning on the way to work.) Inside the plant, I was one of the guys; outside of work, I was determined to remain feminine.

When I first got the job in Mechanical repair, one of the older guys said, "You better be able to carry your own toolbox because I'm not doing that for you." So, I welded a long-handle framed cart with wheels to pull my toolbox. Within a week, that old fart came with his tail between his legs, asking me to weld a wagon for him!

One night, I had to attend a wake after work; grateful we had showers at work, I cleaned up and headed to my car. I was wearing a floral dress with little black pumps. With my pocketbook and duffel bag slung over my shoulder. I grabbed the handle of my car, and my hand oozed blue ink! I couldn't believe it had splattered all over me! This ink was what they called "bluing." They used it to find high spots when machining parts. Nothing would wash this off. My dress was ruined, and the ink took weeks to wear off my hands. The spots on my bag reminded me daily of this incident. Not everyone is your friend.

These types of incidents would happen more often when the big boss would praise me in front of the guys. I silently wished he wouldn't do that so often. Another time, I was walking to my car only to find that my car had four flat tires. At times, there were jealous people who just couldn't handle a woman doing a good job. I had a slogan in my bag that reminded me to persevere; *"a man of quality will never be intimidated by a woman of equality"*. I had to ignore the idiots to rise above it all.

Every shop had their slackers, jokesters, and jerks. For the most part, this was a good gang. The slackers spent more time complaining about a job. It would have taken them less time if they just did the job than finding excuses to get around it while bitching about it! The jokesters would go to the joke store, buy stink bombs, and throw them in the elevator just before the door would close. If you were caught in one of these trips, you had to hold your nose until it stopped on the next floor! That was a *NASTY* smell!

One time, I got stuck in the elevator at Manchester Street alone. At first, I hit the door saying, "Hello? Can anyone hear me?" After an hour, I was banging and kicking and screaming. Well, after 4 hours I thought they'd never find me! This was well before anyone had a cell phone. Just before quitting time, I was rescued. I wondered how long they knew I was there and thanked God for learning how to meditate… It kept me occupied and calm until they finally got me out.

# Shutdowns

Some guys worked for New England Power Service Co. NEPSCO aka "Service Co," came from our "Parent" utility company and traveled to all New England Electric subsidiaries. Service Co guys would move in for the scheduled maintenance shut-downs to help with the extra workload.

One Unit was a complex system of machinery that was precisely synchronized to manufactured electricity; this consisted of a boiler, often 8-10 stories high, a turbine, and a generator with all the machinery, pipes, valves, and many other enormous pieces of equipment, and instrumentation monitoring devices. Each Unit would have scheduled off-line maintenance once a year. This scheduled shutdown lasted six to eight weeks and consisted of a complete overhaul. The entire unit was disassembled, cleaned, greased, blades gapped, tubes welded, and precisely put back together like new. This was done to ensure that everything worked perfectly because each time a Unit broke down (unscheduled maintenance) when it was supposed to be online, it cost the company hundreds of thousands of dollars a day in penalties.

*(At least, that's what we were told. Of course, that was back in the day; who knows what the cost really was. Now that I'm older and wiser, I've come to know things are not always what they seem. People say things for their benefit, and it may not be accurate. Could they have told us that to make us hurry to get it back online? Maybe. It worked. Every emergency shutdown, we'd skip lunch and dinner because getting the unit back online was a priority above all else.)*

When I was a 2nd class mechanic packing valves on the 8th floor of South Street Station, I fell off a ladder. One of the guys caught me and stopped me from falling down the stairs. If he didn't, I would have fallen down eight flights of stairs!

Most of the Service Co. guys were super intelligent and advocates for truth and rights. (*Maybe because they were world travelers?*) Service Co. brothers helped me thrive in the "Plant" and taught me to seek the truth. Through the years, trials, and tribulations, God was with me, always bringing me people to raise me to new heights. *Funny how many, many years later, I can still hear their voices, guiding me with some of the best advice.*

At the beginning of my life at the Plant, one of the supervisors would change rules, and because I didn't know any better, I found myself getting all the crappy jobs. Like when they sent me back into the manhole to work on the effluent pipe. (That's the sewage pipe from the bathrooms to the street). We were supposed to rotate and take turns, but because I was one of the newest, my innocence was being taken advantage of. If our Plant guys ratted out the supervisor, they would have repercussions. Service Co. guys had nothing to lose; they would alert me to these injustices until I was wise enough to see and stick up for myself.

One day, Artie & I were assigned to the manhole; of course, I had to go in. They only had men's size boots and gear, so I still couldn't fit in a size twelve with newspaper stuffed in the toes. But I wasn't about to give in. After I stuffed the boots really hard, I could walk. All geared up in our yellow rain suit and pants, gloves, hard hat, and face shield, I put the harness on, and Artie lowered me from the safety tripod standing over the manhole… down, down, down, I went. As soon as my foot touched the rung of the ladder, there was no grip for my toes (it was newspaper-stuffed). I slid down the entire ladder to the bottom. I could hear Artie snickering as he asked if I was alright. If I were up top, I would have laughed too!

The job was to take readings and clean the instrumentation that measured the sludge (Poop) exiting the plant. In order to clean the instrument, we had to remove the huge pipe clamps on the 8-inch pipe, slide it over, and expose the whole thing. The smell was atrocious. While gagging and gasping for breath, Artie started cranking me up; I wasn't finished. I was about a foot off the ground swinging around, so I started yelling… Only to hear him laughing uncontrollably.

Even as welders, we did all kinds of jobs. We helped out wherever we were needed. There were no "Prima-donnas" back then. I did it and never let on. I almost lost lunch. I was always a good sport, but boy, were they testing me!

Whether it was sliding under the turbine to gap the blades or welding in those tight spaces in the boiler with Eric (the rigger) holding my feet so I didn't fall in, I worked harder than I ever could have imagined and still loved it.

We were considered mechanics in the "Repair Gang"; we kept these Units working in tip-top shape. We were so connected with this machinery; it was as if you raised this 'child' yourself. Each piece of equipment had its own personality; some responded to gentle work, and others needed a sledgehammer. Some would act up when the weather was humid, and others purred like a kitten on rainy days. Just by their sound, you could tell it wasn't well and scheduled maintenance before it broke. Most of us took pride in our work; we were a team. The Plant was a home away from home. You had a purpose, and when something was fixed, you were recognized for doing a good job. When something went wrong, you were happy to rush in to make it right, no matter what time of the day or night. It was a demand that you responded to with love in your heart. I loved that machinery and felt as if it loved me back.

As time went on, I became a sister to the plant guys, earning their respect and friendship. They now knew that I could not only hold my own but I would help them at the drop of a hat. I wasn't afraid of work. I was eager to learn and willing to help. It was fun. I loved my job. When one of the guys needed help painting his house, the entire gang would show up to help. Wakes, Weddings, Parties, everyone was family. It wasn't like a job. It was your life. Sixteen-hour days were common. The equipment was old, and there was always something to fix.

My bag was always packed. Welders were needed around the clock. When the boiler split a tube, they would shut it down, cool it, and we'd have to go inside to weld the "Tube-Leak" split. There was one Foreman who couldn't wait for the boiler to cool down. I can't tell you how often they had to rescue Frank because he climbed in too soon and passed out!

To give you an idea of this, picture the boiler being a metal structure ten stories high. The fire in the boiler heated the water in the tubes, which created steam to turn the turbine on the other side of the wall. When a tube ruptured, it was a big deal. Everything came to a halt until it was fixed. In order to get to the tube that ruptured, we would have to build staging inside the boiler, sometimes 70 feet high, but I Loved it. The dirtier the job, the more fun we seemed to have. The fact that I could not only do my job but was always willing to help earned me respect. I worked hard, kept my nose clean, and stayed out of trouble. Sometimes from 3 am until whenever. It didn't matter what time. I was on call. It was very fulfilling, especially when the head guy, Doc, finally called me his "ACE-WELDER". I was on top of the world. When we'd work those long nights, someone would feed me a hamburger under my helmet while I kept welding. We all took turns. The job kept going until it was completed. We were real-life "HEROES".

My favorite "Plant" story occurred when we were welding in the boiler. The welding job happened to be on the fifth-floor level of this monstrosity of a boiler. To gain access to this section, we entered from the third-floor access door; then, we climbed up the back pass (a section of pipes) and crawled further up by wedging our shoes between the boiler tubes. Like a monkey hand over hand, climbing these tubes for ten more feet before getting to the staging. Staging consisted of a few planks of wood hammered into place so you could sit and steady yourself to weld a straight line. Tools were passed through a six-inch window that opened to the fifth floor outside the boiler. This was certainly not a place for anyone claustrophobic.

Dennis came in to relieve me when I went out for a break. Upon my return, I was riding the elevator back to the jobsite with a man dressed in a suit & tie. I thought 'he must have been important' when he asked, "Hey buddy, are you working on the tube leak?" I was wearing traditional welder's garb: leathers, funky welders cap, hard & all. My welding helmet was tucked under my arm because you never left it behind; the pranksters would stuff it with 'Never-seize' or another greasy lubricant, which made a huge mess. I answered, "Yup!" chuckling under my breath because he, of course, thought I was one of the guys. He asked if I could show him the way because he was the inspector for the Insurance Company. Then I knew he was *very* important. I took him up to the fifth floor so he could talk to Dennis through the six-inch access hole. He explained that he needed a photograph of the "tube rupture" and would Dennis mind getting it for him so he didn't dirty his clothes. Dennis agreed, but I knew something was up by the look in his eyes.

Weeks went by, and I had completely forgotten about that incident. Each of us was standing in the shop, holding our morning coffee around 7:00 a.m. Ira was handing out our daily assignments when Doc came in screaming, "Where is that redheaded bastard!" His eyes were bulging out of his head, veins were popping out of his neck, and he was screaming… "Where's Tony? Where's Tony, that redheaded bastard!!!" as he held a picture of the riggers *red hairy ass*!

Remember that day the Inspector came in to photograph the tube leak???

(Well, Dennis took a picture of the rigger's ass before he gave the camera back to the inspector). That was back in the day when film had to be developed. I would have loved to see that inspector's face when he first saw those pictures!

Boy, oh boy, that is my all-time favorite 'Plant Story'! *I still laugh when I think of it today. You had to be there to appreciate the humor totally. Surely, some of these stories belong to a comedy show!*

The plant was loaded with characters, making for many "plant stories." Another inspector used to say, "Honey, I ain't never slept with an ugly man… but… BOY, have I woken up with some!" Isn't it funny how some things stick in your mind? Every time I hear the name Holly, I chuckle, thinking of that phrase.

There are more stories with Holly, but they belong in her book, not mine! Some are too raw, even for me!

# Bruins

One of the supervisors had season tickets to the Boston Bruins NHL hockey team. When he had to work overtime, he'd give me the tickets. Many times, these games were during the week. Marco was a teenager, and we couldn't resist, so we made a deal: he was to do his homework as I drove. I'll forever remember the deep conversations we had during those rides. He was growing up so fast, and I knew he wouldn't want to hang out with mom one day. I treasured those moments. Al never wanted to go. Work was always his priority, and a good night's sleep was far too important for him to drive an hour to Boston on a work night!

One of my good friends, Monique, had a side job writing for the hockey industry; she knew everyone. Always willing to have fun, we both had the gift to gab; sometimes, we'd even show up with a Lasagna for the Equipment manager, Ken, to share with the team. Being on the "inside" and getting the scoop before it hit the news was always one of the highlights.

One particular night, we had a special invitation to a pub's Grand Opening in town. Monique had completed her interviews, and one of the "commentators," Kevin (who used to interview the players on TV), wouldn't stop staring at my chest. Normally, I'd overlook this because men can be dogs, but he seemed to be drooling. This annoyed me & was something I had to fix! So, I grabbed my right boob & made it talk. As I nudged it up and down, I said, "Look up! Look Up!" The entire bar burst out in laughter. Of course, instead of this being a quiet thing, this was when no one else was talking, and just my luck, everyone just happened to see it! The place was roaring with laughter.

The following weekend, Monique called me, "Eliz, did you watch the game?" I said NO, why?" She continued, "Girl! I taped it; you're *not* going to believe this one". Apparently, during the middle of the game, Kevin was interviewing Ray Bourque when the man in the booth yelled, "Hey Kevin, Look up! Look UP!" Kevin got so flustered that he couldn't finish the interview. The cameras literally had to stop rolling! Oh My! I never expected that joke to interrupt an interview on national TV!

# More Plant Stories

Back at work, every shop had its "accident-prone" man. Of course, none of these were ever life-threatening, so you could always laugh. We had Mac. Every week, something would happen to him. The most absurd was when he called in to say he'd be late because his wife was taking him to the hospital for stitches. He was fixing his garage door and up on a ladder with the door opener and screwdriver in his pocket. Apparently, the screwdriver hit the opener and made the garage door go down with his arm up there, which made the chain cut his arm. He said he got stuck there until his wife got him down. He was always laughing when telling these stories…

One time, he got hit with #6 crude oil. I came around the corner only to witness Jack (one of the cleaners) hosing him down with the fire hose. He was a tiny guy, straddling it like a horse, trying to keep it tame. When the water hit him, Mac went flying like he was on a kid's 'slip-n-slide' oil slick in the hall. All done in his undies!

What a sight!

At lunchtime, Mac liked to take a nap, often lying flat on the picnic table. He would snore so loud the guys couldn't play cards. This particular day, they'd had enough. They duct-taped him to the bench and returned to work without him. That really stuck in my mind. I can still hear him cursing and yelling as it echoed through the entire turbine hall!

Another time, he called in to say he'd be late because he opened the trash can at home to throw trash out, and a raccoon jumped out and clawed his face! He returned to work after that with a row of stitches on his cheek.

It has been said that a book could be written just on what Mac got himself into. He was the world's best fabricator who taught me a lot about working with metal. School can only teach you so much; your expertise will come from working with a Master.

My first year at the Plant, Mac was one of the foremen. He'd have me hone my skills on lunch and breaks by welding community projects. One of his master projects was a "cannon" made of scraps. Ten-inch pipe reduced to six inches with wheels from an old oxy-acetylene cart, a massive chain from the boat docks, and the ball from the old coal yard pulverizer equipment. (The pulverizer was a piece of equipment with solid metal spheres the size of bowling balls, back in the day, used to crush coal). This Cannon was donated to an East Providence VFW (Veterans of Foreign Wars) club.

*I've always wanted to see if it was still there after all these years.*

Gus was one of the guys at Brayton who used to take his dog with him on the night shift. "The Captain" was a huge Airedale terrier. After their shift, they'd go bar hopping throughout Newport. At every bar they stopped in, the Captain would get his own bowl of Kahlua Sombreros. One night, Gus was sound asleep when he got a call telling him his dog was there without him & he needed to come and pay the tab.

During one overhaul, we were changing gears in the turbine. A special hand-cut new bronze gear arrived for #10-Turbine. After replacing the gear, testing was needed before placing the turbine back online. Something went drastically wrong as you could hear metal scraping against metal all over the building. "Shut it down!" yelled Doc. This new special gear did NOT mesh as perfectly as it should. Doc looked at Paul & said, "Run the list. We'll need men to stay overtime". Paul comprised a group of us who would stay an extra shift. We reported to the shop for instructions. This time, my assignment was to operate the crane to lift the turbine cover to gain access to the gears.

Normally, we'd just grab the "old" gear, put it back in, and be home in 3 hours. We were fix-it-men and often created something out of nothing. We always made do with what we had. This time was different. Jon came in with a blank look on his face. "Uh, Paul… the gear ain't there". Paul sternly replied, "Come on, Jon, there's no time to kid around". Jon replied, "I'm not shittin' ya. They're gone." The old gears disappeared. One gear was approximately three inches thick and about eight inches in diameter solid bronze. It was gone! For the next few days, our assignments were to search the plant high and low, inside and out. At this point, most of us knew it 'walked'. It was *off* the property. Somebody must have cashed it in!

Not very often because we got paid so well, but once in a great while, there was *someone* who would help themselves. This was one of those times. The bosses were dumbfounded, not knowing what to do. Finally, one night, a supervisor got a call from a church in East Providence saying a parishioner asked for absolution and could he come to pick up the gear. No one would believe the things that happened down the "Plant". You couldn't make this stuff up! It was really quite crazy. *I always knew there should be a book written about the "Plant Stories," and here it is.*

While Celebrating Nick's wedding, the waitress came over & said, "Eliz, there's a call for you". It was my supervisor, Ira. He said, "Eliz, who's there from the gang?" We got a serious tube leak & you need to come back in now". I said, "We're all here". He said, "Get in as fast as you can". I don't know anyone who would drop what they're doing and run back to work, but we did! Most of us loved our jobs. It was a blessing to be needed, and it felt fantastic to be the hero when the job was done.

I know Al was happy to leave that night… although he respected my place in this "Gang," weddings and sitting in a suit and tie was not his favorite thing to do on the weekend, so off to work I went…

This time, we welded the leak & were done in a few hours. We could have been there all night! I was so happy we punched that job out in a jiffy. I rode my toolbox like a horse down the ramp to the main turbine room. (The ramp was over 200 feet long at a 20-degree angle between the two buildings.) As I approached the end, the chief engineer came around the corner. I almost took him out at the knees! He flipped out, screaming at me. Ira happened to catch this stunt and almost pissed his pants laughing. Thank God for Ira. He came to my rescue, telling Chief they'd be up shit's creek if we didn't come in to bail them out. Thank you, Ira. I may be your ACE welder, but you are indeed one of my Guardian Angels. I could have gotten fired for that one!

Another time, we had just completed working a 'shutdown' with tons of overtime. My car was in the shop so Al came to pick me up. I was so hungry, we stopped at Davol Square pub. They had the biggest appetizer menu around, and they were so delicious. I ordered one of every appetizer, and there were so many the waitress brought over another table. There were shrimp cocktails, stuffies, little necks, fried chicken, buffalo wings, stuffed potatoes, mozzarella sticks, fried scallops wrapped in bacon, fried string beans, calamari, and more. And yes, I ate them all! I was as strong as an ox and ate like one, too! Of course, I could never resist dessert, so I ate carrot cake with crème cheese frosting and a chocolate chip cookie ice cream dessert!

Stuffed to the gills, I slept for 2 days when we got home.

Anyway, being a woman at the plant was not easy. Back in the day, none of the rain boots, gloves, or protective equipment came in women's sizes. They would issue you what they had in stock. Usually, one size fits all—size X-large men! These gloves are what I had to wear to pull fuses when the crane was out of service. Those fuses were so big they were the size of soda cans! With all my strength, I still couldn't fit my tiny hand around those fuses! Years ago, safety was out the window when something was needed. It was GET THE JOB DONE however you can! Just do it! I've seen men pry those fuses out with a crowbar. Then in came safety rules…

One time, I was welding an overhead pipe. They insisted we wear safety glasses. The sides of these glasses were tinted brown. It was hot and humid in that basement, and the sweat made the glasses steam up, not to mention they acted like blinders with the sides colored. As any welder knows, sometimes, if the heat is not just right, your welding rod can stick to the pipe. Well, it stuck, and when I lifted my helmet, I turned my face just enough that the welding rod stuck right to my cheek!!! It was the ridiculous brown-tinted sides that limited my sight. Thank God for Silvadene, a burn crème that (if you can keep it moist until healed) will prevent scars. The key here is to keep the crème moist; if you let it dry out on your skin, you will scar!

Only when the sun shines a certain way can a tiny scar shimmer be seen on my cheek. Every welder should be given his own tub of Silvadene before work!

At three o'clock one morning, I got a call from my supervisor, Ira. He said, "Eliz, we got a leak. Can you come in?" I'll be there in half an hour. I rubbed my eyes, woke up, kissed Al and Marco, and ran out the door. When I got there, # 6-Boiler had a leak in the economizer section. (Every piece of equipment had its own name). This was an overhead weld. I had two helpers, one 1st class and one 2nd class Mechanic, assigned to me for this job. We collected our tools and brought them up to the job site while waiting for the boiler to cool down. Finally, we were set up, the boiler cooled down, and the doors were opened. Of course, I had on the proper safety gear. A welder's leather jacket that was issued to me (welding gear) was one size fits all; this was men's Large. I was a junior size eight!

My helpers were great and stayed with me the whole time. I was almost done welding; the heat in the boiler was steaming up my glasses, and I had only a little more to go. I was forcing myself to finish when a huge lump of metal (melted off and slipped right through my collar.

I was welding overhead, and my welding jacket was too big. This hot ball of metal tumbled along, bouncing in my collar and under my clothing as I jumped up and down. This caused the quarter-sized molten metal ball to singe my skin many times before stopping on my chest.

By jumping around, it was forced to take off again, flip-flopping in its travels as it burned many more times to its final land place right into my belly button.

I was so mad! I screamed and cursed as I was throwing off my leathers, then my denim jacket, then my sweatshirt. Bill and Mikey were right outside; all they saw were clothes flying out of the boiler! These two men were gentlemen; they didn't know how far I'd stripped and were totally embarrassed. Neither of them would look at me. They just kept asking, "Eliz, are you alright?"

Finally, I climbed out and still wore my now 'holy' tee shirt and jeans. Knowing I was okay, Bill breathed a sigh of relief head as I ran down to the shop to get some burn cream.

Ira was at his desk as I grabbed the crème and ran in the back where no one could see; I began to dab the cream on the burns under my shirt, yelling over the wall to explain to Ira what had just happened.

Just then, one of the boiler operators came in with his family to give them a plant tour. Ira was so well-mannered, thoroughly embarrassed at the thought they might see me putting crème on my burn. Ira was someone who would blush at the word 'chest'. Now he was *so* embarrassed his face was beet red, thinking, 'What on earth is Eliz doing back there!!!' Does she have her shirt off? No, I didn't, but *he* didn't know that.

Ira blushed even more when he realized he had to fill out an accident report. He kept stuttering while asking what he should write, and to be a jokester, I said, "Tell them I burned my left boob". "No! No! No!" he demanded, "I can't write that. Isn't there a polite word for those things?"

*To this day, I can still say, "Ira, remember the day I burned my". I don't even have to finish this sentence; he blushes just as red as that day in 1992, and we laugh just as hard.*

By 1995, safety became 'Number One'. Finally, we have women's sizes for all our equipment! And the safety man will issue you a 'ticket' for improper use or non-compliance.

# Closing South Street Station

Many changes took place at work; they closed South Street Station.

As employees, we were issued tickets for our family to watch the implosion of the building. We had to report to a parking garage across from the plant at 5 am. Marco was so excited. Some of the guys even filmed it. It seemed to go "poof" before listing to one side for a bit of hesitation, then finally, a few more explosions were heard, and the whole thing was a heap of debris ten feet high. I was really sad. Working at South Street Station was like a home away from home. We have so many fond memories.

We were Union employees. Depending on where you fell with seniority determined your placement on a bump back. A bump back was when your current location or job was eliminated, and you reverted to your previous job. In this case, I was bumped back to Manchester Street. When it came down to it, the union served all the people.

There were a few men who came directly from Brayton Point. They could not be "bumped back". So, for the good of all, I agreed to take the janitor job for three months. Even though I had NEVER, EVER had that job before. I saved a guy from hitting the street. It was a horrible job, but I knew it was temporary, and I was still the "on-call welder," so I was the highest-paid janitor ever.

Dressed in a full body suit of rubber coveralls with face shield & gloves, that's how I'd clean the locker rooms. I wore the original Hazmat outfit!

The cleaning procedure was to place the cleaner in a jar attached to a garden hose. One day, not realizing there was some bleach in the bottom of the cleaning bottle, I added ammonia and hosed the room down. Oops. They had to evacuate the entire side of the power plant.

(It was too funny; I guess we still have a bit of I Love Lucy popping up here and there).

Yes, it was a bad time, but I had to make the most of it. I worked from 5 am to 1 pm and made the most of a bad situation. I switched my major in school again from Mechanical Engineering to Electrical Engineering. I added Instrumentation classes to the many I already had under my belt, passed the necessary tests, and was accepted into the Instrumentation Department, making top dollar! Things were very good again. Only this time, I didn't have to get dirty at all. This was a job for the elite. I kept my welding certifications and was still on call for welding and overtime jobs. It was the best of both worlds.

Al and I were totally in Love and had the best relationship ever. We each had grown to respect each other; it was like a brand-new love all over again. He felt my sadness when South Street closed, so he built me a welding shop in our backyard. It is so cute. It's a replica of our house, with the little white shutters, brick bottom, and even a porch overhang. Inside was every man's dream. A Miller Bobcat Gas operated, 8000-watt welder/generator with the hi-frequency unit for Tig, Mig, and Stick welding, a giant Air compressor, and a toolbox meant for a master craftsman.

For Christmas, I welded Al a huge brush guard for our pick-up truck. By the time it was finished, it took two men to carry it into my house; it was so heavy. I wrapped it up. Christmas morning, Al nearly got a hernia trying to pull it out from under the tree. I'll never forget the smile on his face. He was so proud of it. It was made from scrap metal, 2000 lb. pressurized boiler tube, and plate. When guys commented on how nice it was, he would smile and say, "My *WIFE* made it," with a smile from ear to ear. Then he would tell me how other men drooled at the fact that I was gorgeous and could weld! They envied him. He loved it. Yeah, it was really neat. Al said I was perfect because I could do anything that any man could, and I was still an elegant lady looking like a goddess". He certainly made me feel like one.

# I Love Farts

My brother-in-law Ray & I used to giggle uncontrollably about passing gas. Yes, you heard it right, farts make me laugh more than anything. Ray could always do them on command, and I was so jealous! One night, I ate a ton of broccoli just to see if I could make the loudest noise, like Ray. It worked. I recorded them on my tape recorder because I was always taping classes at school to help me study and pass all those tests! So, I was excited that I had some Loud, Long, and "Rip Roaring" fart material on the recorder, so when Ray would call, I actually had ammunition to play back to him! Al was NOT amused; he thought I was nuts.

So, one night at school, I was returning from the lady's room, and I could hear my fart material being played loud and clear with the entire classroom in hysterics! Donna was looking for last week's notes & played my recorder. I had totally forgotten that tape was in there!!! Oh my God, I was so embarrassed as I told her it was an April Fool's joke!

*Yes! At 66 years old, I still love the noise of farts! And Hubby still thinks that's nuts. Nothing makes me laugh harder than when we're in church and the little ones in front of me "lets one go." Giggles to the moon!!!*

*One time, Marco had a dinner party for all the guys he worked with. I brought a giant Carrot cake and a huge triple-layer Chocolate cake. His friend Nate and I planned a big joke for the evening. Now picture this: I'm all dressed up like a lady. There is a long dining room table with a white linen set with the proper forks, spoons, and knives in the proper place. Wine glasses are also the proper size for the proper wine. Al sits at one head of the table, Marco at the other, with his colleagues on the sides.*

*Dinner was delicious, as usual, and they just started digging into dessert. I stood up, leaned back, and stuck my tummy out while rubbing it, saying, "Oh my God, I'm stuffed. I don't know if I can fit dessert"!!! At the same time, Nate hit the remote control for the fart machine, hiding under my chair.*

*The look Al gave me was horrifying.*

*I have never, ever seen him so embarrassed in our lives.*

*Al sternly said, "Elizabeth"!*

*Marco's friend Dave nearly spit cake out his mouth as he laughed. Every time I moved, Nate hit the button again and again. That made me laugh even harder. I couldn't catch my breath… All at the same time, the guys were splitting their guts laughing; Al yelled, "Elizabeth, excuse yourself," and Marco yelled at the end of the table, "Mom! STOP it, you're going to shit yourself"!!!*

*I literally could not contain myself. I have never laughed so much in my whole life.*

*Finally, I reached down and grabbed the machine, tossing it on the table, and Al said, "I knew it was that all along." No way. You should have seen his face; he was mortified!*

*Well, I got a lecture and a half from Marco after the guys left about the fact that "not everyone finds farts amusing," and that would not have been funny if his friend Maureen was there. Seriously, I would have laughed even more!*

# Repowering

When upper management made decisions, it looked very different from the worker's point of view. Here's what it looked like to me… I can only speak from my perception.

When the company's CEO was going to retire… he stopped maintenance on all of our equipment. Of course, this lack of maintenance saved the company enormous money. Until the equipment 'shit the bed.'

By then, he was long gone, retired with enormous bonuses.

After that, there was no choice but to repower and rebuild the whole power plant!

Repowering consisted of spending 250 million dollars, converting the old steam turbines to Gas turbines. With state-of-the-art technology, they made us sign a document swearing our commitment to stay at the plant. The power plant was shut down for re-powering, and we reported to school every day, studying and testing for two and a half years to prepare for the new equipment. When the plant was completed, they merged the Instrumentation and Electrical departments. So now I was working at what they call the "I & E" dept.

I really didn't like working with 23KV. That stuff had a particular hum that made your hair stand on end. The people at the plant were human; they made mistakes. Some errors I witnessed put a fear into me that I will never forget. I've seen the damage of a boiler explosion. Did you know that when a steam pipe burst with 2000 pounds of pressure, it could actually cut your head off? Did you ever see the top of an oxygen or acetylene tank break off? 2400 lbs. of pressure can do horrible damage.

It was great working in a brand-new power plant. Management cut jobs, and now there were only thirteen of us in this newly designed department. Whenever machinery went down, the equipment manufacturer was called in for repair. We no longer repaired anything; we were uplifted to higher-paying positions with more elite jobs. It seemed as if we now tweaked equipment to keep it humming perfectly. I was still welding any time they needed me to, which was more often than not, our paychecks kept increasing, and it was pure heaven!

Some things never changed. Back inside the plant, I was losing tools daily. Finally, I painted them with pink nail polish to mark which was MINE. One day, I was on a job, and Paul pulled out a crescent wrench with *my name* in pink nail polish. When I took it back, he uttered something stupid: 'Uh, I needed it.' I had to think of something else! Ah ha! It wasn't until I put a tiny box of tampons in the top drawer of my toolbox that they stopped taking my tools.

I mean, "Who needs a gun? I have a super absorbent!" So true was that statement I learned from a comedian on TV—Thank you, Elaine Boosler, it really works! No one *ever* took my tools again.

Back at home, we needed to expand our little ranch house; it was too small for all our stuff. I drew up the plans for the addition, and Al's brother Ray made the blueprints. Ray has a construction company that builds big, beautiful houses; his work is gorgeous. Al and his brother Ray added to our little ranch house; they put every nail into this whole house. It is truly a work of art.

Mom and I still fought, but deep down, she really loved me and adored Marco. She has been a very sick woman for as long as I can remember. She took lots of medication and was frequently in the hospital. I can't remember how many times she was critically ill. She had a short temper but didn't mean half the things she'd say. Later on, she'd be apologizing. Boy, could she antagonize people! I'd be driving home from work saying I'm not going to fight with her, then next thing I knew, I'd be walking in the house, and whammo… we'd be at it again, yelling at each other. Then, hours later, we'd be sitting having coffee pleasant as pie.

# The Christmas Tree

Weeks before Christmas, Mom and I would start preparing food for that magical day. We'd cook and bake, freezing as much as we could ahead of time. Some of it couldn't be cooked until the very last day, like the fish that needed to be fresh for Christmas Eve. Especially the lasagna; it had to be perfect for Christmas Day. This was our special holiday.

We added to our little ranch house, and the family room was finally complete.

Now we have the biggest house in our whole family. I promised, "From now on, Christmas will be here every year."

I enjoyed walking on the soft plush rug in my bare feet. Everything was so new, clean, and beautiful. Now, I could focus on Christmas.

I called Mr. Jacavone and ordered a Christmas tree. I told him I needed one that was over twenty feet tall. He laughed and thought I was nuts. I had always dreamed of a huge tree, and now we had the space for it. I asked him to ensure his sons deliver it "after Al leaves for his business trip at 10 am" on Sunday.

Sunday morning, Al stood at the front door in a suit and tie, waiting for George to pick him up. Mr. Jacavone's boys pulled into our driveway in a flatbed truck with a HUGE tree. You should have seen Al's face. He ran outside, telling them they had the wrong house. When I ran out to say no… His first words were, "What the hell are you doing???" When I explained that I wanted to surprise him, he said, "Are you crazy?"

With limited time, he convinced the boys to put the tree in a huge bucket out back and tie it to the V of a bigger tree so it wouldn't fall. I was ordered to water it ONLY, and we'd "talk about it later." I was forbidden to touch that tree until Al came home.

He was so angry!

While he was away, Al called to tell me, "We can't even lift that tree, and I'm not moving it until we can." With these words ringing in my head, I brought the question to the guys at the plant. Mark told me of a story about how his father was a perfectionist and would drill holes in the tree trunk if there was a bald spot and then glue the branch back in place. Bingo! What a great Idea! I borrowed a one-inch drill and bit from work and took it to the backyard with a saw in hand. I shaved off four feet of branches from the bottom of the tree with the plan to replace the branches later… Yes! Now, we should be able to move that tree.

Meanwhile, we had a massive snowstorm. With this huge blizzard, the tree and all the shaved branches sat outside, frozen, waiting for Al to come home.

Back at the plant, Mark and Tom helped me make a Christmas tree stand to hold this mammoth tree. I welded a ¼" thick boiler plate, 36" round with a 12" base, 4 heavy-duty bolts, and a spike in the middle to hold this sucker. Nothing is going to tip this tree over! Yippee! What a great tree stand, and it doesn't even leak! It was so heavy they followed me home to help me carry it into the house.

When Al got home, it took lots of sweet talking just for him to calm down. Finally, he talked with his brother next door, and Ray said, "Let's try it."

We prepared the space by protecting the new rug with a clean white sheet. Then we put the stand on it, and Ray and Deb came over to help. Marco waited patiently at the top of the stairs with the Camera. The four of us had a plan. Thank God the top of this tree was still tied with a rope. We got it halfway through the door, and after an hour of pushing and pulling, it made its way through the doorway with a thud! We all went flying! Deb got pinned under the tree, Ray hurt his back on the stairs, and I ended up on the other side of the room. It took a little while for us to get our bearings. Then, with another rope, Ray guided the top up the staircase while the rest of us stood it up in the stand. By the time we were done, we were sweating, covered in pine needles, and sore. I plopped back into the rocking chair to look at this monstrosity.

Everyone was standing in awe. It touched the ceiling, and I was so excited!

Marco continued taking pictures the whole time.

Just when we thought we could relax and admire this beauty. It sounded like it was raining. Al said, "What's that noise?" We all stopped talking to listen. What? What is it? Oh My God! It's raining inside the house! Oh My God, it wasn't raining, it was the tree! The Tree started thawing out! "Sap was running down the walls. The rug was getting wet! "Marco, quick; get the towels," I yelled as I began wiping the water. We used every one of our towels and all the linens in the house to try to wipe it off the rug. I thought for sure it was a temporary thing. We were at the point of using blankets when Marco came out of the basement with the lasagna pans—when I said; enough is enough, "GET IT OUT OF MY HOUSE!"

Al and Ray looked at me with astonishment. Then Ray said, "Are you sure"? I cried yes! They used a saw to cut the tree into five pieces to get it out of the house.

I stared at the $200.00 lump of evergreen in the snow, crying, "My rug is ruined. Look at the wall. Sap is running down the walls; Christmas is ruined".

Sixty people were coming for Christmas in less than five days, and now we had a huge mess and no tree. I was so upset. I just cried.

The next day, Al called me and said he had a surprise. He returned with a $9.95 special from the Ann and Hope department store. This tree was 17 feet tall, with 3 feet between branches and little fuzz balls in between. It was a riot! It looked like the Charley Brown tree. This was the Christmas we'll never forget. We still have sap running down the wall (no one can reach it to clean it). And we still laugh about it today. We pull out those pictures every Christmas and tell the great Christmas Tree story.

*As years went by, we finally had that room painted, and the sap is gone, but the stories remain.*

Since the Christmas tree incident, I've been forbidden to touch anything about Christmas. Al and Marco now get the tree and put it up. I am only allowed to decorate it. The good thing is that Al really liked the idea of a tall Christmas tree, so he now finds a tall, skinny one every year. We tucked it in the corner of the family room, which is reachable from the top balcony of the dining room. I decorate from that corner above and with a BBQ fork duck taped to one end of a broom handle. I have just the knack of hanging the ornaments on the tree. Marco stands below to catch the ones that fall. Year after year, I got better at it and dropped less and less. One year, I almost took out the picture window with the end of the broom... Marco ran and grabbed the duct tape and foam rubber to pad the back end of the broom handle. Now I've got a good cushion, and the window is safe.

*Since our first year with the new addition, we have had over 60 people for the Christmas Day Celebration! Al's dad is always the first one there at noon, saying, "Where's the soup?" family and friends continue coming in all day long. Some eat, leave to see their in-laws, and return for dinner later. My nephew is a fireman, and my niece is a nurse; even their colleagues stop by to make dishes to return to work.*

*A delicious buffet is set up in the Dining room. Antipasto, Italian wedding soup, a whole stuffed Turkey, prime rib or ham, Lasagna, Meatballs in red gravy, Eggplant Parmesan, Sausage & Peppers, Veal with peas in red gravy, Chicken Marsala, roasted garlic & onion white & sweet potatoes, vegetables of all kinds, and too many deserts to mention here. It is the grandest party of the year and continues to this day. We have enough food to feed an army, so we do it again the next day until all the leftovers are gone. It's the best holiday celebration ever.*

# Aerosmith

Al had a business venture in Memphis, Tennessee. He told me to go buy a fancy dress because there was a "black tie" dinner we would have to attend. I went kicking & screaming because I didn't want to go. I really didn't want to go! I kept saying, "What the hell am I gonna do in Memphis?!" (On these types of business trips, Al was in meetings from early morning until late at night; most of the other wives are a lot older than I am, so I am usually left by myself).

Bags in hand, we arrived in the land of Jazz. At the counter of the fancy hotel, the concierge' told us to always be careful if we went outside of the hotel to always travel in groups because it was not a good area. Wow, I thought this was really weird. Al and I checked our bags because our room was not ready, then we went out for a walk. It was a beautiful small town with lots of tiny shops. We found Beale Street, famously known for popular Jazz bands, and made a note to get back there for nightclub fun later. After a bite to eat, Al whispered for me to stay close; he thought the four boys in the restaurant were watching us. He was right. On the way back to the hotel, we were followed by this group of hoodlums who surrounded us and began to make cocky remarks when two policemen just happened to appear out of nowhere. The group disappeared. With a sigh of relief, we were safe at the hotel.

Al could sense trouble right away. I have always been a naïve person who always thought, 'No one's going to hurt you if you don't give them a reason to.' This was the rose garden I grew up in: Mom's protection. Al was raised in reality. He had to learn how to fight when he was eight years old & the big boys went after his sister. He grew up in the rough part of town that my Mom wouldn't even drive through. We were so different. I am so blessed for him; He is exactly my "complimentary opposite."

Back at the hotel, we settled into our suite, and then Al had to report to a meeting. I ventured out to explore the hotel. There was an elevator with a red carpet that went from there to a huge fountain (all the way through the lobby to the other end of the hotel at the lounge). Once a day, bus-loads of elderly women stood in a line along both sides of this carpet. Then, with a loud, sharp whistle, the marching band music began with the elevator door opening to the sight of several ducks led by the leader of the marching band. The ducks followed this man all the way down the carpet to the fountain and jumped in. It was quite an astonishing sight. All of the women were clapping as if a man landed on the moon. I wondered 'what the hell that was all about' as I pulled up a chair to the bar. The man next to me just happened to get a kick out of my comment as we began to chat. Beyond all amazement, the entire band entered the lounge & bought us all a drink. Well, that was it. God just put Aerosmith in this hotel 'just for me!' How wonderful is that?!?!? My weekend was a blast. We ate, drank and even sang with the band in that hotel. I shared all of my funny stories and had everyone laughing!

OOPS… Did I say that aloud? Well, this was back in the days when I was "one of the guys working at the Plant." I had the best jokes and 'Plant' stories out of anyone.

This little ditty is a rhyme that got the most laughs that weekend…

There was an ol'man from Alas.

Whose balls were made out of brass.

In stormy weather, He chained them together

And Lightning shot out of his ass!

Saturday night, Al in his tux & me in a full-length gown; we looked like the perfect couple. The room was elegant & the people were charming. Jamie was sitting next to us when Al took his position at the podium. He was making his speech in front of hundreds of people when Jamie asked me, "Hey, did you know Aerosmith is having their concert tonight?" I replied, "Yeah, so we're stuck here." He laughed. Being one of the 'big shots' in the wholesale industry, I now know why he laughed. When Al came back to the table, Jamie said, "Let's blow this garage"! Al said, "What?" Jamie said, "I want to go to the concert; come on, let's go"! Al made a few stops to speak with his colleagues, and the next thing I knew, we were running down Beale Street to catch our Limo. Laughing with glasses of Champagne, Jamie made a toast to Al for being the hero of the night. Not only did we get to see the Concert, but the band also took us backstage, we had a blast!

# Somewhere Around 1992

One evening, Al picked me up after working a double shift. I was so hungry & tired. We went to this little bar across the street from the plant. They had the most magnificent appetizers. They had two pages of appetizers: potato skins, baked stuffed shrimp, shrimp cocktail, nachos, empanadas stuffed with beef, chicken, pulled pork, and snail salad, and I had to have every one! I ordered one of everything on that menu. My husband just sat there in amazement, watching me eat all of it one by one. The waiters just stood there with their jaws hung open because they couldn't believe this skinny little thing was eating all that! There was so much food they had to pull another table up next to our table because the dishes kept coming. And I kept eating, and eating, and eating because I had not eaten a decent meal for three weeks straight. I had just been picking, and often, my co-worker Dennis would feed me a hamburger under my helmet so I could keep welding! We did whatever it took to keep the job going. Coffee through straws & you just kept welding. But it was fun, it was really fun.

# Mom Died

In April of 1992, my mother passed away. It was a shock. We were at a dog show, putting a deposit on a new puppy, to later drive to New Hampshire to pick him up. On our way home, we stopped to tell my mother. When we pulled into the driveway, Al said, "Stay in the car." He sensed something was wrong. He had more intuition than I could have ever dreamed of at that time. Marco and I sat in the car. Al came out and said, "You need to go in." Marco stayed outside. Mom had died in her sleep. I was in disbelief. I grabbed her shoulders to move her, saying, "Mom, wake up." She was stiff. I was in shock.

To reiterate here, we did not have the best relationship. She needed help when my dad died, but in 1959, you didn't go to a shrink. She had thirty-five surgeries by this time. She had lots of health issues, yet still, Dr. Rocchio had always saved her. She always made it through surgery. Dr. Rocchio said if she had only gotten to the hospital, she would still been alive. I can still remember the eeriness in the house. I didn't want to stay there. I couldn't cope with a dead body. I wanted someone to come get it right away. The Ambulance drivers wouldn't take her. They called the funeral parlor, so we had to wait even longer. I went to our neighbor Dee's. I didn't know what to do. I only knew I couldn't be in that house with that dead body. It totally freaked me out.

*If I only knew then what I know now, I would have embraced that dead body and sent the luminous body up to the White Light of God. I would have prayed and done a ceremony for her. I would have embraced my Mom and told her I loved her. I regret that I was so cold and ignorant of what life and death were all about that I did not carry her to the Light that day. Please forgive my ignorance, Mom; I do Love you. I thank you for the life you have given me. I thank you for all you have done for me. I know now all that you have sacrificed for me. It makes me wonder. Why did things have to happen like this?*

*If my mother died now, I would have been such a different person. I would have embraced our differences. I would have treated her with respect and love. I would have done for her as a daughter should have. God Forgive me for what I have done.*

The next day, Al called the woman about the puppy and said we couldn't take him. My life had turned upside down. We had to deal with the house full of mom's stuff. We had to deal with the undertaker, the funeral, and all the things that go along with it. Thank God for Al and Aunty Irene. I was not much help with any of this. They took over and made all of the decisions. I was in a fog.

At the funeral, people came from all over. Everyone loved my Mom. There were cousins I hadn't seen in many years. There were lots of strangers introducing themselves to me, saying who they were and how they knew my mom. I just stood there in a daze, hugging and letting everyone kiss me on the cheek. I can still see the dress I had on, but the rest was a blur.

The day after the funeral, Mark and his wife Mary came to visit. I was upset that Al & Marco were so late for dinner. We began to eat without them when Marco ran into the house and handed me a puppy. He was so cute. He was a fawn 'Boxer'. Al & Marco had driven to New Hampshire to pick up the exact puppy we had picked out last week. We named him Mack. Mack thought Dukie was his mother. They would cuddle up together. As Mack got older, he was so intelligent he would go round up Dukie when he'd wander. I could tell him to "go get daddy," and sure enough, here they'd come. We never had to tie him. He was so smart. He knew things without speaking. He could communicate with you better than someone who talked! I think it was Mack's intelligence that made every dog near him look stupid.

# Arizona #1

My buddy Monique lived in Florida and had a job writing for a hockey magazine, so we often combined hockey with vacation. She called me from Arizona one day and said her boss gave her an extra week in Phoenix with a car as a bonus. She added, "Can you join me?" Al was such a peach and said, "Go, enjoy!" Within three hours, I was packed and on that plane. She was waiting for me at the airport. Everything happened so fast my mind didn't have time to catch up to what my body had just done! It felt as if I was dreaming. We jumped in the car, giggling and talking about how there was nothing to do in Phoenix, so we drove to Sedona, and the Grand Canyon.

I remember driving up that long road to the Grand Canyon; it was so dark. I kept saying, "Where's this *Canyon* everyone's talking about!" We got to the hotel, and there were only dim lights in their parking lot. I couldn't see beyond them. Everything outside was pitch black. Monique said, Eliz, go to bed; we'll find it in the morning." Good thing I stayed in the room that night. If I had ventured another ten feet from the hotel door, I'd have fallen 5,000 feet down! The Grand Canyon was literally RIGHT THERE!

In the morning, we hiked down into the canyon on the South rim. Every rock I touched talked to me. I felt as if I had fallen into the history of ancient days. I felt as if I was one with each particle of sand. Something was really happening, and It was beyond amazing Each time I closed my eyes, I could see beings that had crossed over. They began communicating with me, and I understood the details they were describing. "History written in the books is not always accurate," a young Indian man with a long braid described to me. He said, "We will show you when the time is right." It was amazing. How could I tell Monique? She surely would think I was nuts.

The trail was no bigger than three feet in width, and every time the mules needed to get by, you had to get out of the way! Many times, there was nowhere to go, so you'd squish your body up against the wall of the canyon, never going to the outside side where you could so easily slip way down below! I couldn't get over the fact that there were no railings and people didn't watch their little kids! I thought for sure a little one would have gotten killed in there! Later, we found out that really does happen; a guide told us people die all the time. What a beautiful yet dangerous place. One of these days, I'd love to take the mule trip to the bottom of the canyon; they say you can stay overnight, too!

It was recommended to spend at least twenty-four hours there because of the sun coming up at different times makes the walls of the canyon change color from purple to orange to beautiful red colors. I've seen pictures before but never like this. From the very first moment I laid eyes on the canyon, I felt as if I was an ant that had stepped into a humongous painting! The glory of this place is beyond words. It is truly God's work. I never dreamed this would be so beautiful. The colors are so vibrant; pictures, for sure, do not do it justice.

On our way back to Sedona, we hiked up to the top of the Red Rocks. I had heard that these rocks are "energy vortexes" of the world. Although I did not know exactly what it meant, I wanted to experience it firsthand. We climbed up as high as we could, and then we just sat there to take a rest. This is when it happened. My spine began to vibrate from my tailbone up to my sacrum, then higher and higher past my neck up to my skull. It was an amazing feeling I did not want to stop. Monique felt it, too. We just sat there until the sun started going down. Without a flashlight, we were forced to leave. We went back the next day at sunrise to do the same thing. We stayed there as long as we could. It was amazing. I couldn't explain what happened; I only knew I wanted more. It felt so good, as if my spine was heated and vibrating on the inside. We had two days in Sedona before we had to drive back to Phoenix. I knew I'd be back there again.

# Arizona Again

On one of my trips back, I dragged Al, kicking and screaming, to Arizona. He said he couldn't take time away from his job, blah blah blah… He was now Vice President and part owner of the Company. I didn't care; he had to see this! He was always on the phone with work, and the stewardess had to tell him to turn off his phone for the plane to take off! I knew I had to make this trip short, so we went on the long Columbus Day weekend in October, three nights and four days.

We landed in Phoenix, rented a car, and then stopped at Walgreens to get a cooler. We filled it with ice and drinks, then headed straight up to Sedona. As soon as we got to Bell Rock, we pulled over and climbed up to say a little prayer. I thanked God and the land for bringing me back there. I made Al sit there and see if he felt what I did. He said "NO". I had him sit a bit longer, "do you feel anything now?" I asked. "No," he said. I kept asking, "Don't you feel that?" My whole being was vibrating; it was like euphoria. Two hours later, he said, are you done yet? I realized I could not push it, so we went to check into the hotel. Once we unpacked, he asked if we could climb another one of those red rocks. Ok, I thought, *now* we're on to something.

The next day, we drove up 89A to the Grand Canyon. When Al first saw the Canyon, it was 3:00 in the afternoon. He began running down Bright Angel trail towards the base of the canyon. I got nervous and said, Al, remember what they said: one hour down is two hours back up! He said, "I'm fine." I could NOT keep up with him. He was running so fast. It was getting dark, and there were NO lights out there! I began climbing back up, and of course, Al was more physically fit than I was. He passed me and said, "Come on, don't let the mules get in front of you!" I said, "I don't care if they shit on my shoes! I am climbing as fast as I can." Sure enough, the mules passed me. I was out of breath, leaning up against the dirt wall of the side of the path. I began to pray, asking God to help me get up the canyon. I saw a Buffalo and surrendered. Next thing I knew, I was at the top of the canyon. I don't even know how it happened; it was like *poof,* "in the blink of an eye." One minute, I was far down below in a panic, and the next, I was on top of the trail with Al. This was my first experience with a power animal; the strength of the Buffalo surely came in and took over without a doubt.

We spent the night at a hotel near the rim. I rose with the sun and opened our hotel door to find a bunch of baby deer standing right there. There were so many of them we couldn't believe it. They were not afraid of people. Even though there were signs saying don't feed the deer, it was obvious that people did.

We headed to the airport and found the helicopter rides were $150 per person & Al thought it was too much! By agreeing to stay behind and read a book because *I had already been before*, Al agreed to go without me. I had given the woman my credit card number, and just before the helicopter took off, I told her to double it & I jumped into the chopper. Al couldn't argue as we flew off; he just shook his head.

Regulations had changed just weeks prior to this that now prohibited helicopters from flying below the rim of the canyon. Our pilot was against those rules & agreed to dip far into the canyon for us to get spectacular pictures. He kept saying, "If you were here last week, it would be like this!" The experience was beyond words. I expected to get a song & dance for spending the extra $150, but all I got was smiles.

I knew one day Al would like to meet the Hopi Elders; ancient history is in his blood. I was also told that you needed an escort to go on to an Indian reservation. So, I made arrangements for Ms. White-cloud to take us there. The base price was $500 for her to guide both of us all the way up and back to the Hopi Elders. We met her in the morning, and she jumped in our car. We stopped at a market and filled our trunk with groceries, water, and gifts for Grandfather Martin and his family before driving up to his home. We were told that some of the "young bucks" (younger tribe members) were fighting with the elders. They locked the water tower, and food was scarce. Before we got to our destination, she took us to a small neighborhood and introduced us to all her friends on Second Mesa. Their artwork was beautiful, but their stories were so sad. I wanted to give them my wallet; I felt so guilty for having such a good life.

I couldn't believe that our government had given these people land that had absolutely nothing on it. I had never seen the true meaning of barren land before. There were tiny little clumps of dry grass approximately every three feet. The rest was all dry dirt, and they call this land? Nothing could be planted here; nothing grows! Wow. There was not a tree in sight, and you could see for miles! I was ashamed of what our forefathers did to these beautiful Native people. What a shame. I wish I could change that.

Finally, we were able to meet Grandfather Martin, his wife, Grandmother Mina, and his grandchildren. They welcomed us with open arms. Al and he spoke about many things. Grandfather brought out parchment papers with drawings on them. Al and he were discussing these drawings, and I didn't know what they were talking about. We were there for over eight hours. Some of it was over my head, some of it I could understand, like when they spoke of Moses and Jesus, and the wars, and what is to come. We were there so long that I couldn't focus on their conversation the whole time. I was drifting in and out of consciousness. It felt as if I was on another planet. Something was happening to me that I couldn't explain. My body was vibrating again.

It was there, on Second Mesa that Grandfather told me, "I was to be a healer *if I choose to accept what God has planned for me.* He said

I would be put through a "QUICKENING; learning very much—very quickly, once I agreed to follow my path." I thought, 'this guy must be nuts. I'm a Welder!'

*Little did I know how true his words would ring! This trip was less than one year before I began studying Shamanism!*

We thanked Grandfather and his family, and Ms. White-cloud drove back with us to Sedona. I realized what a great thing it is that she does here, escorting people to the Hopi Elders. I was humbled and grateful that I could give her money because now I know where it is going. I only wished I had more to give.

We spent two more days in Sedona climbing one red rock after another before we had to fly home. Al never said he got that "feeling" that I get when I sit on the red rocks. All I know is he *did* want to keep going up there to sit. That's good enough for me.

On the plane ride home, Al said, "You know, Elizabeth, I really didn't want to do this, but now I can honestly say it was amazing. I didn't expect it to be this good. If you want, when we retire, we can live six months here and six months at home". Now, that is something serious to think about. Could I, or would I ever live anywhere but Rhode Island?

Since returning from Arizona, I began to enjoy the energy at the Plant. On Lunch and breaks, I'd spend time with my hands on the generator. The vibrations of this enormous equipment would fill my being with a song that reverberated throughout my body. It seemed to awaken the energy in me that was awakened on the red rocks of Sedona. Those vibrations were feeding my Soul. I would talk with the Generator in my mind, asking it to send "good vibrations" out to every home it touched. Sending a prayer with it for the good of all, I was unaware of the magnitude of these prayers. It just felt like it was the right thing to do. My connection with God was stronger; I knew there was more to life than I was taught in every school I ever attended. There was something that we were not being told; I had a glimpse of it, and I wanted more.

# White Water Rafting

Monique and I planned to meet in Denver, Colorado, for a White-Water Rafting adventure. We only had one weekend to accomplish this because we were both working so much. She was flying from Orlando, and I was flying out of Boston.

Something was wrong. I couldn't pinpoint it. My plane was delayed twelve hours. I was supposed to leave at 11 am, and finally, at 11 pm, we were boarding the plane. I noticed a drunken man, maybe in his late twenties, with a dirty grayish-white tee shirt, long, greasy hair, and filthy pants boarding the plane. He looked like a street bum and was very loud and obnoxious.

When the plane took off, he was sitting one row in front of me on my right. He vomited on two women sitting next to him. I could see them jump up screaming while rushing to the lavatory. The smell was overpowering. I thought the flight attendants should do something Quick! One ran up, threw a 'barf bag' at him, and then disappeared. It was horrible.

We landed in Chicago. I was expecting to find my connecting flight when we were informed that our flight had been canceled. It was 1:30 am. Thank God for Cell phones. Monique was at the hotel in Colorado waiting for me. I had reserved the room on *my* credit card, and the hotel was booked! I finally gave them information over the phone so she could get the room and sleep.

There was a church group with children who were also stranded. We were all in an airport without food, drink, or a place to stay and no attendant to help. The airport was closed! I ranted and raved about getting my luggage and finally found a security guard who helped me find it in a back room. With luggage in hand, we were guided to a limo that seated 8—there were 18 of us. We all piled in, and I had a stranger sitting on my lap! I didn't care; I was not getting out of that limo! They took us to another airport in Chicago for a connecting flight.

What they neglected to tell us was that the airport was also closed. A security guard gave me a cart, pillow, and blanket and told me to sleep. What?! I was scared shit! The airport looked like it was a refugee camp. I was so naive and, of course, being the material girl that I am—had on my spike hi-heels, dressy dress, and wearing my best jewelry! I was seriously scared. I began praying! After an hour, the guards came to take the carts, saying they had to clean up the airport for opening; it was only 4 am! I went to the ATA counter and sat on the floor, waiting for them to open. When they finally opened at 5 am, I expected to get on the 1st flight out of there. I was informed that all the flights were full and that I would be put on standby. I couldn't believe it! I called Al—screaming—"Do something! You must have connections!! They can't do this to me!" I thought, surely, they HAD to put you up in a hotel! I thought surely, they HAD to give you food, vouchers or SOMETHING!!! What are all those fancy private rooms for? They treated us like cattle. They should have done something! We paid good money for these tickets! No-one cared! They got our money and couldn't care less about us!

I finally arrived in Colorado at 3 pm on Saturday. (Monique and I were supposed to go white water rafting at nine that morning.) As soon as I walked out of the airport to summon a taxi, a man came up to me, telling me he had my taxi. Totally exhausted, I jumped in his car. "Hi," he said. "My name is Tony. I'm sorry you were delayed, but I was unable to pick you up yesterday—I have a message for you." Shocked and not knowing what on earth he was talking about, something urged me to pull out my notebook and start writing. I didn't even know why. I just wrote.

He explained that he was a Ute Indian and had messages for me, and one day, I would go back there (when I could take the bite of a rattlesnake), and he would take me up to Ute Mountain. His message was much like the Hopi Elders had told me in Arizona. I was mesmerized but somehow *knew* he was right. He told me things about my past that he couldn't have known. About my adoption, my dad, my life, and how it was all about to change, he explained that I was a great Healer and my powers were just under the surface. He said many magical events would take place to give me what I needed to put me in the right place at the right time. Totally blown away, I took his information and thanked him, not even knowing if I was still here on earth. It was beyond anything I'd ever felt or heard before. There was a knowing, a knowing that I knew his words were true. I felt it in every core of my being. It was as real as the hand at the end of my arm.

Tony dropped me off at the hotel with a hug as if we had been old friends for many years. He did not charge me. He said my service to the world was payment enough, and he was honored to be able to be a part of it.

I got to the hotel room, and Monique was still sleeping. I banged and banged on the door. It took a half hour to get her to open the door! She had arranged for us to go rafting on Sunday, so our trip was not a complete loss. I told her what happened in the taxi, and she thought I was nuts.

White water rafting is an experience everyone should try. I certainly thought I was stronger than Monique, and if she could do it, then surely I could. Oh My God, I held on for dear life! There was an introductory safety course before getting on the raft in the water, stressing how important it is to HOLD ON TO THAT OAR. Once we got into the rubber boat, I held on so tightly you couldn't pry my hands off it.

Monique was very relaxed. Each time she took off her helmet, swinging her hair in the wind, the guide would bonk her on the head with the oar. He continued stressing how important it was to keep your helmet on. It was so funny! Then the guy sitting in front of me seemed to have butter on his ass. Every time we went over a wave, he slid off the seat and bounced right into my lap! At lunch break, a couple of lovebird honeymooners tried to venture off to be alone when they both fell down an embankment into a cactus bush. The rest of the lunch period was spent picking (cactus) prickers out of their asses. Romantic, eh?

White water rafting was in Canyon City, Colorado, and quite a haul to Denver, but we made it back just in time to catch our flights home. Monique caught her flight to Florida. Finally, on my plane, I was so exhausted as I plopped into my seat heading back to Providence. I fell fast asleep.

Forty-five minutes later, I woke up. We were on the ground. I asked the woman next to me what happened, "Why did we land?" She said, "Honey, land? We're still waiting to take off!" Oh My God. All I could think about was the horrific experience I had Friday night trying to get *to* Colorado! I went into a total panic! I kept thinking, "Get me out of here. I've got A.T.A. a-phobia!"

I ran to the front and demanded to get off the plane! Ironically, it took them one minute to find my luggage. Here I was, back in the airport with luggage in hand—*without* a ticket to—anywhere! What *was* I thinking? It cost me SIX more hours and $1100.00 just to fly home with another airline. Lesson learned = THINK long & hard BEFORE YOU ACT. *After further investigation, we found that the plane never made it back to Boston. I'm really happy I listened to my intuition!*

# Corvette

One of the guys at the Plant had a very severe accident. It could have been me. I had been working right next to him all week. A 600 Volt switch gear blew up! He was only 27 years old. Brian was one of the best electricians in the gang. He was called to fix the switchgear because it kept getting wet from a temporary pipeline leaking overhead. You see, they were getting ready for the 're-powering' of the power plant. Temporary revisions were taking place. A six-inch water pipe ran overhead and continued to drip down into the basement onto this electrical switchgear. Each time the switchgear would trip, it would be turned off, isolated, dried, and repaired. This time, when they re-energized it, it held for five minutes. Everyone thought it was clear, so they began to clean up the work area. This is when it blew! Brian was the closest to the explosion and burned 33% of his body! He almost didn't make it. He was in the hospital for over six months.

This was another turning point in my life. I realized how valuable life is and how it can change in a minute! With mom just passing and now Brian's accident… this made me think differently about many things. I looked at everything differently.

At this point in my life, I became so *materialistic* I had our financial advisor crying, especially on the day I told him I bought *my own* Corvette. You see, Al and I went half on a 1979 Stingray somewhere around 1990. Then we went to a Corvette show in Carlisle, Pennsylvania, with our friends Rondelle and Dave. They had a beautiful Black and Red 1964 Stingray convertible. Al and Dave combed that fairground with a fine-tooth comb; as Mom would say, they didn't miss a thing. When we walked by a white 1964 Corvette Stingray convertible with a red hood scoop, Al began to stare. He circled the car once, then twice. I knew we were in trouble when he and Dave went under the car with flashlights and mirrors. I didn't care. I was making the big bucks and was used to getting anything I wanted; why shouldn't he? Yes, it was on a Sunday. We purchased the car using three credit cards just to get it home.

I drove the '79 Vette while Al drove the '64 in front of me, and Dave drove his '64 behind me. It was great until the rain came pouring down so hard it took us eleven hours to get back home. I'll never forget that ride. I learned the true meaning of the word "hydroplane" because I spun around three times, and I was only going 40 mph! We finally got home, and within a week, the '79 was sold; this was fine. We went half on the '64. Or so I thought…

One beautiful fall day, exactly one month after returning home. I jumped in the '64 and was backing it out of the driveway. Al came flying out of the house, jumped in the car, and frantically said, "Where are you going?" I said, "I'm taking the car for a ride." He freaked "NOOOOOOOOOOO"! I said, "I *thought* we went *half* on this car." Ah, he said, "*Your* half is the passenger side!" Seriously!!! I *DON'T* THINK SO. He should have never put me to the test.

The very next day, I called my cousin Danny (He owned a Chevrolet dealership). I told him I wanted my OWN Car, a car that makes me go, "Wow." He said he'd look and call me when he had one. The first call came in for a 1992 black Corvette with a black ragtop. I took it for a ride and went home to think about it. Danny called me to tell me I left my pocketbook in the passenger side of that car and he'd get it to me.

*The moral of this story is if the car keeps your pocketbook, chances are you're going to lose a lot of money! As life went on, I would soon see how important symbols are and what they mean. This was one symbol I did not pay attention to. Although I declined the black car, it was obvious that it was NOT the "Wow" car. I still didn't pay attention to the symbol that would ultimately cost me a bundle.*

Within a few days, Danny had my dream car. When he called, I was welding at the power plant. Danny said, "Hey, Eliz, I found it; she's a beauty!" Within one hour, I was driving that beauty of a car down Metacom Avenue when the police pulled me over. In the excitement, I hadn't waited for Danny to put a dealer plate on the car before taking off on a joy ride. I got a police escort back to the dealership. You had to see Danny's face! I did have the *"I love Lucy"* reputation even with family. Danny just shook his head with a grin.

YES! She was a beauty! She was a six-speed, 1992 white Corvette with a red interior, black rag top, console, and dash. She even had an extra white hard top for chilly days. What a classy car! Sign right here on the dotted line! Oh, MY God! What did I do? I just signed a loan for $36,000.00!!! I didn't care. Nothing mattered. Life was short, and I believed you had to do whatever made you happy, especially after my Mom died and what just happened to Brian. I mean, that *could* have been me! This was the thing that made me go, "*Wow.*" I wanted it, and I got it. You should have seen Al's face when I drove it home. I got the lecture of all lectures about saving money for our future… blah blah blah. It went in one ear and out the other.

# Intro to Shamanism

As with all big businesses, the Electric Company was no different. They were on a mission to do more work with fewer people. We were once a huge company that employed more than forty-five people in the Mechanical department, and now we have five.

It was a cold winter morning, and no one had plowed or shoveled any paths. The company had cut back so much. No one sanded the parking lot or paths like we used to when it snowed. In my opinion, people have become bitter because they don't even respond when the Company calls them in for overtime. Those days have gone. The employees have become very selfish—it's now every man for himself. The snow had fallen on top of sheets of ice.

This particular day, our welding job was outside and, of course, another 'rush' job. I was carrying more than my fair share of welding supplies when—Ka'Plow! There I went, flying—up in the air and twisting my body before crashing down and banging my head. I fractured L4 and L5 with bulging discs on L4, 5 and 6.

I was out of work and in severe pain for ten months. I was literally crawling out of bed to reach the bathroom each morning. I went to doctors all over New England, with the most intense procedures being done at Massachusetts General Hospital. Finally, the Ultimate Pain Clinic unsuccessfully injected me with huge needles. Dr. Onofrio told me that surgery would be a 50/50 chance that I could end up in a wheelchair. *What?* I would be nuts to take those odds. The pain was constant and interfered with all parts of my life. I wasn't meant to be in a wheelchair! Something must be wrong!

Driving home after this meeting with the Doctor, Al handed me a magazine to distract me from crying. It had an Advertisement for

Shiatsu'. I didn't know what it was but felt compelled to call for a session. A very nice woman answered the phone and explained the first visit was $90.00. *WHAT?!?!?!* I have health insurance. I couldn't justify spending all that money for my health when I had a $5 co-pay. I hung up the phone in the kitchen, crying again at the lack of choices I had, when Al opened the door to the Garage. I could see my car right there, not six feet away as I thought… 'I can't drive my Corvette. I can't even get in it! I am willing to spend THAT much money to fix my back!'

Shiatsu is a Japanese acupressure massage, and it is quite wonderful. Nancy, the practitioner, worked on me for two hours at a time. She had me walking normally within six weeks and continued to work on me to remove the pain. After three months, she said, "We've come a long way, but I think you really need to see a friend of mine, Judy." I made an appointment with Judy immediately because Nancy helped me so much.

When I walked into Judy's office, there was a fuzzy rug on the floor, feathers on the wall, and several colored clothes on a table. There was a sweet smell I couldn't identify. Judy told me to lie on the floor. I said Lady, if I get on the floor, I may not be able to get up, she assured me, "I'll help you." As I was lying on this long-haired fuzzy rug (later, I'd find out it was an Alpaca), she shook a rattle over me, said some words in a language I didn't recognize, and sprayed something all over me from out of her mouth. Then she said, "Stand up. How does that feel?" I had NO pain! The pain was gone… completely!

I said, "Lady, I don't know who you are or what the F--- you just did, but I gotta learn that shit!" She was less than impressed with my choice of words but realized working as a welder; I had earned the *cursed* mouth. She said, "Honey, first, you learn new vocabulary; then I will teach you"! I immediately began studying Shamanism with her from that very weekend.

I thought… 'No one ever has to be in pain again; when I learn this—I can fix the world!'

*This was the beginning of a mentorship that turned into the deepest friendship two women can have. Our conversations are never mundane and always level up to the most magnificent ~ enlightenment. I can't ever thank Judy enough for all she has taught me. I am forever grateful for her wise words of wisdom.*

# Bull

We knew Dukie was getting older; he was now twelve years old and showing his age. We didn't want Mack to be alone, so it was time to look for another dog.

Marco, Al, and I were in the car, sitting at a red light in Smithfield. At the same time, we all said, "LOOK!" We saw this dog looking out of the window in the car next to us. His head was huge. He was so unique! It was an *American* Bulldog. Al was on a mission to find one. Within days, we were at a breeder picking up a puppy. He was the cutest brindle puppy with half white on his head and his paw in his water bowl. We took him home and named him "BULL."

(The ironic thing was that Dukie had been sluggish the past year and would often lie around. After we brought Bull home, Dukie came back to life—chasing the puppy and stealing his toys for over two years before he had a stroke and passed.)

While at a Shiatsu session, Nancy told me I should have a mammogram. She sensed something was going on. She was good at reading energy and felt there may be a problem just by what she sensed. I was new to understanding that people could actually read energy and find such things. I went to my doctor to have this checked. Nancy was right. Within a week, I was scheduled for a biopsy.

At the same time, Al's father had open heart surgery at RI Hospital. Doctor Singh told the family, "He's eighty years old. Let's send him home, make him comfortable with morphine," and basically wait for him to die. My sister-in-law contacted her dad's surgeon in Boston and faxed records to him, and within an hour, Dad was in a rescue squad headed to Boston for open heart surgery.

Because of this incident with Dad, I wasn't going to take any chances in RI. I headed up to the Brigham and Women's Hospital, the best breast clinic in the USA. The doctor was a peach and thought I was a riot because I was always making jokes. He finally agreed to perform surgery without anesthetic and let me take flower essences for pain. I had surgery and calmed the pain by taking my herbal remedy. The only problem was that I talked through the whole surgery. I had all the nurses laughing and even made the nurse take the lump out to the waiting room to show Al what I had "just given birth to." I had to make fun of it all; I was so scared! A few days later, pathology results came back, and I was diagnosed with cancer. The doctor called me at home and said we had no time to waste; we must schedule the second surgery right away. We picked a date, and the second surgery was in two weeks.

I called Judy to tell her I was going in for another surgery. She said, "Come over. We need to talk." She again did that spray thing with her mouth and a few other movements, which had me wondering what she was doing. Then I went to see Nancy, and she had me put an obsidian rock in my bra and said more prayers, asking the rock to remove the poison in my body. In the morning, I had to pray with the rock as I ran it under cold water, praying that the toxins would go to a place that did no harm. I had to continue my herbal remedy and add essential oils to this ritual faithfully every day. Even though it was weird, I would have done anything Judy and Nancy said; after all, they helped me so much, and Judy really created a miracle with my back pain!

On the day of the second surgery, I had a nurse write on my breast with a big arrow saying, "Cut that boob," pointing to the right one, and another note saying, "Remember *dimple*-NO-DENT"! It was a joke I had going with the Doctor about not deforming me! This time, it was major surgery; they were going back in to remove ALL traces of cancer and do a complete mastectomy if needed. I even had a plastic surgeon on hand, just in case. When I was in recovery, I can remember waking up, trying to look to see if my breast was still there. (The bandage seemed huge; I was so scared.) When the Doctor came in, he said, "Ah, Mrs. D, I'm really sorry we must have made a mistake. There was NOTHING there. I'm so sorry for putting you through all this."

It was amazing. The cancer was completely gone!

*"We must have made a mistake" became a phrase I'd get used to in the Shamanic/Spiritual Healing arena; it often happens when doctors can't describe how healing miracles take place. I'm so blessed to have been a witness to these miracles over and over through the years.*

During the whole recovery time at home, Bull never left my side. I swear he thought his sole purpose in life was to protect me. He was my "Velcro dog". Later on, if Al would rough-house me, fooling around, Bull would try to nip him in the butt. He was my special dog. As a puppy, he was really calm. I kept telling the Vet something was wrong. He doesn't play like a puppy. They kept telling me he had leg aches because his bones were growing faster than his muscles, and vice-versa. When he was one year old, we took him to the vet to be neutered. I insisted on a set of X-rays on his hips. They told me he had hip dysplasia so bad he probably wouldn't live to be three years old.

*Bull was one of my best clients. I practiced all of my healing techniques, starting with Reiki. He loved it! And I'm sure that is why he lived to be almost ten years old!*

# Reiki

Nancy called and said she was having her friend teach a class called "Reiki." Hands-on-healing, I was told. I witnessed miracles with Nancy and Judy's healing work, so I signed up for this class. At work, I was telling my buddy Lucy about it, and my supervisor, Joe, overheard me. Later, at the copy machine, Joe asked if he could join this class. I thought it was funny that he was so secretive about it, but I respected his privacy and called Nancy later from home to sign him up.

At her house, Joe and I sat in chairs in a circle with six other students. The teacher did this prayer over us one at a time. My head and hands began to tingle and vibrate. I thought this was really weird and couldn't wait to know more about it. This was what they call an attunement. They explained that attunement is teaching your body to recognize the vibrations from the Universal Life Force, which is actually God's healing energy flowing through you.

I thought, "What on earth is Universal Life Force?" In class, I asked the question. The answer I got was "Creator". I said, "Creator? As in GOD Creator?" They said yes. "Wow," I thought, "why are they afraid to say the word "GOD"? I didn't understand this. I have always had a special connection to God. I mean, that is where I come from, and that's where I'm going when I'm done here on earth. Why wouldn't they just say God? So, I asked again. The answer was, "We use Creator so as not to offend anyone. Creator appeals to all religions." Hmmm, this is something I had to think about. I never thought the word God was ever offensive. I mean, if someone said Jehovah to me, I wouldn't be offended; that is their word for God. I can respect that. There is just too much political correctness in the world and not enough respect. It still pisses me off to think they won't let God in Schools; maybe if we had God in school, there would be more respect and less murder!

In an attunement, the Reiki healing vibrations are transmitted from Teacher to Student by what I call a prayer. They call it something else: an Attunement. Basically, it is just that: a prayer. Call it what you will. I liked it a lot and practiced on Bull, my plants, and situations that got better with every prayer!

Nancy was giving Shiatsu sessions at the park in Newport for the Japanese Black Ships Festival and asked me to come to do Reiki. I asked, "Me? I don't think I can do this—*touch a stranger?*" She convinced me it was the best practice to just do it, so I joined her at the festival.

It was my first time doing Reiki on strangers. Reiki is a session that is performed with the client fully clothed and lying on a massage table. You place your hands on their head, then in various positions as you connect up to God (act like a conduit) and, as teachers say, "get-outa-the-way" to let the Reiki—healing energy flow through you to the client. Reiki energy goes to where it is needed. At the very least, the client feels balanced and totally relaxed. Since then, I have seen it create miracles when performed in Prayer. Reiki energy transmitted with true Unconditional Love is truly God's work. I am blessed to be a conduit for God's healing energy to flow.

I remember my first client. An older Japanese man jumped on the table and said, "Reiki me." When I was done, he hugged me and thanked me for *"the most amazing energy healing he ever had."* He was so nice! Later, I found out he was the director of the whole festival. He knew Reiki, and his comment to me led me to have confidence that I was doing it right. What a blessing. Since that day, I Reiki'd everything I could get my hands on. The dog, Al, my plants, even the birds and deer in the yard and watched the healings happen.

Two weeks after the Black Ships Festival, Judy called to say she was teaching Reiki 1 and Reiki 2 next Saturday. *Would I be interested?* Interested? I was so excited I practically jumped through the phone.

There were ten students in the class. We started with textbook information. Then she had us lie down while she did an Attunement on each of us. When she touched the top of my head, my crown chakra, I saw a rainbow of colors swirling over me. My whole body began to tingle. It was like nothing I had ever felt before. I didn't know exactly what it was doing, but I knew I LIKED IT. I liked it a lot. After the lunch break, she explained these energies. We would harness and use them for healing, not just ourselves and other people, but situations as well. It was amazing. It totally changed my life. She said there would be a 21-day adjustment period for our body to integrate the Energies.

Immediately after the attunement, I could smell everything, I could hear better, the food tasted so much better, and even my sight, my eyes seemed to see everything with clarity and brighter colors. When we practiced hand positions on each other, I could even feel the energy. It was amazing as if I was shown life with a better enthusiasm. It was difficult to put into words. I was very inspired.

The next Saturday we went to a wedding. Ut oh, I couldn't NOT drink alcohol. Not even a shot glass of wine. Two sips knocked me on my ass. After my Reiki attunement, my Body went through many changes: Physically, Mentally, Emotionally, and Spiritually. I was super sensitive to everything in a good way.

# Bio Mom

After Marco was born with platinum-blonde hair and sky-blue eyes, I wondered where he came from. Everyone on Al's side had light hair but not *that* blonde! And all of them had dark eyes except his mom, but even she did not have sky-blue eyes. My hair was very dark, and my eyes were very dark brown. Marco did look exactly like my Grandpa when he was born; however, that was my Grandpa in the family that adopted me, and there were no blood relations.

My friend Rondelle and I were talking about things in the world that didn't make sense. This was around 1992. We talked about how much I wanted to increase my intuition. She spoke of her friend Tony, who had a gift, and said he was a really good psychic; I should go see him. I loved and respected Rondelle, so I made the appointment. Tony was an older man who lived in a retirement community. Not many people knew he was a "psychic," so discretion was a must. When I went to visit, a neighbor was looking out her door. Tony greeted me as his niece who came to visit. He asked if I wanted a cup of tea, and we sat at the kitchen table while he shuffled cards. He asked me to write my name, then some numbers and colors as he explained he didn't read the cards; they were to only prove what he was saying was accurate because he read from my handwriting on the pad.

He told me I was adopted, my adoption father was *accused* of committing suicide, and if I wanted to know more about my biological mother, I should go to the RI Historical Society on Brook St. in Providence. He gave me names to look up with street addresses in the late 1950s and '60s. He told me my bio-mom's name was Teresa, and she got married three years after my birth. I paid him the $50.00 for the reading and left. I sat in the parking lot in awe.

Rondelle did not even know I was adopted. We had never talked about it because we had only been friends for a year. It wasn't that I was trying to hide it; it was just so far out of our conversations that I never thought to bring it up. Now I'm really shocked by the information Tony said. Wow, I wondered if it was true. I really didn't know much about my bio-mom, especially not her name. I was so blown away by this information I wrote it all down and stashed it away for another day. It was too much to deal with just now.

A couple of years went by. My uncle Sonni (an alcoholic physical therapist living in Puerto Rico) called to say I should know about my bio-mom. He said her name was Teresa, and my Uncle Mike used to work with her. He also said he didn't know anymore. I called Uncle Mike. He said he didn't know what Sonni was talking about, "he must be drunk." This coincidence of the names gave me enough curiosity to go to the RI Historical Society and look up what the psychic Tony had said. Interestingly enough, I did find Teresa, her last name, of Silver Lake in Providence, Rhode Island, and both her parents' obituaries with the list of all their siblings. I also found that Teresa married H.M. three years after my birth. I shared all of this with Al and filed it away. It was, again, way too much to handle at this time.

When I finally decided to check into this, Al said, "I'll make the call; this way, if she doesn't want to talk with you, I'll be able to help." He called a phone number that we found with that name in our local phone book, and it ended up being a male cousin. When he answered the phone, Al said, "I'm looking for Teresa ---." The man said, "Why do you want Teresa?" Al said, "It's private. We need to talk with Teresa." The man got huffy on the phone, and there were a lot more words, and then Al said, "She might be my wife's mother!" and hung up. I thought! Oh No! That is NOT what we wanted to do. What if she didn't want to know me? I want to give her the opportunity to be discreet!

A few minutes later, our phone rang, and it was a young woman who said, "This is Teresa's niece. My brother told me what you said, and we want to help. (This was at the time when 'Caller ID' was brand new. We didn't even know we had that.) Within a minute, the phone rang again, and this time it was an older woman with a deep, raspy voice, and she said, "We don't know no Teresa, and Teresa don't want to know you! Don't call here again!" and she hung up.

I said to Al, "Bingo! We got the right family, and *that woman knows all about my birth!*"

That was probably around 1995.

When I was telling Aunty Irene about this, we all laughed and said we don't need another family; they're probably dysfunctional just like ours, and we laughed and laughed.

Two weeks before Christmas 1997, Al came into the house from getting the mail. He had a small envelope, which he opened and handed to me, saying, "Elizabeth, what is this?" The writing on the front of the envelope looked like a child wrote it, and it was addressed to him with our address. Inside was a small piece of paper with the name Teresa ---- and her address, in Warwick, RI. Then underneath it said "Gaspee Point," a neighborhood in Warwick. Al looked at me and asked, "What's this"? I said, "Oh my God! That's my biological mother's name". He said, "What do you want to do"? As I took the paper to my Mesa/ Prayer Altar, I said, "Let me meditate on it and see what I get."

By this time, I had been meditating and receiving clear communication with God's guidance. I connected with God, filled myself with the light of the Holy Spirit, and Anchored the light through me and into Earth, just as I always do to ensure a pure connection to God; then I began to ask questions, and God showed me the answers.

First, I understood, "There was no phone number; do not call; you must go there." It was a beautiful, sunny Saturday morning. I came back out to the kitchen and said to Al, "We must go there."

Al said, "Are YOU sure? I support anything you want to do. Are you sure?" I said, "Yes, we must go."

So, we jumped in the car and drove as I continued to *pray to God, asking God to give me a sign* that we were doing the right thing. On Warwick Avenue, Al said, "Ooh! I gotta go to the bathroom," as he pulled into Wendy's burger place. I thought I might as well go, too. We don't know what this day will entail. As I opened the door, right there in front of me was a five-foot by three-foot sign saying, "Dave Thomas Supports Adoption." OH MY GOD! A SIGN! AS BIG AS ME ~ RIGHT THERE STARING ME IN THE FACE!!!

My prayer had been answered. I asked for a sign, and we got a physical sign ~ I *knew* we were doing the right thing.

We proceeded to a tiny house in Gaspee Point. I rang the doorbell, and this sweet man answered the door. I immediately thought (he may not know about me because they got married three years after my birth, so be discreet) I said: "Is Teresa here?" He said wait a minute, "Teresa, someone is here to see you." This woman came into the kitchen, and I was shocked. She looked so much like my mother, Jennie, who raised me from birth, her body shape, hairstyle, glasses, and even her mannerisms. It could have been my mom, Jennie, standing right there.

I had the envelope in my hand, and I said, "Hi Teresa, my name is Elizabeth, this is my husband, Al; did you send me this?" As I gave her the envelope, she looked at it and said, "Why, no, they spelled my name wrong. We don't dance," as she laughed. (There was a famous dance studio with the same last name as her but spelled differently).

In my head, I was screaming for God to help me, to put the proper words in my mouth because I didn't know what to say. When I opened my mouth, it was as if someone spoke through me. I said, "Teresa, my mother was Jennie L., and she always said I should find you because she loved you so much." At that moment, Teresa grabbed me, hugged me, and said, "Ooooh, Jennie, she was my good friend. Please stay and have a cup of coffee."

We sat and shared small talk until her husband invited Al to see his clock collection. When they left the room, she grabbed my arm and said, "Thank you for being discreet. He does not know about you." I said, "I don't want to make trouble. Please call me any time. I gave her my card with my phone number on it. I could tell Al did not know what was going on when we left. We were sitting in the car putting seatbelts on when she ran over to us. She reminded me she would call me at another time.

Al drove around the corner from the house; I broke down crying and released all that had been built up for forty years. I had no control, and I cried for days. When I meditated on this, I knew. *It was as if God said, "Every cell of your body knows she gave birth to you. Every cell of your body has cellular memory. You are releasing all of the trauma from the moment she rejected you while you were still in the womb".*

Three months later, Teresa called. She apologized for not calling sooner, and she said they had to go to Oklahoma to settle her brother-in-law's estate. We made a date to go for lunch.

It was a nice, warm Saturday afternoon. Teresa answered the door, all dressed up with her pearl necklace and little pocketbook. She was quite impressed by the '92 Corvette I drove as we headed off to lunch. As soon as I was about to drive on the on-ramp to the highway, she screamed, putting her foot and hands both on the dashboard, yelling, "OH NO! I DON'T DO Highways." *What!!!* Now what do I do? I planned on taking her to a nice restaurant and had to now figure out how to drive all the back roads from Warwick!

On one visit, Teresa told me my biological father's name was John. The only John I heard her talk about was a family member. By now, Teresa had been showing signs of dementia (a decline in mental function). At another visit, I asked about John. She said, "Oh, we don't talk to that side of the family anymore."

On another visit with Teresa, I asked her to tell me more about my biological father, John, and she corrected me and said his name was Ron Charpentier.

Then, on another visit with Teresa, I thought she was speaking clearly and it was the right time to ask. I said, "Teresa, first you told me my biological father's name was John, then you said it was Ron. Which is it"? That's when she said, "Oh no, no! Your father's name is NOR-MAN! Norman Charpentier. We worked at Speidel, and he drove me to work until we retired."

Teresa had been forgetting a lot, so I didn't know what to believe. I resorted to never knowing who my biological father was. Nor does it matter; I consider my adoptive parents, John as my dad and Jennie as my mom, and that's it.

Al & I continued to visit Teresa and her husband. Everyone called him "Father". His birth certificate only had initials on it, so he has gained the nickname "Father."

One day, Teresa, 'Father,' Al, and I were talking over coffee while sitting in her kitchen, and a man came around the corner. Oh my god, he looked exactly like me, with very little hair! It was so weird; I felt like I was looking in the mirror! He was Teresa's son with 'Father,' and he was born six years after me. They also had another son who was born three years after me. We have had several visits with this family, and they're really a humble, special group of people. On one visit, I told Father, "You treated me as if I was your daughter." He replied, "You gave me the strength to tell Teresa I also have a daughter in Wisconsin out of wedlock. Her name is also Elizabeth."

*When Teresa passed away, Al and I continued to visit with Father and enjoyed his wisdom. He was such a kind, gentle man, and at 94 years old, we just heard of his passing. A woman, Carol, sent me a message via Facebook, saying she was at the funeral and her aunt Anna told her about me. Anna is Teresa's sister. Anna was the only one who knew Teresa was pregnant with me. Teresa told everyone she had a tumor and went into the hospital to have it removed. Carol is 74 years old and would be my cousin. We're due to talk tomorrow. Surely, there will be more stories for the book. All the puzzle pieces seem to be coming together.*

# Fourth of July

The family gathered at Aunty Theresa's beach house for our annual Fourth of July holiday. My cousin Maria's husband was a police officer, and he always had the best fireworks display in the neighborhood. The kids were overly excited, amplified by enormous amounts of sugar as desserts lined the kitchen table.

Of course, I had just returned from the market with them, allowing each one to pick their own half-gallon of ice cream with all the candy toppings they wanted. Felicia was most surprised as she questioned, "Aunty Eliz, are you saying we don't have to agree on one ice cream? We can each have our own?" Yes, of course, five half gallons of ice cream, Reeces's peanut butter cups, almond joy bars, three musketeers, M&M's, and more filled our shopping cart for over $100 worth of sugar, and I was the favorite aunty.

The breezeway couch was loaded with everyone's jackets/pocketbooks and excess baggage for the day. As I walked through the breezeway, I noticed a pocketbook with its contents, including a tampon, spilled out onto the floor. I tossed the tampon back into the pocketbook and placed it on the couch. Eight-year-old Felicia screamed at me. "That's my dad's! Give that back to my dad!" I couldn't help myself laughing. She ran to get her mom, and she burst out crying louder and louder. Maria came in to see what was going on. After I explained what I had done. Felicia said, "No! That's Dad's fireworks!" Maria said, "No, Felicia, that's not fireworks." Felicia insisted, "Yes, it is! It even has a wick!"

# Cousin Bobby

We were driving up to Connecticut every weekend with Aunty Irene to see my Uncle Vic. His emphysema had worsened, and he was hospitalized. We all need to remember that Healing is not always living; it may be crossing over without pain.

The bed next to Uncle Vic was empty. The next thing I knew, I was doing Reiki on my cousin Diane on that bed. Later, I opened my Mesa right there and began doing a healing on Uncle Vic. The priest had closed his Chakras after doing death rites, and Uncle Vic was having trouble breathing. I held his hand and asked his permission to open his Chakras. He squeezed my hand and looked right at me, which he had not done to anyone in days. Within an hour of opening his Chakras and calling in the angels to guide him, Uncle Vic peacefully crossed over. It was a peaceful passing, and the entire family was there to see the smile on his face.

On one of these trips from the hospital in Connecticut, Aunty Irene blurted out, "Elizabeth, what is a dildo?" I couldn't contain myself and burst out laughing. Al was so embarrassed, but there was nowhere for him to run. I almost fell out of the car laughing. We were on the I-84 highway with another hour left to drive home. Al motioned to me to be nice and please hold this answer until he was not there… You had to see his face, thinking I'd explain more with him still in the car! I am still giggling as I type this. He was *so* embarrassed!

You see, one of my Uncle Vic's sons has a booming business. He sells "adult things" on the internet. And the funniest part of this is that Uncle Vic was doing the books for the business at 78 years old! This is hilarious. In our family, no one *ever* talked about these topics, and now all my cousins are having fun talking about it! Crazy as it is, that made one of my cousins the wealthiest of all. God Bless you, Cousin Bobby!

A few months later, we're at Aunty Irene's 75th Birthday party. We sat at a table with Aunty Irene's friends. Aunty Ida is 78 years old. Norma is 84, and her daughters, Pamela and Paula, were sitting next to her. Norma asks, "Hey Ida, is that Bobby, Victor's son? What does he do for a job?" Aunty Ida answered, "Oh, yes, that's Bobby… he has a *CON-DOM* factory." Well, Pamela almost choked. I swear she had macaroni come out of her nose as she said, "*WHAT* did my mother just say?" This has to be one of the funniest situations we've ever been in, or as Al says, "you just HAD to be there" to appreciate the humor.

*Years later, I was visiting cousin Bobby & he asked if I wanted to go for a boat ride. I looked at this enormous speed boat with the lettering on the side extending from end to end, taller than me, advertising the name of his adult toy company. Surely, this book must be a comedy series for TV~*

# Family Reunion

From our very first date in 1972, Al and I hung out with a bunch of his cousins. It was a fun gang, and we always had a blast. Every July, Al's mother's side had a family reunion. Al is one of seven brothers and sisters. They're all married with children, and now their children are having children of their own. The cousins come from all over the country with their husbands, wives, and children in tow. Everyone loves to have a good time, and there are plenty of fun things to do, such as ping pong, swimming, and jungle Jim. There is always an enormous amount of food, from little necks, steamers, and Italian calzones to venison, pasta salads, burgers, and sweets. Everyone brings their favorite dish to outdo each other. This particular year, they rented a huge blow-up castle for the kids.

Alice is one of the funniest people I have ever met. She will have you splitting a gut with laughter. (The very first day I met her, I was 15 years old, and she was wearing a tee shirt with "itty bitty titty committee" written on the front of it.) She and Elaine threw the little kids out of the blow-up castle, and we adults marched in. We were acting like children and totally embarrassing our children. While we were bouncing, one of the guys would run to the corner on the outside and dive at it. This sent the inside person flying like a slingshot as if they were shot out of a cannon! When I saw this about to happen, I yelled. "Look out!" Everyone came to my side, bouncing in one corner. When we all jumped at the same time, the roof collapsed down and the sides gave way. Oh Damn! We thought we broke it!

Picture this: the center section stayed inflated, and when the roof came down and the sides let go, causing us to get stuck in the sides of this monstrosity! Our legs were sticking straight up, and I couldn't gain the leverage to move one way or the other. I landed on top of Al, who landed on top of Alice. All I could hear was screams of laughter. We were all stuck and could not get out. One of the cousins laughed so hard she peed her pants! I didn't have the strength to move the wall that had fallen on me to get myself out. I was literally wedged between the massive wall structure and the inflated bottom floor.

Finally, a huge arm emerged, and I reached to grab it; thankfully, Ernie dragged me out!

At this time, I could hear Al screaming with laughter and realized he was still stuck inside. It took two guys to pull Al out feet first. He and Alice were pulled out, laughing so hard, yelling about coming down the birth canal and being born again. It was the most laughter I'd ever witnessed in my entire life. We were all *screaming* with laughter when the others realized they weren't the only ones who peed their pants!

When we were all finally pulled out, Al's mother was holding her side, laughing with tears in her eyes, and one of the other cousins was recording the whole scenario! The little ones were crying, "You *broke* it". Another cousin was yelling, "Get your credit cards out; we have to pay for this." Thinking we broke it, we started seriously thinking we broke it… only to find out it was Gerard who pulled the plug on one of the fans, causing half of it to deflate! It wasn't broken at all!

# Dr. Norma

Dr. Norma Milanovich is a co-author of several books. One of my favorites is "The Light Shall Set You Free." After reading all of her books, I placed an order for her "back newsletters." I really enjoyed listening to her CDs sitting on the porch with our dog Bull & my Mesa (portable prayer altar) opened. One morning, I was relaxing with headphones in my ears as I listened to Dr. Norma. My cell phone rang. I was so into the CD that I reluctantly removed one bud plug to hear who was calling. It was Dr. Norma on my Cell phone.

In disbelief, I said, "Whooooo, Dr. Norma? I have you on my cellphone in my left ear and on my CD in my right ear!!! Wow!" Now, how funny is that?!?!? I had recently ordered more of her CDs. Dr. Norma was calling to tell me her "secretary is out of town, & my order could not be mailed out until she was back; would I mind waiting?" This led to a wonderful conversation for over an hour in which I asked, "What do I have to do to get you to come to Rhode Island?" And she replied "Invite me". I said, "Okay, you're invited." She replied, "OKAY, I'm COMING." We booked it; Dr. Norma was coming to teach a workshop here in RI.

Two weeks before Dr. Norma's scheduled workshop, I received a call saying Don Martin & Marco Nunez would indeed be able to accept my invitation to come to my home again. I thought, oh my, how funny this is. I surely hope they come on a different day than Dr. Norma! With God's help, it all fell into place beautifully. The Shamans from Peru came in with plenty of time to enjoy and complete everything we wanted to before Dr. Norma.

The Shamans worked side by side with me to see clients for Readings and healings at my home. Then, we held a wonderful

Shamanic workshop at the Smithfield Senior Center. Then my brother-in-law, Paul, and Sister-in-Law, Josie, made a farewell Thanksgiving dinner from soup to nuts for everyone to enjoy.

I had one day to clean the house and prepare before Al and I picked up Dr. Norma at the airport. As I cleaned, I'd throw excess into my bedroom, thinking I'd get to it later. Well, time ran out & next thing I knew the whole house was neat & tidy except our bedroom… I figured it would be okay because no one would go in there to see.

Dr. Norma came in on Thursday night. Friday, she saw clients, and at night, we prepared the room at St. Alban's church for Saturday's workshop, "The Seventh Golden Age".

On Saturday morning, Dr. Norma and I were talking as she followed me into my bedroom and stated, "OH MY! Looks like you need some Feng Shui in here!" I was so embarrassed for a minute, but then I had to laugh because, really, I'm not a messy person. I just needed more time between workshops!

On the morning of Dr. Norma's workshop, I received a phone call from the Pastor of the church. She informed me that we had to move the workshop to another day. She made a mistake. They were having a ham and bean supper in the hall we were going to use and needed to cook in the kitchen next to our workshop space. When I conveyed this message to Dr. Norma, she calmly said to tell her that it was unacceptable and ask her if we could do our workshop in the church.

The Pastor agreed, and everything went off perfectly.

I met the most amazing people at this workshop; they flew in from all over the USA. As each person called to sign up, I found myself involved in the most spiritual conversations. What a delightful experience it was, once again beyond my wildest dreams.

Amazed, I couldn't believe how calm Dr. Norma was with the Pastor… She then explained, "Honestly, Elizabeth, if we asked to anchor the Light in the church, the pastor probably would have said no." Surely, God's still in charge. We are only the conduits for his infinite Light and Love.

# DEEP into Shamanism

From my first Inca Shaman class with Judy, seven of us graduated. Those classes consisted of two years of intense Shamanic training; we had many life-transforming events. I loved and embraced this Inca lineage; they work with a Mesa (a portable prayer altar). The Mesa is the medicine bundle that holds objects of power that represent places, things, or events of transformation that took place in that Shaman apprentice's life.

Judy is an amazing healer. She was teaching us how to do what she does. She heals people from all over the world. From that very first class, I knew this was my life purpose. That year, I went on to study with Judy's teachers and then their teachers in Peru. It truly was a "Quickening," as Grandfather Martin said only one year ago!!!

I studied everything they taught in every Mastery class to perfect my healing work. Then, I expanded my studies with other Shamans and Master healers from all over the world. My thirst for knowledge became brighter than ever. I loved it. Spirituality and healing work truly feed my Soul.

*This is bigger than the "wow" I got from sitting in that Corvette many years ago. This WOW has never gone away, unlike the material. Wow, I'd have to renew time after time.*

*The wow from the diamonds lasted months, then dwindled, and I needed the Corvette, then that lasted months… and something else was needed… When the QUICKENING began, the spiritual Wow has never ended; this is the wow we all search for… not the materialistic things. It is our connection to Spirit that completes our being and feeds our soul with never ever ending wow.*

One Saturday morning, Al went dirt bike riding with his brother Ray and his two boys. Later that afternoon, the kids came running over yelling, Aunty Eliz, "You had to see Uncle Al; he went off a ten-foot cliff!!!" Oh My God, they were carrying on and on about how he shouldn't be alive! When Al finally came in, he said he was just bruised; his thigh and knee hurt.

The very next day, it was beautiful, 80 degrees and sunny. Al was sitting on the porch reading a biker magazine. I asked if I could Reiki his leg; he bruised it badly yesterday. He said, "What do I have to do"? I said, "Nothing, I'll do it right here." I placed my hands on him and channeled the Reiki Energies, asking for special healing and extra strength in that leg. I also performed prayer as I was taught in my Shamanic classes.

Within two days, he was fine and back riding again. This time, he was on his Harley, riding up Cherry Hill Road behind a woman in a '72 Corvette. She obviously thought the street was on her left and proceeded to turn. She must have noticed the street sign on the left led to a parking lot (the street she wanted was actually on the right); she pulled a quick right turn, cutting off Al. He hit the "Stingray" label on the side of her car with his leg. It was the same leg that he hurt last week. His leg was stuck in the fiberglass of the car and dragged him 200 feet. Witnesses said they were "amazed he was alive and never even dropped the bike!

I was at the kitchen sink washing dishes when he came home, dropped his pants, and yelled, "Look at my leg!" I thought he was nuts. I thought, *why was he doing this?* I said, "It's red. Why?" Then he told me the story. There was over $800 worth of damage on his bike, and he only had a red mark on his leg. We couldn't believe it!

*Yes, I had asked for special healing and extra strength when I prayed Reiki IN THAT LEG. I knew that was why he was fine. Pretty wild, eh?*

By this point, I was doing Reiki on clients. One of my regular clients is my 90-year-old father-in-law. He is a strict French catholic.

He Loves Reiki. The first time I did a Reiki session on him, he asked, "What God are you praying to?" I said, "Dad, the same God you do; there is only one." "Then why don't I hear you?" he said. From then on, I had to repeat the "Our Father" and "Hail Mary" over and over again for the entire session. He is a peach, and I would do anything for him!

Most of our family didn't even know what exactly was going on back then. On my way out the door to another class, Al would say to me, "If you get weird on me, I'm going to make you stop." Then, one day, I was practicing "*spraying* Florida water" and having it dribble down my chest, and he said, "Come on over here and do it like this," as he took me on the porch, making this noise as if to spit off the porch. I yelled, "NO! It's not like that… it is a soft spray from your bottom lip. A *gentle* spray. The Florida water is sprayed from your lips because the sweetness added to your breath gives it the power behind the intent to summon God. It's like incense used in church. Prayer with the Holy Spirit, likes sweetness, and this is a way of honoring God to create a sacred space".

There were many ceremonies and many different ways of doing the same thing. There is a phrase, "*many paths lead to one God.*" This is true. Very rarely, a good healer will teach you how to do what they do. Some want to be a guru and have you become dependent on them for everything. The first notion of this was when I went to Judy. She said to me, "Let me teach YOU how to get YOUR OWN answers". She truly wanted me to do for myself, for me to learn for myself, get my OWN answers, and be able to be a good healer. Why? She would say, "Because THE WORLD NEEDS HEALERS". She is one human I knew that is closest to being impeccable, without ego. I wasn't used to this. I was used to going to a doctor, getting a prescription, and going back for every ache and pain. This was amazing. I was being taught how to heal myself. She called her first class "The Medicine Wheel," the life-transforming teachings of how to heal yourself. It was the beginning of Shamanism and later, more intensely, can be further studied as the path of the Healer. Once you transform yourself and know that you truly are one with God, then, and only then, can you begin to heal another.

I wanted more; I couldn't get enough fast enough. Judy sent me to Denise, who used to teach Shamanism for one of the Shamans in the USA, "Alberto." Alberto was responsible for bringing the Inca teachings to the USA many years ago. I did a two-year program of Medicine Wheel with Denise and Oscar Miro-Quesada, and with Alberto, I studied every one of his classes and all of the master classes. I also studied with Alberto's teachers here in the USA and in Peru, including Don Manuel Quispe and Don Martin Pinedo Acuna and the famous Twin Shamans, Ysabel, and Olinda. *I hosted many of these amazing Shamans healers right here at my own house for over fifteen years.*

This is when things really started to move quickly. Miracle after miracle happened before my eyes. I watched my buddy's heart attack vanish without a trace. And as long as I remained humble, more healing happened. I watched other healers get a big head, and their healing powers vanished; when they said they no longer were interested in doing Reiki, I knew it was not a lack of interest. God took it away.

*When I first began this journey, Native Americans refused to teach me time after time… asking me, what tribe are you from? When I would reply, I was adopted, they'd say, well, call, so and so. I called and left numerous messages. They would never call me back. Al and I went to pow-wow after pow-wow to search out medicine men and women locally who could or would teach me. There were none. So, I continued my training with the Peruvian Shamans. That was many, many years ago. I have since learned that the Native Americans are now opening their hearts and are sharing their knowledge. This makes my heart sing! Thank you, God. I am glad now that people have many places to learn this good medicine. I have found that it doesn't matter where you study, whether it is in Russia, Venezuela, or Peru, the core traditions are the same: Many paths, One God. It's good that so many are now sharing.*

One of my teachers, Don Manuel Quispe, a Q'ero elder, told me, "We will teach anyone who wants to learn and will keep the medicine sacred to their heart so the teachings will not be lost. Our grandchildren do not want to learn, much like you did not want to learn Italian from your grandfather." Yes? Yes, you are so right! They teach us, so the stories, rites, ceremonies and rituals will not be lost. I will hold them sacred to my heart and teach them as I have been taught to honor and obey God. It's in my Blood.

*It wasn't always easy for me. I studied really hard. But in the beginning… I messed up. As I recall some of the first shaman classes. I remember the first time I studied with Oscar Miro-Quesada; he was teaching us to face the directions and command that our guides come in. Calling upon Angels, Saints, Spirits, & Guides, it came to my turn. Crazy and nervous, I yelled at the top of my lungs, "Come, Come to me, Leonardo, Michael-Angelo, Donatello, Rafael… Oh Shit! I just called in the Teenage Mutant Ninja Turtles!!!" Unable to believe I said all that aloud, I doubled over laughing hysterically. The entire room stood silent, just looking at me!*

# Clara's Medicine Wheel

I arrived on Friday morning for my first Shamanic weekend with shaman Elder Clara.

This workshop was in a building that used to be a church. All that is left are the walls, rugs, and the Altar. It had amazing energy and was really a neat place. The grounds were beautiful. The church was up on a hill; woods lined the road, and down below, next to the lake, where we had a fire ceremony. I unpacked and met Dona` Clara. I was surprised to see a woman who reminded me of me. She had a definite Human aura/energy to her, unlike the "God-like" energy I felt when I was with Judy.

(A few months prior to this, I was packing my car to drive to this class. That day was so weird because I couldn't seem to get out of my driveway. I kept forgetting things, such as taking my vitamins, feeding our parrot Jose', going to the bathroom, putting the cans in the garage, and packing my sleeping bag. I literally went into the house and shut the alarm off four times. Wow, that was really weird. Something kept me from traveling. The last time I got into the car, my phone beeped with a message on it. It was Chris calling to tell me that the weekend workshop was canceled.)

Finally, I'm here for the workshop that had been previously canceled. Dona` Clara spoke wonderfully. I didn't daydream ONCE the entire weekend. She had my full attention the entire time. It was a beautiful learning experience. She was a wonderful teacher and kept you enticed with a lot of stories.

We performed breathing exercises and worked with past lives using stones. We made Mandalas (sand paintings), representing our lives and who we are, and after each session, we would update and check it. We made a prayer offering for fire to honor the issue being healed for each stone and danced to remove the luminous threads of each.

Then, on Friday night, we did a Sacred Fire ceremony. We burned offerings and cleaned our past lives so they would no longer be attached to our souls. We were asleep by 1 am. The next morning, I noticed Lola had some negative energy. She looked angry. She was dressed in an old Harley Davidson ripped shirt and dirty jeans. When she talked, her mouth seemed black with nasty grey teeth. She had lots of long key chains hanging from her baggy pants with a lot of noisy clanking jewelry. She said she had Gnomes and Leprechauns talking to her. She told me stories of her spirit son (who's not really her son but wants her to be his mommy). She explained, 'Don't get worried about the changes in her voice and the way she walks, etc...' She continued to say, this is the boy coming through her as he held his rabbit, and she tucked her hand under her chest. I told her I didn't think it was good to have dead beings attached to you like that, "They should be released to the light." She gave me the creeps. But I was seriously trying hard to be a better person and not pass judgment. Her energy was so HEAVY and very hard to ignore. I could FEEL IT!

Another girl, Helen, and I got cornered again at lunchtime. Helen rolled her eyes and walked away. I continued getting really bad vibes from this girl. I thought Dona Clara was blowing her off when Lola asked too many questions, especially when she repeated those same stories during class. Later, I realized that was because Clara really needed to attend her privately. I understood that "things aren't always what they seem." When we took a break, and everyone had gone outside, Dona` Clara called me over to tell me, "Don't get caught up in her stories. She likes to suck the energy out of people." Now, I was sure my initial gut feeling was correct.

After supper, we were back in the Ceremony when Clara mentioned that she was feeling tired. She asked for the energy of the group to pick up so we could make it through the long night. We were doing a Sacred Despacho Ceremony, a prayer bundle, a package made of leaves, flowers, and candies put into paper prayed upon and burned or buried as an offering to God. After all the Kintu's (Leaves with prayers blown into them) were placed on the tissue, Dona` Clara folded it up. Although I didn't see her get up, she attempted to go to the door of her room, which was directly behind the Altar. She never made it. She collapsed right there, hitting the piano face-first as she came down. I got up immediately, and her assistant, Chris, was already there, turning her face up. There was this death stare on her face. It was so shocking! Her body was limp. It seemed to take a long time for me to get there, but I was there right when Chris turned her over. She began to come around. When she started to move, she said, "I'm going to be sick". We grabbed a bucket, and she kept vomiting a black bile; the stench was so strong! It looked like black tar!

I got a cold cloth and kept wiping her face and neck, holding her hair up. When she seemed to stop, we helped her crawl into her room, where Vicky and Chris went with her, and she slept. I then turned to look at the girls. Some were crying, while others were terrified. Chris was a nurse, and she stopped one of the girls from calling 911. I immediately knew it was Hutcha (heavy energy). Somehow, I had the strength of the Jaguar within me, keeping me steady. After Dona` Clara was taken to her room, I told the girls, "It must have been something she ate that didn't agree with her. She'll be fine." We hugged and gave each other support. I am amazed at how strong I was at that time.

Vicky came out and said, "No, we're going to finish the ceremony and burn Despacho at the fire the way it was originally planned". Dona` Clara was now sleeping in the back room. As part of the ceremony ritual, Vicky cleansed all of us off with the Despacho, and then they all went down to the fire. Chris stayed with Clara.

When they left, I snuck off to the outside of the building in prayer and called Judy. She was the only one I knew of that I could talk to about this. She would know what to do, I was sure! I don't play with the dark side! I was sure this "scenario" was of that Dark, Negative side, and I wanted no part of it!!!

I explained everything to Judy. She *connected up* the way she talks to God. She said Dona` Clara had a seizure, and she needed to work on her for me to call back later. Judy would stay up all night and wasn't going to sleep. She said this was her stuff, not mine, and there was nothing to be concerned about. I was just witnessing it for the lessons to be learned. Judy said I had to continue with the girls to the fire ceremony. She would send extra protection to the group. I maintained calm as I walked through the woods to join the others already down by the lake. When I joined the others around the fire, the sky opened up, and it poured. Ironically, it felt like a blanket of warmth as the rain was so warm it cleansed us all. When I looked up through the trees, I saw God's face. I felt absolutely safe, knowing that God was in control and protecting all of us. It totally blew my mind to see a face up there through the trees in the sky. When Kathy and Heidi also saw it, I knew it wasn't my imagination!

We finished up at about 1:30 am. After everyone was sleeping, I checked the messages on my phone; it was Judy, saying to call her if I wanted. I did. She wanted to make sure we were all alright with what happened. Everyone was ok. She explained what I felt… that I knew 911 would have only made things worse because *That* was NOT of this world. Only God could conquer evil such as that. Judy was good at summoning God for work such as this, and she was teaching me how to do just that.

These four-day workshops were done several times a year. Dona` Clara pushed me to new heights. Every time I was in her company, something dramatic happened. The first time, she had that seizure right in the middle of Despacho. The second time we did the workshop, a big black figure hovered behind her and another girl at a fire ceremony. We all had to leave, scrambling out of the woods like scared little chickens! Getting lost, it took us three hours to find our way back to the old church.

That incident really pissed me off because I was thinking, why don't we stop and confront this thing? Nothing is more powerful than GOD, and if we are God's people, we will be protected! Later on, I realized that I would have definitely been okay with that—however, there were many people in that workshop who had only done a couple of classes. They certainly had a lot to learn, and it was safer for them to leave. Dona` Clara was looking out for the entire class by making everyone leave.

Dona` Clara always put me in situations that were uncomfortable. I now know it was to toughen me up. I was no longer afraid of the dark side. I know God is more powerful than that, and there is nothing God cannot fix.

*Your power comes from God. God is the power within you. Use this power for the good of all to be in service for all of humanity, and it will be strengthened forever and ever.*

*You must take responsibility for your life. No one has any power over you. We are never the Victim; we only call to ourselves that which we need to learn. Each of us is born with a blueprint. This blueprint includes many lessons for our Soul's growth. You placed every person in your life.—exactly—they are there to trigger certain lessons for you to accomplish. If you recall, some people come into your life for a minute an hour, and some are there for a lifetime. Some push your buttons so badly it drives you crazy. Next time you see that person, remember this paragraph… Think about them as a mirror to show you that which you need to heal in yourself. Once you learn the lesson, the issue no longer needs to present itself; it goes away… or that person no longer "pushes your buttons" because you made peace with the issue.*

*If you get nothing else from this book, remember this paragraph, for it can be the biggest lesson you have ever learned, and may you take this information and use it as the wisdom needed to catapult yourself to the next level in your soul's growth.*

# Disrespecting Despacho

One of the girls I work with, Lina, begged me to do Despacho at her home. She heard me explain what Despacho was many times. It is a prayer offering to God to petition him on your behalf; this is when powerful prayers are needed. It must be done for the good of all & harm none.

I explained this to Lina many times. Finally, we picked a date for me to go to her house to do Despacho. Despacho typically takes 3 to 4 hours & is quite intense. I asked Paula to come with me as my assistant weeks before. At 3:00 pm on the day of the Ceremony, Paula called me & said: "I changed my mind, I can't come". I couldn't believe it! Two hours before we're going! I told her, I'm going, if you don't want to, no problem… It was too late to cancel now. I won't let Lina down. I always keep my word. These women waited months for this.

Yes, I was completely pissed! I couldn't believe Paula backed out at the last minute. When I got to Lina's, the women were all in the kitchen drinking wine. Many lessons to be learned here!

NEVER do a ceremony when you are not balanced! Alcohol is never allowed at a ceremony! You can drink or celebrate after the ceremony.

When we sat on a blanket on the floor, I began to explain how Despacho is performed. One of the women said, "Well, I don't believe in God". I should have said right then & there, "Then WHY ARE YOU HERE?" But, in an effort to show everyone that they CAN connect to God, and it is such an amazingly beautiful thing, I said, "Connect with that source which gave you the breath of life that which you believe put you here on earth…" Because that is God.

This woman was confrontational. The rest of the women were very respectful & nice. Lina was really excited & a gracious host. Her husband even built a beautiful fire for the ceremonial burning of the Despacho.

When we went to the fire, I was opening sacred space & that woman began rolling a joint. That's when I heard loud and clear, "Get out of here!!!" Another lesson… When anyone disrespects the ceremony—LEAVE! I should have left immediately when I saw the wine before the ceremony. It took three strikes for me to get it! This falls into the category of "Never try to prove that shamanism works," and when things are not going smoothly… meditate to see why! This was a severe lesson, indeed. When you are doing Despacho, you have a responsibility to hold sacred space for the entire energy of the group. Never, ever do Despacho or any kind of Ceremony unless you are 100 percent balanced!

# Freaked Out

We have a friend who received a Hockey scholarship for college. Derek is an amazing friend and a great hockey player. Once, he told me a funny story I like to share. (I love to see people laugh!) He shared a house with four of his classmates. One day, they locked him in his room, which was in the basement of the house. He had to go to the bathroom, which was upstairs. He tried and tried, calling and yelling, and they still refused to let him out. He was so desperate he looked around, found their hockey equipment, and pooped in one of their helmets.

It still makes me laugh when I see his face as he tells the story. I always wanted to keep a book of the funny stories I have heard in my lifetime. Writing this book is how I will savor my favorite ones here. I love to laugh, and most of all, I love to make others laugh.

By now, I've been studying with several Master Shamans, and I'm working with clients daily, having great success. Derek called me to tell me he hurt his back "really bad" playing hockey and could not move. He was at his house in Michigan. I asked him if I could do a healing for him. He said what do I need to do? I said, "Just lie there and connect to God. Ask him to heal you." I said I'd call him back in about twenty minutes. I opened my mesa and sent Long Distance Healing to him with the strongest intent I have ever used. When I called him back, he was upset and sounded like he was crying. I immediately thought, what did I do wrong? He said, "Nothing, the pain is gone." I said, "I don't get it. *What* is wrong?" He said he was scared, and it freaked him out. Of course, it *did* work! I have been shown the power of healing. I have been shown the power of prayer so many times. Even though for only a minute, I did wonder if I did something wrong. How could I ever doubt that this would work, especially when I know doubt sabotages the results?

Ok, so he was freaked out. That's okay, I thought. The pain was Gone! That's what we needed, and he's fine now, or so I thought.

An hour went by, and the phone rang. It was his girlfriend, Jen. She asked, "What did you do to Derek? He's really freaked out." I explained Long Distance Healing and thought she understood by the conversation we had. The next day, Derek's mother called. She wanted to know, "What did you do to Derek?" OH MY, Now what!?! I spent the better part of the next two hours explaining what I did. Why weren't they happy that the pain was gone??? I just don't get it. It turned into a really weird situation.

After the healing, things with Derek were never the same. He looked at me as if I had four heads. Then he stopped visiting us. I'd get a sporadic e-mail to say hello, but things dramatically changed. It made me sad. His pain was removed. Why wouldn't they all look at this as a good thing? I just don't get it.

In the first few years of studying shamanism, I got mixed feelings from a lot of friends. Especially the ones closest to me that I used to hang around with. After all, they knew me as the "I Love Lucy, Welder, hot-shit joker." Some thought I'd joined a cult, others just thought I was weird. None of them saw the serious commitment I put into study. To them, I was just "away" doing something. No one knew how serious this was. They expected me to stay with the same personality, with the same level of knowledge that I had when we hung out. If I had been in college pursuing a Doctorate degree, they all would have respected me. Shamanism studied in the mountains of Peru didn't award those types of degrees. I've done many, many Long Distance Healings, and confirmations are nice. But I realize if I search for confirmation, my ego is flying, and the healing will suffer. I can actually sabotage the work; I must Let Go & Let God. When I trust that it is always God's work, thy will be done, then it is perfect.

"Let Go & Let God" is kind of like ordering a couch. You go to the store, pick it out, pay for it, and go home & continue your life. You don't sit there thinking about it, waiting for it to come. You trust that the couch will come because you've done your part and paid for it… You forget about it until it shows up in the truck being delivered. When we put our prayers out there, we must trust that God will follow through with whatever is in our highest good. God knows us better than we do & he knows what will fulfill our divine plan, for he can see the original blueprint we came into life with, of the life we need to live to get our soul to grow to the next level…

*Now that I am thinking about this, years ago, I never called my Doctor to say "thank you" after a visit. Now, I make a point to say thank you.*

*In Prayer and in God's work, I am learning more every day of my life.*

*I accept all that God wants to teach me. I also know that when I get messages, whatever they are, at whatever time… I must listen.*

*I must strive for impeccability in everything I do. I MUST follow my guidance no matter what it is about. I MUST walk in alignment with God, trusting and thanking every moment of every day. God helps me on this path of Divinity.*

# Engineering

I don't get caught up in politics and can't even tell you why the Company had to de-regulate, but they did. This meant that the Electric Company could not both generate and sell electricity. The (Power-plant) generation end of the company was being sold. I was given the opportunity to stay with the Electric Company and maintain my 20 years of service or go with the new company (that just purchased the Powerplant) as a new employee. After weighing my options, I elected to move back to the offices and stay with the mother company. They were in the same building where I was originally hired in customer service. I went back to night school again to obtain the necessary education, which would enable me to transfer to an even higher-paying job in Engineering.

I was one out of twenty employees who passed the four-hour tests given by an outside consultant company. Out of a possible 105 points on the test, my score was 105—(there were 5 points for the bonus question). I must confess that I connected up & conversed silently with God during the entire test. I literally heard the answers. I was then accepted into the Engineering Department, and with continuous education, I was promoted to Senior Engineer. So, now, when someone was building a new house, I designed the job so the Overhead line guys could build it.

It was a beautiful job because many times I'd be in the woods, taking notes with nature, the fox, raccoon, deer, and all her babies. One day, I'd be in the field measuring to see how much wire was needed, how many poles, and where to locate the transformer; next I would be in my office entering the jobs into the computer. Often, talking with customers on the phone and scheduling more appointments. It was a pleasant job, not like the Customer Service of years ago when everyone was crabby. I honestly loved my job.

Because I was no longer on Eddy St, near the Ear, Nose, Throat clinic, I could no longer run across the street to get my allergy shots. I was allergic to everything from grass, trees, flowers, and even cats and dogs. Their office was open 8-4, and my office had the same hours. While complaining to Judy, because now we've become best friends and we talk all the time… she said why don't you do bee pollen? "WHAT!?" I yelled. Then she explained that it *must be local* bee pollen… (Take 1 granule of bee pollen today, 2 tomorrow and 3 on the third day. If you get a tingle or funny sensation on your tongue or anywhere in your body, STOP (some people are allergic to bees and cannot take this remedy). If not, if there is no funky sensation on your tongue, then… continue adding a granule for 30 days; this is approximately 1 teaspoon. Continue taking 1 teaspoon of bee pollen a day forever. This builds your immune system so much that your body will be strong enough to resist most allergies. Wow! Within a month, I had no allergies, not even seasonal sinus infections that I suffered through my whole life! I can't even count how many antibiotics I had taken in all those years.

I had a great relationship with our family doctor, Amoretti. He was fun and talked Italian to all the little old ladies in the office. I could call him and run in before office hours for my seasonal sinus infection, grab an antibiotic prescription, and still make it to work on time. On my annual visit, he wanted to write me another prescription. I said, "No, thank you. I don't want that anymore. Isn't there something herbal or natural I can take?" He got very upset with me, said I needed to find another doctor and walked out of the room. I seriously thought he was joking until he left the room and slammed the door. In my jonny, I jumped off the table and ran after him asking… "Hey Doc, you're joking, right?" He said, "You need to find another doctor". I was in shock, dressed & sitting in my car when I called Al. His immediate response was, "What did you do to piss him off"? Thank God I found Judy, Bee Pollen, and now I am on a mission to interview doctors who would work for me, not the pharmaceutical industry!

It took a few months before I found Dr. Shah. This is a doctor who listened to me and then said, "Elizabeth, I trust you will do your research because I cannot advise you on Essential oils or herbs, but I will work with you."

*Dr. Shah respected my wisdom as I continued to travel the world, studying alternative medicine, shamanism, and oils. When he opened his new office, we were honored to bless it with the elders of Peru. What a blessing to honor all traditions and all religions, for we are truly working in ONENESS, for there is truly only ONE Creator. He has since moved to Arizona and is still a great resource of wisdom.*

# Nipmuc Rd

It was a chilly day at work. I had on my comfy green suede jacket, jeans, and work boots. Rae and I often went out on the road together to work because when we teamed up, we could bang out a ton of jobs. Rae would drive, and I'd write detailed notes and have the sketch drawn before we got to the next job. This particular day, we were on Nipmuc Road. Last month, we completed a job for Mr. Bucci, which consisted of installing eleven poles. His driveway was unpaved and went from Nipmuc Rd all the way through to Carpenter St. in Foster. Today, we had just finished a job on Nipmuc Road, and it would have taken another half hour to go all the way around to Carpenter St., so Rae said, let's go through Bucci's property to cut through. Good idea! Well, it had rained for the past few weeks, and the path was muddy and quite slippery. We drove past Mr. Bucci's home and were halfway to Carpenter St when our little yellow truck started sliding. It was as if we were slipping in chocolate pudding when the truck slid sideways and tilted down a foot. Rae kept rocking the truck back and forth, flooring it. Mud was flying everywhere! We were so stuck! I had to crawl out of the window because I couldn't open my door. The mud was a foot over the door panel. I climbed out and grabbed some sticks in the woods and put them under the tires for traction. When Rae gunned it, the sticks went flying, covering me in mud! "Stop!" I yelled as I jumped back in the truck and said, "Try it again!" the truck went deeper and deeper into the mud. The truck became impossible to move. Neither of us wanted to get on the dispatch radio and call for help. The guys would never let us live this down!

We finally got a cell signal and phoned one of the foremen. He took this opportunity to razz us and said, "Stay there… we'll come get you tomorrow". We called another, one of the linemen who said, "Call someone who cares!" They thought it was a hoot! Finally, after an hour of calling everyone we could think of, against all our will, with our tails between our legs, we radioed dispatch for help.

They sent a tow truck for us! It was so tiny it looked like a matchbox car. He couldn't pull a log out of there, let alone our truck! The driver walked up toward us and yelled, "Ladies, I can't take my truck in here. You're on your own," and left.

It was just starting to get dark when we saw a huge black, brand-sparkling-new GMC Dually with huge Monster Mudder tires! Mr. Bucci, the owner of the property, was yelling out his window, "Who are you, and what the hell are you doing on my property!" Rae yelled back, "Lou, it's me, Rae!" Shaking his head, he walked over to our little truck, hooked up a chain, and pulled us out. Mud flew all over and made a mess of his beautiful truck. Finally, we were free.

Just as we thought, we were the laughingstock of the office. Everyone knew we were stuck, and everyone was laughing. We took the brunt of this episode big time!

The next day, I took my car for inspection at my friend David's. Upon entering the garage, I noticed this huge black, brand-spanking-new GMC Dully all covered in mud. Ut oh. I asked, "*Who's* truck is that?" David said, "Oh, that's my buddy Lou's truck; he pulled some bitches outta the mud yesterday and BLEW HIS TRANNY!" Oh My God,

I looked at him and said, "Ahhhhhhhh, David, I was one of those bitches…"

Sorry, Mr. Bucci, we didn't mean it. We were trying to cut through, to do more jobs in less time because we had so much work!

# The Healing Engineer

Back at work, my Shamanism and Reiki came in handy. I'd actually Pray over the phone to keep it quiet so I could concentrate on typing my jobs into the computer. It worked wonders. The phone never rang until my computer work was complete. I had a special prayer that I used when angry customers called. I said it silently in my head, and the customer would calm down within a minute. It worked every time.

A few of my co-workers knew what I did, and sometimes they would request special prayers to "cleanse" the office of "heavy energy." The Cleansing would "clear" and shift the attitudes of everyone. Immediately, you could feel the difference. Even the angry people seemed to be pleasant within minutes.

I continued working in engineering. Nights and weekends I'd see clients helping one by one. I continued traveling to study with Masters from all over the world. One would think there weren't enough hours in a day, but when you love what you do, it's not like work. And I truly loved helping people. I seemed to have a knack for helping people get out of their slump. Whatever the issue was, of the mind, body, or spirit, they were always moved forward with joy in their heart. Eventually, word got around, and I couldn't hide it anymore.

Rae was famous for sending everyone who seemed out of balance to me to get "fixed." One night, we were working overtime; I'd just come back into the office when Jerry, the Overhead supervisor, was just completing a 24-hour shift. He tossed all the papers off the desk, laid on it, and yelled, Eliz, come Reiki me, my head is splitting! Within fifteen minutes, he was up and ready to work another shift.

A huge lepidolite rock sat on my desk. Lepidolite is a mineral with lithium in it (years ago, it was said lithium was used to calm mental patients)—as time went on, everyone in the office knew when they were "stressed" to come *rub that stone*. Sometimes, that is all that was needed; other times, they'd be relieved with rubbing the stone and a little conversation. One of my favorites was the black stone obsidian, its volcanic glass (obsidian eats heavy energy and replaces it with positive rejuvenating energy).

I had always loved rocks and would always bring one home from the sacred places I visited. Studying shamanism, I also incorporated crystals, minerals, and meteorites into my practice. Each one has their own personality, and I watched them transform energy daily.

*As time went on, God brought me all around the world. I was guided to pray on the stones and bring them back to sacred places… for example, my Macchu Picchu stones that were prayed on daily in my Mesa for many years, I had to bring to Mt. Washington, Haleakala, The Mayan temple, Belize, Narragansett, RI, and other sacred places… and then I had to return to all those sacred places to bury those sacred stones. It was as if God had me build a network of his infinite Love & Light around the world.*

My intuition was honed and getting better and better. I was able to watch the energy of solar flares and predict mandatory *overtime* within 36 hours. Every time we had a solar flare, we would have power outages. So, I could warn the line guys to pack extra lunch because they would be working overtime soon.

God, I loved my Work. I was no longer an Engineer by day and a Shaman part-time. I had integrated both of my careers together to follow my Divine life path. It was like walking hand in hand with God every moment of every day. The Divine Guidance never shut off.

*I know that when I am working in alignment with God, opportunities happen for me that I never could imagine. Things that are happening are so good; it was not even in my wildest imagination to dream it like this. And, even when I think it can't get any better than this… IT DOES. It just keeps getting better and better every day. Thank you, God; I am truly humbled by your presence in my life.*

# Symbols

One day, I was reading a book that my cousin Danny wrote about *'Financial security.'* My eyes started doing something weird, and I thought I was going blind. In the upper right-hand corner of the page I was reading… it was like lightning was going off in that small space, about the size of a dime. First, it began on the page of the book; wherever I looked, it was there, in the upper corner of my vision, on the wall, in the window, on the TV, on the desk. It wouldn't go away. It continued for over an hour. I began to freak out and panic.

I called Judy. She said that it was *"psychic surgery"* and "Didn't I ask to be able to see, hear and feel as the Masters do???" She said to sit comfortably and relax; the information will come when you 'settle into it.' I focused on it. I could see a symbol. I wrote it down. It was my first of many symbols.

Later on, when I sat with each symbol, I began to get information on what to do with them. Some are used for empowerment, some for healing, and some to remove obstacles for my clients. Oh My God, I'm in amazement once again. Each time I think it can't get any better, it does, and I give thanks, then it gets even better than that. It's a circle of reciprocity of thanking and receiving, over and over again, more and more amazing things. To this date, I continue to get symbols. They come in one at a time and download information to me, sometimes for ½ hour to one hour at a time. They are amazing, and I am not to discuss them or show them to anyone else for 120 days. I must honor and sit with them for them to settle in and align me with the 100% Pure White Light of Christ/ God. I continued my Shamanic studies, branching out into many healing modalities, including Holistic Health and Alternative Medicine, and studied with every Master healer that I could. I did as many workshops as I could afford and charged those I couldn't.

One day, after completing many years of training and finally seeing clients of my own, I got a phone call from a woman who said she was an Abenaki Indian. She wanted to meet a 'real Shaman'. I wondered if she was being sarcastic and if she wanted a confrontation because years ago, many Native Americans would not talk about Shamanism. They treated it as a big secret and thought some were bold to say they were a Shaman. Thus, I said a prayer and headed out to meet her at Applebee's. We had the most amazing conversation over a cup of coffee and dessert. Now we are good friends. She has taught me the true meaning of the words "Let Go and Let God." Trust in God, for he will bring you on amazing journeys. Thank you, Grandmother Gentle Wolf, my friend.

# HRS ~ Ancient Wisdom, LLC

Al was watching more people come to our home for healing. First, it was family and friends, then friends of friends. When it came to seeing clients who were people I had never met before, he became very concerned. He is a businessman and suggested we go to a Lawyer to make sure we are legally protected.

Thus, the business "Healing, Reiki and Shamanism, LLC" was born.

After submitting an application to the town, I received a letter requesting me to appear before the Town Council. It was a cold, rainy February night, and the roads were very icy. I was not afraid; I had the legions of Angels by my side.

The town council meeting was being held in the High School Auditorium. When I arrived, I noticed many TV cameras. One of the nightclubs in town was applying for a Liquor License. There was a lot of controversy over this club because it was going to have topless dancers. Go Figure! I thought the *I Love Lucy chapter* of my life was over, and here I am promoting spirituality in the same place as a group of Porn stars. This was just too funny! God certainly has a sense of humor!

Our town is mostly of Italian heritage, and just like any other, they don't want their dirty laundry aired out in front of everyone. This time, they didn't exactly keep it discreet. There were protesters and angry mobs both outside and inside of the school.

I said prayer to keep me out of the limelight and just let go and let God take over. The next thing I remember was them calling my business name and asking me to come to the podium at the front of the stage. I felt as if I wasn't even in my body as something came in and took over to speak for me. The members of the Town Council asked many questions. The first being, what is Shamanism? What is Reiki? The words came out of my mouth as if they were being spoken from another source. I heard my voice say, "Shamanism is not a religion; it is a way of life. A way of getting back to prayer and nature to heal the way our ancestors did before we had physicians. Reiki is an energy channeled from God through the practitioner to assist the body's own natural healing ability. This tradition is thousands of years old and has been proven to accelerate healing and well-being." It all happened so fast; the next thing I remembered was the gavel being slammed on the table and the board saying, "Congratulations and Good luck."

I was approved for a business license. Then, I got a State Tax I.D. license. Then, with the lawyer's request, I filed, paid for, and received the necessary legal documents for the business, *Healing, Reiki & Shamanism, LLC*. All I could think was, "Wow, this is all surreal. It is really happening now. Clients are coming every week, and I'm witnessing healings every day."

*As the years went by, our work included many other modalities. God guided me to make a name change and told me it had to be "Ancient Wisdom, LLC." Since Ancient Wisdom, LLC was born, we have traveled the world working with the best of the best as we continue to bring the teachings to those who will keep the teachings sacred to their heart.*

# The Elders

My favorite Shaman *Elder* teacher was Don Manuel Quispe. Some spell his last name Quespi or Qespi, but his son Nazario told me his ancient name is "Quispe"; he prefers that I use this name here in my book. (Quechua was an oral language, which is why you will see many different spellings for the same words). Nazario said he is happy I will write about the ancient teachings and his father. He knows that I will honor and keep his father's teachings sacred. Don Manuel was believed to be 99 years old when he crossed over to the other side in 2004; I say *believed to be* because he had no birth certificate. I know the veil is very thin, as they say, for I have seen it. Don Manuel comes to me often. Sometimes to slap me upside the head when I was doing or thinking something I shouldn't. He was a very humble man and also a lot of fun. He had such a cute little laugh, and I can still hear him giggling.

To this day, I also have a special working relationship with a Master Shaman, Don Martin Pinedo Acuna. He is my shaman brother. He was the apprentice of one of the greatest healers in all of Peru, Don Benito Corihuaman. Don Martin married Don Benito's niece Maria (because he did not have any children). Don Martin inherited Don Benito's Mesa (medicine prayer altar). He is the 'keeper' of Apu Pachatusan, one of the sacred Mountains of Peru. People come from all over, from sunrise to sunset, each day for healing with Don Martin. They bring him gifts of guinea pigs, chickens, flowers, or whatever they can afford for payment for their healing. Many groups from the USA visit him every year, bringing the American form of reciprocity—money. Don Martin uses this money not only to educate his children but to give back to the community as well.

I honor his teachings, his humor, and his friendship. He has taught me how to slow down and to "be." To "be" in that place between the worlds where the unmanifested lives. He taught me how to go there to bring it into manifestation. Here, we call this "co-creation." Where we actually dream the world into being. Daydream the way you want life to be and make it happen.

In my thirst for Shamanic wisdom, I studied with as many Shamans as I could. One of them was Oscar, a middle-aged Shaman who came to teach in Rhode Island in the summer of 1999. The group was made up of twenty-five people from all over the world. Oscar had a surprise for us. His father made a brew of Plant Spirit Medicine for us. We were told it was a mix of seven plants—Plant medicine was what they called it. It had—Ayahausca- San Pedro- Peyote- tobacco- and three other ingredients that I cannot recall. We were to drink one small glass in the prayer ceremony. We prayed and fasted for three days, eating only bland liquid soups and drinks. The ceremony began at 7:00 pm. The anticipation was high, for you could read it on everyone's faces. I had never done plant medicine before, and because of my dance with cocaine in the 80s, I was really nervous. I prayed and prayed to see if it was in my highest good to participate in this ceremony. I got a definitive YES; this would not harm me in any way because the brew was just a "taste." One by one, the glass was passed as everyone held space for each other in prayer. The energy of the group was high and peaceful. Then I saw others that went back for seconds and thirds before puking their brains out. It seemed to take over their bodies and turn them inside out! What *were* they thinking?

I did everything in prayer with God's guidance, honoring, and talking to the plant. I'm sure this is why it was really beautiful for me. Oscar guided the rest of us outside to the fire ceremony. The ceremony at fire consists of each person approaching the fire to give thanks and pray with it to take away their fears, health issues, and any heavy energy they have. After everyone had a turn, we could then sit and talk. By 2 am, most of the people had gone back to the main house to sleep. Oscar and I talked about many things. He answered all of the questions I could think of asking. I had so many. Then it got to the point where he didn't have to speak; it was all telepathic. It was *that* knowing of anything that ever was or will be—that inner knowing when you just KNOW it to be true. Like the fingers on your hand, that truth that you *know* is yours. This was my first glimpse of this knowledge; then, even more information came in. It was the absolute truth. It was then that I knew what it was—I could hear— and yet no one was speaking.

I heard, "What is it you want to know? Do you have any unanswered questions?" I thought about my father's death when I was two years old and asked for the truth.

Then, I saw it with intricate detail; I saw the man enter the house up two stairs into the kitchen. He looked at the bananas wrapped with green tape on the counter. He wore a knee-length, tan camel hair jacket. With a darker brown hat on his head with an even darker brown ribbon around it, even the scarf on his neck was different shades of tan to brown. He went through the living room, up the stairs, to my father, who was reading in bed. He said John, I wish it didn't have to be like this. My father got out of bed and signed the man's paper with a force so hard it scratched through into the pine bureau. Then he ordered him to get into bed. I saw my father slip his hands under the sheets, thinking, *Jennie must know I didn't do this.* Then the man shot him twice! The first bullet hit him in the forehead (a little off-center to the right); the second one hit the wall just above the bed. The man put the left glove on as he held the other, walking down the stairs. He walked through the living room, into the kitchen, broke the green tape on the bananas on the counter, took a banana, went down two stairs in the hallway across the lawn, and jumped into a car that was waiting for him on the side of the road.

As long as I can remember, I recall being a small child thinking, "Daddy has a boo boo" with a bloody forehead every time someone in the family would mention his death. This time, I not only saw the murder, but I also heard the conversations that took place before, during, and after. That was in 1959. I knew my Father *was* murdered!

*While reading and editing parts of this book with Aunty Irene, she recalled 1959, being at Lowes State Theatre with Uncle Dan, Aunty Theresa, and Uncle Sal. The owner came down the aisle to get Uncle Dan for a phone call. Uncle Dan returned and said, "We have to go. John is dead." Aunty even recalled what movie they were watching. She explained, "When we got to your mother's house, the policemen threw the mattress out the window and were burning it in the backyard." Uncle Mike was there and added, "Yes, I helped the policeman throw the mattress out the window, then me and Uncle Joe cleaned up the room; it was a bloody mess"! The shocking thing here was that this is the first time they are recalling this from over fifty years ago… both with the same detailed story. I can't even begin to tell you how I felt. It was so bizarre!*

My friend Sue is a lawyer. She said there is no statute of limitations on murder; she'd help if I wanted to pursue it… it was too overwhelming, and I couldn't go there. And who would she interview? They're all dead! I prayed and knew God would guide me accordingly.

# Arizona w/Girls

It was a beautiful day in June. I had organized a group of girls to meet the Hopi Elders in Arizona. April was still the guide and liaison to Hopi Elder, Grandfather Martin.

Doris, Shelia, Lisa, Ann, Cindy, and I flew into Phoenix and drove to Sedona. We stayed at a beautiful "roundhouse" off the main road. It was quiet and serene, with a view of the 'red rocks' from every window. We were the only ones in the house, so everyone got to choose their room. After settling in, we opted to walk along the main street and get a bite to eat. The girls were in awe. The scenery of this place is beyond belief. The feeling of the dry air, the sight of the red rocks, the smell of the flowers; One can describe, yet it will not be understood until you truly experience the energy here. It has been said that Sedona is one of "the energy vortexes" of the world. Much like the human body has chakras—energy centers that spin in connection with meridian lines—like electrical pathways of energy throughout the body. Sedona's vortexes are one of the many (energy centers) chakras of the earth. The energy is amazing, and this was my 6th visit, so I knew all the best places to go.

When we approached the first of the red rocks, Dora said, "That's too high; I'll never make it up there." I said, "No, we're not going all the way up. Just follow me…" I walked to the left, then to the right, slowly climbing; Dora was in such awe she never realized we were indeed walking to the top. I knew she'd make it, and if we zig-zagged, we could get up there. It worked. She was so happy. I had brought the girls to my favorite spot up on Boynton Canyon, opened my mesa, and did a prayer to thank God for bringing me back to this sacred space once again. Each girl found her own sacred spot and was in complete silence. There was a slight breeze, and the sun was warm overhead. As I sat on the enormous red rock, my spine once again began to vibrate; it vibrated into each and every one of my bones, then my cells, until it came up to my crown. Once it reached my crown chakra, I connected up and felt the oneness with God. It was as if I was connected with Christ's Consciousness and brought the light from the heavens into my body. It is this Oneness that there is absolutely NO separation from God. This oneness that we are all connected to all of everything. Realizing that we are like a blood cell in the veins of the body of God. We are no different than the plants, the rocks, the trees, and each other. It is the breath within each one of us—God is that breath—We are connected to each other in every single way—we are truly all ONE—all One with GOD.

I built an Appuchetta—a stone prayer altar on the top of the red rock that day, giving thanks to God and yet anchoring this Oneness to my soul so I would never forget. An Appuchetta is a stone altar made in prayer at a sacred place; later, when you are in prayer, you can call upon this Appuchetta to connect with those sacred energies and bring them into yourself from wherever you are. Medicine people build sacred prayer altars at all of the sacred places they wish to connect with, like a gridline (web) all over the world; it becomes a power object for connecting and praying with the world.

*Never Ever Forget the Oneness I am with God. I AM Elizabeth. Elizabeth means "one consecrated by God". I AM.—do people realize the meaning of the words I AM?*

*It is stated in the bible I AM who AM—the "I AM" are the most powerful words you can say, so when people say I am sorry, they will stay sorry! The I AM before any words give such powerful essence to the words after it—So, it should be consciously said I AM and make positive words follow… such as I am a Divine being of Love and Light.*

*I AM Happy, I AM Healthy, I AM Love. Ponder upon this for a moment. This is very empowering…*

Jennie and Jen were friends of Ms. White-cloud, who also joined us. Everything was going as planned. We met at Grandfather Martin's granddaughter's house to enjoy cultural food and song. It was here that Ann flipped out. She wanted to get out of there and go back to the hotel. It was a four-hour ride. I was afraid for her to leave because we were told we needed an escort to get onto the reservation because they said it was especially "*dangerous*" because our laws do not pertain to them. They are a government within themselves. Ann was a tiny blonde, blue-eyed girl with an unusual fight-or-flight attack that was going on. She put up so much fuss that Lisa felt bad and left with her. I thought this was horrible because we paid so much money to see the elders, and now Lisa would also miss out. Ok, so it was some past-life thing. Let the Shamans work on you. Ann refused. With this said, then acknowledge it, get over it, and realize it is NOT in this life! If we had stuck together, she would have been protected, but by leaving, she was running into the lions' den. I was so worried for her safety! This was so difficult for me because I put this trip together, and now it's splitting up; how can I secure the safety of everyone if I am not with them all at the same time?!? This put me into such a predicament.

I excused myself to the bathroom to gain some privacy and prayed for guidance. It was then that I realized I had to let go and not get caught up in this drama. I specifically heard these words as if God was standing right in front of me. *I am not responsible for Ann or her actions. She is over 35 years old.* I prayed and let it go.

Grandfather Martin's relatives made lunch for us. There was delicious flatbread with taco sauce and vegetables and desserts of all kinds. Then they told stories and sang songs just for us. Many thanks and lots of hugs; we were blessed and on our way.

We continued driving, and alongside the road were many natives selling crafts along with native silver and turquoise jewelry. One of the girls spotted Ann & Lisa, who obviously stopped on the side of the road to purchase something. My worries were over. It has been confirmed that they were fine.

Later that night at the hotel, I was woken up at 3 am by Dora and Ann, saying there was an *incubus* in their room trying to suck their energy. I was rooming with Lisa. Cindy was alone in another room. All of these girls were in my very first shaman class many years ago with Judy. I guess it was because I continued training with more teachers; they figured I knew more. I had not dealt with an incubus before. I opened my Mesa, connected to God, and got specific answers to make this thing go away, so I proceeded to work on it, sending it to the Light for healing and transformation through God.

In the Inca tradition, we do not send anything negative back to where it came from. That would be keeping the negative energies earthbound. It is best to send them to God, in his Light, for healing and transformation. All of this work must be done with love in your heart. Not many can accomplish this because thinking of these bad things as bad or the enemy will, in fact, keep them earthbound and give them more power.

The maintenance man was a sorcerer, trying to suck energy from our group. By performing shamanic work with the girls, we were safe. We had not included Shelia because she was still asleep. We thought she had not been affected. Obviously not, because she refused to come with us the next day and said she was told to jump off a cliff.

Oh, Joy! This is just great. I was forced to step up to the plate again. I needed to get into prayer to put protection around Shelia, our entire group, and the land. Shelia still refused to come with us for the day. I was torn between the fear of leaving Shelia alone and going on to the scheduled group Prayer Ceremony at Cherry Creek with the others.

After prayer, I had the knowing that she'd be fine. I knew that my fear could attract more fear, so I had to 'let go & let God,' even though it was quite difficult to leave Shelia when the last words she said were, "I'm going to jump off a cliff."

I couldn't keep thinking of Shelia because if I did, that is the attachment shamans talk about: NOT letting go. If you stay attached to the outcome or stay in fear, it could sabotage the results. It could have been very dangerous. Once I let go, God took care of everything. We were all fine. It was a huge lesson for all of us.

We were home for one week when Dora called me to ask why I was *not* going to Judy's. She was doing a class on 'How to maintain focus in the midst of chaos'- Dora added, "Sat night, we're going to discuss in detail the stuff that went on in AZ."... I proceeded to say, "That's exactly why I don't think I should go because, in prayer, I received a very strong message; a scolding if you will; that I should trust that God took care of it and leave it all alone! Don't talk about it anymore because I am feeding negative energy when I talk about it!" and feeding it calls it back to us.

# Sacred Rose

My best friend, Becca, called to tell me her father died. Her Dad was my good buddy, Mr. Mitchell. I loved Becca's parents like they were my own. I could sit with her mom for hours, listening to her wisdom. She had such a love for nature; it was as if she could talk with the squirrels. Their home was a farm on top of the hill with its own pond. When we went up there, it was like going to another state. You couldn't even hear any cars. He was a skilled blacksmith who used to shoe the horses at a race track in New York.

One summer, he taught me how to make horseshoes from metal in a forge, hand-cut copper roses, and other beautiful crafts. I was so deeply saddened by his passing.

When I was younger, I begged Mr. Mitchell to teach me to make the copper rose. He reluctantly said, "Well, okay." He was a stern man of few words: "be here bright and early." I took vacation time out of work for two weeks. I was so excited I got up early, grabbed coffees at our local Dunkin Donuts, and as I was walking to the barn, I could hear Mr. Mitchell say, "Well, good afternoon!" It was 9:00 am. He had been waiting for me since 4:00 am! He explained how beneficial it is to work with the sun. Sun up to sun down and sleep when the sun is down. I finally learned how to make that copper rose; it took me eight full hours to do it myself, and when I was done, my hands were a mess. They were all cut up and sore for days after, but it is my treasure. One of the guys at work offered to sell them at his store; he wanted me to make him a dozen and offered me one dollar each.

I have two copper roses, the one Mr. Mitchell and I made and the one I made by myself.

They are priceless, and I would never, ever sell them.

With Mr. Mitchell's passing, I cried so hard. When I finally got my composure, I did Sacred Ceremony Death rites for him. I could actually hear his voice. He told me he was at peace and he was no longer in pain. Although he felt sad to leave his family and friends, it was his time. He also agreed to come to talk with me in the future, and I promised him that I'd help him here on this three-dimensional earth plane.

# Mack

I always seemed to study with several Shamans at the same time. The teachings were feeding my Soul; I just couldn't get enough fast enough! I was in one class or another every weekend.

West work is about stepping beyond death and facing your fears. Mack came down with a heart condition. I had all of the Shamans I knew in Peru as well as America working on him. Within a month, his heart was fine. He was off his pills and running around like a puppy again. The Vet was shocked. A month later, his hips went. One day, he was fine; the next, he was dragging his back legs. We brought him back to the Vet for evaluation. He said there was nothing we could do; not even surgery would help. We bought him a sling so we could hold his back end up so he could walk outside. It was so pathetic! I connected up in Prayer, and because of my attachment to Mack, it was so hard to listen to the information I was getting. I did not want to hear it. God was letting me know it was his time to cross over. I refused to believe this. God, you MUST do something. 'You *must* save Mack,' I demanded. How could I fight Mack's divine path? It is Thy Will Be Done. This is God's work, not mine. I was devastated. Mack was a member of our family.

I couldn't believe the information I was getting, so I called Judy. She said, "Elizabeth, you know it is his time. You can heal his hips just like you healed his heart, but then he will manifest something else. *It is his time to go.* He can be more help to you on the other side." That was exactly what I kept hearing when I connected up; however, it was NOT what I wanted to hear. It was so difficult to hear these words.

We all loved him so much. I spent the day with Mack and Bull lying on my bed. I kept asking Mack if it was true that he wanted to go. Asking time and again, "If you want to go, please let me have a sign, lick me on the nose. He licked me on the nose. "If you really, really want to go, lick my left hand." He licked my left hand. I did not want to believe it was so. It hurt so much. I could see it in his eyes. He was ready. By the time Al came home from work, I knew without a doubt it was so. It was Mack's time to cross over, and the least I could do for him was to support his decision. I had to stay with him until the end. We took him to the Vet. Chuck and Nancy were there. They worked for Dr. Zeke for many years. After he retired, it was taken over by another vet. I didn't know this new guy, but at this critical time, I explained to him that I needed to do a Shamanic Ceremony, Death Rites, after Mack died. He agreed. All I kept thinking was that Mack deserved the best, and I was doing this for him. God gave me the strength to get through this. Losing Mack was like losing a child.

When I got home, Bull (our 80 lb. six-year-old American bulldog) was sitting up against my bed. He knew. He hugged me and held my hand like a human. He always interlocked his paw 'fingers' in mine. I cried with Bull the whole next week. He sulked and was really depressed with me. We totally understood each other. Mack took a piece of my heart with him. The Bach flower remedy "hornbeam" and Joy Oil from Young Living really helped me at this time. In two-weeks-time, I could finally think about him without the pain of that giant hole in my heart. Bull and Mack always lay down with their heads right in the middle of my mesa when I'd do prayer. Now, Bull is physically there, and I can feel Mack's Spiritual presence. I can hear his nails as he walks on the tile floor, and I can still hear him drinking water in the kitchen. I know Mack is still with me.

One morning, I was driving to a job in my little yellow pickup truck, and I heard a huge sneeze, and I saw Mack sitting on the passenger seat with snot all over the dashboard. I know it was real—I HAD TO CLEAN IT UP!!!

Mack's gift:

In fact, the veil is so thin… It's been a mess here since Mack passed away. Bull is still walking around sulking. Marco is sad, and Al, well, you can't even mention Mack's name in front of him. He leaves the room. I told him he needed to cry, and it was ok. He just walks away. There is no discussion.

Me? Well, I just keep crying.

Thursday, I picked up Mack's ashes from the Vet; I couldn't stop holding them close to my chest. I just sat there in the truck crying. Oh God, I miss him so much! It hurts!

There was something special about him. I had such a strong connection with him. Al brought Mack to me the day after we buried my Mom; his life brought me comfort at such a traumatic time.

I walked with Bull every day. It was so pathetic to see him like that, sad and sulking.

Each time we walked, I would find a feather. Then it was everywhere; I knew they were from Mack because *he* knew I liked feathers. I got feathers from all kinds of birds: Canadian Geese, Blue jays, Sparrows, Robins, and Ravens. EVERY Day, everywhere I went!!! It was undeniable that they came from a source beyond Earth because I had never seen this many feathers in all my life! There were thousands. I know it was Mack sending them to me for sure!

A few days after Mack passed, I saw a whole goose fall out of the sky right onto Route 10, fully intact. I questioned if I really saw this. Surely, I must be dreaming. The next day, it happened again. I saw this dark object coming down from the sky right in front of my truck. Sure enough, it was a goose, a whole big Canadian goose. Once again, as I was driving on Route 10, it landed right there on the side of the highway near the middle median. I called Denise, and she said, "Eliz, it's a message; you need to pick it up and meditate with it, then bury it. If not, they will keep coming." This is too weird. I called Judy to see if she had any ideas. I thought, "There must be something easy I can do instead of picking up a dead goose off the highway." I was hoping she had something better to say! Not so, she confirmed what Denise said, that this is what I need to do.

After my own meditation, I confirmed, "I MUST pick it up if it happens again."

The very next day, I was driving to work, thinking *this is nuts*! Here comes ANOTHER GOOSE. Oh my God, right out of the sky! This one almost hit my truck right on the highway of Route 10. It landed on the middle median. Oh my God!!! Now my heart is beating so fast, I'm shaking, and I know for sure I have to go get it! What the heck is going on? Geese are falling out of the sky!

I went to work and got my little yellow truck to start my day, knowing I must get this goose, or they WILL KEEP COMING. As Judy said, "*How many more must die before you GET IT.*" I continued to think, "Oh My God, this is just too much!"

I pulled over with flashers on, put my gloves on, and, with a big bag in hand, headed out to the middle median of Route 10. My heart felt like it was going to beat out of my chest! I was so nervous and breathing so fast that I began to hyperventilate. As I touched the goose, it was warm. I began to get the dry heaves. I thought it must be bloody and gross. I took a deep breath and prayed that no one would see me trying to put the goose into a bag. I couldn't believe it didn't fit! Who knew a goose would be that big?! I quickly put it in the back of the pickup and drove off, hoping that no one saw me. Surely, they'd put me in the nut house.

I called Denise. She said "I'll meet you at home". I explained to her I had to finish my job. "I will drop off the goose at home; meet me there after work."

She advised me to put it in the freezer (it won't fit!). Denise said, "Wrap it in several bags and put it in the coolest place you have." It must be 98 degrees out. It was the hottest day in July! The only cold place at my house was in the garage under Al's '64 Corvette. I had to call Al and tell him not to touch the bag under his beloved car. Of course, he wanted an explanation. I don't need to tell you *exactly* what he said. (He flipped!)

*(Let me see, how many years ago was it that he said, "If you get weird on me, I'm gonna make you stop"??)*

Denise and my friend Pam met me at home after work. I also called Richard, Al's cousin. I knew I needed to save something from this gift, maybe feathers? I just didn't know what, and I had never done this before. Having Richard standing by with his hunting tools was a plus.

The weirdest thing was that there was NO blood anywhere on this goose; he was fully intact. Al and Richard inspected the entire goose because neither of them could believe there was not a blemish on this bird. All they could see was that his neck was a bit limp, possibly broken. Really weird, a whole goose. No blood, no damage, not even a broken feather.

I opened sacred space, sat with the goose in prayer, and meditated until I received the information. The messages were so beautiful. It was Mack honoring me and thanking me. Oh my God, it was so intense the words came as if he were talking to me.

Then he told me I could use the wings in ceremony only if I chose, or I could bury the whole bird. I chose to save the wings for ceremony.

Richard cut the wings off for me. I cured them in borax and had to bury the rest of the Goose body by myself. No one could do this for me. It was my gift. It was my message. I must honor this by pushing my limits and taking hold of it as sacred.

I walked into the woods and found the perfect spot. It was still over 97 degrees by 5:00 pm. As I dug the hole with the shovel, I kept hitting rocks. Denise and Pam stayed with me for support. They coaxed and cheered me on, so I continued digging. After digging down about six inches, I looked up; soaking wet from the heat, I was sweating like crazy. Denise said, "Deeper, you don't want animals to dig this up!" It seemed to take forever. I was so thankful that Denise & Pam were there to continue talking and supporting me through this most difficult event.

On Thanksgiving morning, we were heading out the door for dinner with family at Jeanne's house. Al ran inside, yelling, "You better come here! There's something here for you!" I followed him over to the side of our house, and lying there was the most beautiful, perfect Raven. I put gloves on to inspect and found that his neck was a bit crooked. This beautiful bird was perfectly intact, and his feathers were most beautiful.

I instructed Al to wait in the car; I'll be out in a minute. Never could I let him see I was wrapping it up and placing it in the freezer downstairs. He would have shit! Because of my love for all God's creatures, he often brings them to me. My friend Scott is a taxidermist in town, and he taught me to put them in the freezer as soon as possible. This time, I visited Scott with a bird in hand when he asked, "What do you want to do with it?" He was thinking about mounting it on a branch to post in our family room. NO! "I want to hug him". You should have seen Scott's face. Now, we've had some very interesting conversations over the years, but he's never been told someone wanted to hug a dead bird. I always get what I want, so within a week, I was picking up Raven. Scott made him better than I could have dreamed, spread his wings, fluffed up his body, and cleaned him so perfectly that I could hug him any time I wanted.

A month later, one of my Reiki students was so appreciative he called me and asked if I liked Bear. He said he had a present for me from Canada. When I arrived, he handed me a frozen box, about 18 inches by 18 inches square. This student had fallen out of the tree after shooting this bear and became paralyzed from the waist down because of it. Although he paid his Karma, praying and connecting with the spirit of the Bear, he finally made peace with it. It was a huge gift that I continue to pray with every day of my life to balance the lives of all Bears throughout the entire world. Once again, I took it to my friend Scott, the taxidermist, and he cleaned up the bear and kept it all natural. He gave me the skull with teeth along with the tag to prove it was all legal. Scott recently passed away, so along with all my critters, I add prayers for him daily. Scott was such a blessing and enlightened Soul. I know he prayed with every animal the hunters brought him; it was his gift, and he is still guiding animals, now from the other side.

So many things came to me. I finally had to pray and thank Mack and tell him it was not necessary to send me whole birds and animals. I appreciate feathers just as much. And still, to this day, I get feathers. Yesterday, there was a huge raven's feather as I opened the back door. It truly amazes me.

*Little did I know I am from the Bear Clan of Lake Huron (1590) confirmed by my DNA (2023).*

# Al's Company

One cold Saturday in November, we were having the storm of the century. We already had a foot of snow still left on the ground from a few days ago, and another foot was predicted before midnight tonight. I went to work with Al because he was having his annual flea market. This was his once-a-year event when his wholesale company opened the doors to the public and allowed them to purchase selected items at discounted prices. Al is such a perfectionist when it comes to his business. We were open and ready for business, but because of the snowstorm, no one was coming. I was secretly delighted to have him 'alone, all to myself.' I relished the opportunity as we got into deep conversation. It was time for me to tell him, "That corner of the warehouse" space is really negative.

There is a real dark corner in the back of the building where they stash "rejects" (damaged goods that must be sent back to the manufacturer). That corner is cold, damp, and has the energy of a rat! He said, well "fix it." I really don't think he knew what I was going to do, and I didn't ask… I just did it.

I started upstairs in the office area. With sage in hand, chimes, Rattles, and Florida water, I went into one room after another. Praying and releasing negativity, cleansing and filling 100% Pure White Light of Christ / God into each and every corner of every room, closet, bathroom, and stairway. From the floor to the roof, without missing a spot.

Within 1/2 hour of completing the ceremony, a man from a nearby store came and bought several thousands of dollars worth of snow shovels. There was no denying how this happened.

At the end of the day, we were packing up to head home. Al's friend George called. He was on his way home from Florida with his wife. Just as the phone rang, I heard God loud and clear. "They would spend the night in a hotel if they got on that flight; tell them to stay put…" (I repeated what I heard out loud) amazingly, Al suggested to George that they get a hotel for the night. The flight was indeed canceled, so they avoided the chaos and spent a nice night in a nice, warm, and cozy hotel.

When I first learned how to connect to God, it was connecting UP; I'd do it everywhere. Al said my eyes looked so far up—it looked like I was going to have a seizure. Once, we were at a party, and a woman fell, and people ran to her side. I immediately connected up to God to see if she would be alright. I was getting an answer that she'd be okay, and a man came up to me to ask if I was alright; he saw the whites of my eyes. This was exactly what Al was talking about. Seizure? No way, I was alright. I was better than alright… I was connecting up and getting answers with God.

*Even though connecting up worked, it is not like today, where I connect with God. I've actually fine-tuned this now & can connect without anyone knowing I've done anything different. I also have Divine Guidance now, where I allow God to Guide my every move. It's much easier now, discreet, and much more accurate.*

# Hawaii

In 2004, I began to hear messages about Dolphins, Lomi-Lomi, and Hawaii. I didn't even know what Lomi-Lomi was at the time, so I searched the internet to see what it was. I found it was a Sacred Hawaiian massage, a beautiful dance over the body. I found a website and printed the page. It was about a woman, Tammy, who held workshops for people to swim with the dolphins and taught a certification class in Lomi-Lomi massage. I thought—nice, *but I was broke.* I had spent so much money studying shamanism/ healing and traveling the world, but even though I was working and making a lot of money, I could not afford this trip.

The message kept coming. Every day, it would interrupt my morning prayer ritual. I only had so much time in the morning to pray, shower, get dressed, and get to work on time. I printed out the brochure and put it on my Mesa (Prayer Altar). When the message interrupted me again, I sarcastically yelled, "If this is what you want me to do! SEND ME THE MONEY!!!" Within two days, I had a check for $600. *(It was a dividend check from a retirement fund. I didn't even remember requesting them to send me the checks—I thought I had them roll it over back into the account.)* I had a feeling, and I told Al, "I *think* I have to go to Hawaii." He said, "Are you nuts? Pay your bills." Friday, I received a check for *$770 (In Rhode Island, we have TDI (temp. Disability) taken out of our checks every week and put into a fund; then, when you are out sick for any length of time, you can collect your TDI—it's the state law. Well, at work, the company elected to reimburse this amount annually—as an incentive not to go out sick.* Once again, I said to Al, "I *really* think I gotta go to Hawaii."

He answered, "YOU'RE READING THIS ALL WRONG, GOD WANTS YOU TO PAY YOUR BILLS!"

On Saturday, I was sitting at the kitchen counter, and Al came in with the mail, handing me an envelope, stating, "Open this now." You could see through the envelope that it was clearly a check. I opened it, and it was a check for $1700.

At that time, Al just looked at me and said, "When are you leaving?"

*(I had surgery in 2003. I had forgotten that I had insurance on my car loan. I continued paying the loan when I was out sick. So, the credit union issued me this check for my overpayments because the insurance company had already paid them. The sources of money came from places I totally didn't expect. It was a shock when I received each check. That is how I knew it was from God, and I knew I had to go to Hawaii!)*

It astonished me. I didn't want to go to Hawaii, but now that I got the message and demanded, 'Send me the money.' I knew I had to go! I booked the flight and workshop with Tammy.

I really didn't want to go alone, and surely God knew this because a week before I was to leave, Nancy called me and said, "I heard you're going to Hawaii… I'm coming too!" This was another one of those times where I think things can't get any better, and then they DO! I couldn't have even dreamed it this good!

I was plucked out of my comfy little life here in Rhode Island and inserted into the native life in Hawaii, doing exactly what they do, eating what they eat, and sleeping on a Futon on the floor. I thought I would be fine. Reality slapped me in the head when I realized there would be no dairy, meat, chocolate, caffeine, or sugar. Sleeping on a futon on the floor was next to bugs so big you could put a saddle on them! By the third day, I was exhausted from not sleeping and detoxing like crazy, starving for caffeine and sugar. At this time, I was used to cramming 7 tsp of sugar into a Dunkin' Donuts medium iced coffee daily. Hawaii was a humbling experience.

On the first day of our Lomi-Lomi Massage, Tammy had six natives come in for us to practice. They each stood there in their tan bronzed skin with a sarong on. When the teacher said, okay, get on the table, each one of them, in unison, dropped their sarongs and lay naked on the tables. I looked at Nancy and whispered, "They're *f---ing naked*"! She laughed and said, "What did you expect? *This* is a massage!" I had NO idea! I never expected it. I was *shocked*! I neglected to investigate details about massage when I got the message. I just knew I had to learn Lomi-Lomi. Getting over my shock, I learned one of the most beautiful massages ever. Lomi-Lomi is a sacred Hawaiian massage, literally a dance over the body with healing energies that are very powerful.

After graduating with Lomi-Lomi, we took a boat and headed to the Island of Lanai. It was breathtakingly beautiful. The sun setting on the water was precious. Nancy & I swam out from shore for 20 minutes before I had my first encounter with the Spinner dolphins. We were surrounded by at least 25 of them. They were so playful, swimming with us, touching us, and letting us pet them. When I got back to shore, Nancy told me my leg was bleeding. I looked down at my calf, and I noticed that the huge MOLE I had since I was a small child *was gone,* and that's where the blood was coming from. I had heard that the dolphins possess certain healing frequencies that could raise your vibration if they choose to "zap" you. Oh My God, I've been 'Zapped'! What a beautiful thing.

*That mole was gone until I was 60 years old ~ I guess it's time to go back for another zapping with dolphins!*

I ran back into the water to play with the dolphins and say thank you. I realized that as one kissed my cheek, the diamond earring that my mom gave me for my confirmation (and had never taken off since I was twelve years old) slipped down my neck and into the water. Immediately, I accepted that it was given to the dolphins in reciprocity for their electrical act of kindness. Each and every day since I look at the one diamond earring I have left, I remember this truly spectacular experience. Now, as I write here about this experience, I realize that these mere words can't do it justice. Thank you, God, once again. Thank you, Dolphins. Your vibrations are forever embedded within my soul.

# Rainbow

Just as I entered the on-ramp from Route 10 to 95 while driving in Al's White Grand Prix, a huge rainbow from overhead actually appeared on the hood of the car! It came through the sunroof onto my hands, on my body, and all around me, as I could see it in the rear-view mirror. I stopped right there on the on-ramp. I was engulfed in the Rainbow; the colors were everywhere around me and within me! Thank God—no cars were behind me. It was as if I was frozen in time. I breathed and embraced this rainbow within me. (In 1995, I was given the Native American name "Rainbow Dancer" by Hopi Elder Grandfather Martin. April, the woman who took me to the Hopi Elders, used to call me Rainbow Warrior because when I accepted my role in life to be a healer and studied with so many teachers, I was on a mission. Grandfather Martin claimed I was Rainbow Dancer because my heart danced when I saw the rainbow, so from then on, I was Rainbow Dancer. As I sat there on the on-ramp engulfed in the rainbow, it seemed timeless. There was no time, no space. I was one with the rainbow. Truly, I now know what it is to be; "I AM ONE with God." I am Rainbow Dancer.

That year, I must have seen a dozen rainbows within a three-month period. They were everywhere. One afternoon, as I drove up Hartford Ave, I witnessed a huge double rainbow. I wished I had a camera with me. It is still embedded in my head, and I will never forget that vision. I've been blessed with so many beautiful experiences.

Another day, I saw the sun coming in through the front door. I ran to open the door and stood in the doorway to embrace the Sun, and it was so beautiful. As it hit me in the third eye, I let it fill every morsel of my being as it fed every cell of my body. I was enjoying the sun setting when my son called. He told me to "hurry, look at the Rainbow." I ran to my back porch and was able to embrace the rainbow once again. I was once again merged with the rainbow.

*To this day, I'm 63 years old, and I have had so many amazing experiences with Rainbow, Thunder, and Lightning. I can seriously tell when it's coming; it's like I 'smell' a rainbow before I see it.*

I understand that you must be thinking, all Elizabeth has to say here in this book is, "Oh my God, it's amazing…" I must have repeated the word amazing a hundred times by now. I can't help it… for just when I think it can't get any better than this…

It does. And it keeps getting better and better, and there are no words to describe my amazement with these experiences that I keep having. Bear with me when I cannot find the perfect words to describe these magnificent moments in my life. If only you could feel what I feel, the power of God, giving me gifts day after day, week after week, year after year, better than I could have *ever* imagined it. And to come to this from the I Love Lucy, clumsy, swearing Welder is beyond anything I could have ever dreamed.

Some of the things that happened to me… well, they were so wild… you couldn't even make this stuff up!!! It's not in my wildest imagination to even dream it like this. It's simply marvelous.

# Hypnosis

I figured if I was taking people on Shamanic journeys and getting into people's heads, talking them through meditations, etc... I must know what I'm doing. I signed up for NLP (Neuro-Linguistic Programming) and Hypnosis classes in Maryland and flew there several times over three years to study with one of the top hypnotherapists in the country. This was a class for medical professionals from all over the world.

One day, a woman from Tibet stood up and gave a speech: "You Americans think you can inject the cow with hormones and things that make him *fatter* faster, so you can have meat at a *cheaper* price, and then you wonder why you all have cancer." She reminded us of how we "GREEDY Americans" have meat hanging off our plates when, in all other countries, meat is a delicacy, the smallest portion on the plate. I wish I could have that speech on video for everyone to see. It was very accurate.

I think of this often when I'm in a Chinese buffet and watch the enormous amounts of food people ingest. I knew she was right. Why do we hurt ourselves like this? It's the American way. Our Medical *industry* seems to be there only to put a band-aid on our problems when in other countries, the medical people will teach you how to be healthy. Our system seems to be one to give you a pill that will help *this*, and with the fine print, in reality, it is harming *that*! I promised myself I would not get into bashing the medical industry here; there are far too many alternative practitioners already doing that. I realize I can do more harm by adding to that negativity. What needs to be done is to "hold prayer" and hold the vision for the Alternative and Conventional Medical people to join hands and work together for the good of all. Realizing it is *not* about the money; it is about life and the generations to come.

In Maryland, there was plenty of practice time. Hypnotherapy helped me to identify my love for Italian Bread with my Grandfather. As a small child, I would walk from the store up the hill to Grandpa's house with a warm loaf of Italian bread… God, NO, don't ever take away my Italian bread! I am so glad I followed Judy's recommendation to study this class. Once again, she's guided me to perfection! After every class, we would all gather and share stories at the local lounge for coffee and dessert. Pam was talking about my healing work. It was a hoot when the bartender jumped over the bar to have me work on his knee. He told everyone to help themselves as he pulled up his pant leg for me to work on it. Within a half hour, he was out of pain and telling everyone about it.

Once word got out that I did Shamanic Healing and Lomi-Lomi Massage, everyone wanted a session. Betty and Pam helped me rearrange furniture, piling one mattress on top of another to make room to work on clients. One by one, they came for lunch, dinner breaks, and after class. We worked until midnight every night.

As a graduate of the American Hypnosis Training Academy, I am highly trained in the Art and Science of Clinical Hypnosis and NLP. These trainings added to my resume and enhanced my wisdom beyond anything I could have imagined.

# Lightening

Al and I Love to watch the lightning storms. He went to get chairs in the back of the garage as I waited under the canopy. Ka-boom!!! There it was; it hit the ground right in front of me. I watched as I was one with the lightning; I was frozen—standing there. Then I watched the lightning follow through the wires through to my house and hit the main control box. It was absolutely beautiful. Al ran to me, throwing the chairs aside, and yelled, "Are you okay?" I was better than okay; I was in amazement and so very excited! Although I was completely engulfed in the intense lightning, I was not burned as many are. I felt as if I had touched a million volts of electricity without being harmed. That night, I could still feel the vibrations throughout my entire body. I was buzzing. It fried all the computers in the house, and the alarm system, and we lost power for the rest of that week. Now, every time I even *think* of thunder and lightning, it makes me vibrate with intensity all over again. And when we have Thunderstorms and lightning storms, the vibrations are magnified even further, in a good way. It's like an intense meditative state of higher consciousness.

I always had a strong connection to lightning. When Danny & I were small, Mom would sit us on the porch to watch so we wouldn't be afraid. When I was nine years old, walking towards my mom, not three feet away from her, when a Lightning bolt came in through the kitchen window on my left and traveled right between us before it exited through our living room window to my right, not twelve feet away. I could have reached out and touched it as it passed between us. Each window was open about two inches; it was a rule mom always had when it was lightning. She'd open the windows. I often wondered if this is why… did she think it would break the window?

This was my first lightning experience, and I was in awe. I could never understand Mom's friend Melinda, who used to hide in the closet when a storm came (She had lived in Italy at a time when they were at war, and she was terrified) because I had come to love Thunder and Lightning.

I was taught early in my Shamanic career that some people work with power animals. I not only have precious power animals; I can now call upon the power of the Rainbow along with Thunder and Lightning. I call upon these magnificent powers to cut through negativity or to intensify the healing results as I work with Christ's Pure, 100% White Light of God.

# T. Parker Rd.

At work, a job order request came in for an overhead line to be built on Parker Road. The last pole currently standing was over 1/2 mile away from the four *'for sale'* lots. The Verizon engineer, Henry, met me at this location so we could work together, measure, draw diagrams, and map out the newly projected eighteen-pole line extension. (You see, Verizon sets poles in certain areas, and Narragansett Electric (now NGRID) sets poles in other areas. This was a Verizon set area.

At the end of the day, when our work was completed, Henry left. I was intuitively called to go over to a rock on Lot #1. It pulled me like a magnet straight from my heart. When I walked closer, I noticed it was a Prayer Altar, much like the Prayer Carnes the Ancient Indian Tribes built. It literally brought me to my knees. In awe, I immediately began praying. I have never before been taken to my knees in this manner. It was humbling. In prayer, I asked God why I was brought here and what it was I needed to do. I didn't get an answer right away. I knew it was going to be big because the sensation within me was so intense. It was as if I was renewed with a sense of purpose and direction. Within two days, I received information in detail; about a Healing Center. I drew pictures of it. I was shown the entire building, the grounds, interior, and exterior, with specific details. It was absolutely beautiful.

A few days later—I returned to Lot #1 and its prayer altar. The owner of the property was there. We spoke about many things. I was guided to tell him of my vision. He completely understood what I was saying. He explained that his wife wrote mortgages and could help me obtain one. It seemed very promising. He said, "Have you seen the *ridge?*" I replied, "No," as we walked deeper on the side of the woods. I confided to him all the information I had received, as well as the sketches of the Healing Center building and how it is built into the *ledge*.

The *ridge* that he showed me was the *ledge* in my sketches! I never before knew this man, and now here we were, on this land, both with tears in our eyes for the revelation. We both knew it was true, for I had never before seen the ridge, and I now had a picture that I had drawn only nights before. He hugged me and wished me well. I thought for sure God was leading me to buy this land.

Back at home, I spoke to Al about this. He said, "Oh, Really? And where are you going to get the money to buy this?" I know that if it is meant to be, God will open doors for me that I never thought possible because he always does. I will let go and let God do what needs to be done for things to happen.

The price for the land was set at $150,000.00. It was almost all ledge, and we probably wouldn't be able to put a foundation *in* the land; we'd have to build on top of it. It is one of the highest (altitude) properties in all of Rhode Island. I thought it was perfect; Al thought I was nuts.

After a few days, I was meditating and told to let it go. The land was sold.

A few weeks later, I was called to write a job on Lot #2, and I could see it was completely bare. The owner had cut all of the trees down, throwing shrapnel from the cuttings all over Lot #1. The trees were crying, the land was crying, the sky was dark grey, and you could hear the land's painful cry. I sat in my little yellow truck and cried with them. This is a place so far out there I never have any cell service. My cell phone rang. It was Al. He said, "What's the matter?" I told him. It is so sad the land is crying. All the beings here are crying. He said, "Take them home." *WHAT?*

I could hardly believe my ears; *this* was Al. I never expected this from him. I didn't think he had a clue about my work, and here he was, telling me to take these beings of light home with me. I must have totally underestimated him.

I went to the Prayer Altar and prayed. I asked the *Beings of Light* of T. Parker Road if they wanted to come to my home. It is not as much land as they are used to, but it is all we have, and they are welcome here. I am sure I felt them jump in the truck. There were elves, fairies, tree spirits, gnomes, water sprites, birds, coyotes, foxes, deer, raccoons, etc… I could feel them in the back of the truck as I drove home. To this day, I can still feel their warm presence in our yard. They are wonderful. As I told them, they are not allowed in the house. I could hear them laugh. They even hold space when I do a full moon fire ceremony. I am never alone. I honor them and thank them for keeping our land sacred. We have more deer, birds, foxes, raccoons, and coyotes than ever before. And they all get along.

I have a vision. To have a church where everyone of all religions, races, creeds, or colors is accepted—to come, meditate and pray with God. It will be a place where everyone can come for Healings, Classes, Ceremony and Sharing. I call it the Ancient Wisdom Healing Center. I shall hold mass every Sunday morning. I will have ceremonies and healing sessions, drumming circles, classes, and prayer. I will marry people in love, baptize newborns, and perform death rites to carry souls back to the creator. This will be a happy, healthy, gratifying church of wisdom, working with Angels, Saints, Spirits, and Guides of 100% Pure White Light of Christ, making miracles happen every day."

"I Love this life. Thank you, God."

*As I edit this book, which was started in 2006, it's now 2023. It wasn't time for this book to be published; now it is. The years went by so quickly that I find myself here looking back on all these details. I realize the healing center was not a physical building, even though I have detailed drawings of it as a round building with a 360-degree porch and a cupola on top with a prism. God had other plans. The healing center was me. That's why I had to travel so much, to reach people who couldn't come to me. It's been wonderful, and I got to see the whole wide world.*

# Mr. Sacco

Our good friend Bobby called. He said his "dad took the whole family to Disney World for a vacation and had a stroke." Could I please do something to help? Al and I were just going out to dinner with our friends Carole and Steve. I asked them to hold on; I had an important call. They sat with Al while I escaped to my room and did long-distance healing. During such healing, I go into prayer, connect with the person, ask his higher self for permission to continue & then, with my higher self, perform the healing. Many times, I am shown exactly what is going on as I follow God's Guidance. Sometimes, it is so personal it is not for me to know; during such times, I summon God to rectify the situation while I just stand by as a conduit for the energy to flow through me. It's always in Divine order to be just what the person needs to let their soul jump to another level in their healing progress.

The next day Bobby called me, and thanked me, saying his dad was much better, his fever had broken. He was alert, and they were making arrangements to get him home. His mom got on the phone to say thank you. I felt it necessary to explain that it is not me doing the work; it's all God's work. I cannot take credit for such work. I'm only a conduit for God's healing energy to flow. Mrs. Sacco truly understood, and it was such an honor to talk with her. What a blessed woman.

For months after this incident, I would run into Bobby and he would again thank me. His dad was coming along fine.

A few years later, Mr. Sacco again became very sick. I didn't wait to be asked this time, as I had promised Mr. Sacco I would help if he ever needed me again. In my prayer ritual I connected with him and knew now it was his time to go. I talked with his higher self. It was very difficult knowing that Mr. Sacco could not be healthy again in this lifetime. He was in the nursing home for quite a while. It was hard knowing I could not intervene. It was especially hard knowing that the family could only pray, wait, and watch the deterioration of their loved one. He said I knew he was on his path and had many reasons for lingering on his deathbed the way he did. It was not for me to say or to judge. I had to keep this all inside. Sometimes, the life of the Shaman can be very lonely because there's so much we cannot tell. We must hold "the confidentially" sacred. I prayed for Mr. Sacco and his family that they all find peace on their journey. Each morning, I would connect with Mr. Sacco and God to check on him to see if there was anything I could do.

He was added to my morning prayers for the entire time he was at the nursing home. Then, one morning, I felt complete peace for Mr. Sacco. I was led to check the newspaper. Yes, it was true. Mr. Sacco had died.

At the wake, I could see the white orb between Mrs. Sacco and the casket. It was spiraling there over the enormous bouquets of flowers. It was then my job to touch each family member on the arm as I stated my condolences. As I touched them, even for a brief moment, I spoke the appropriate words; God's love and light shined through to them in the specific way that they needed. The room shifted as if all were brought a sense of peace and relief. Now, they truly knew Mr. Sacco was no longer in pain. He had completed his journey on Earth and headed now for Heaven, for he had another assignment with God, all was in divine order.

I returned to my car in a state of wonder. I could not believe what just happened, how God came in and took over. Speaking through me the perfect words for each and every person I touched. I felt so humbled by the presence of God and Mr. Sacco. I am so honored to be a part of this healing work. I am also reminded at this time of the statement, "Healing is not always living; It may be crossing over without pain."

Normally, when someone crosses over, I perform death rites. As a shaman, these are the rites of passage how one leaves this earth plane to follow the white light up to Heaven. It is my honor to be able to guide someone who has crossed over, to show them the way straight up to heaven (also known as the white Light). When I asked, Mr. Sacco did not want to leave this earth plane right away, so I held off, understanding that many times, the soul wants to stay around for the funeral. I told him I would do Death Rites later in the week. He agreed. He is such a blessing to work with. I made a deal with him that if he ever needed me, he could contact me & I'd do my best to help him. I meant it. He is a peach.

It was exactly one week to the day when Mr. Sacco interrupted my morning prayers. "Elizabeth, he said, I'm ready now." I prepared a sacred space for Death Rites with flowers and candles. Then began to prepare him for the journey; reminding Mr. Sacco that he could contact me at any time. I saw his smile as he thanked me & asked me to pray for his family. He knew they would hurt from his loss. His Grandmother and Grandfather came to greet him, along with family and friends that had passed from long ago. I could see him smile as they led him home while I watched his luminous body ascend with the White Light of Christ to the heavens.

# Flood

In October of 2005, it rained so much that we got fifteen inches in two days' time. Al's mother and father lived with his brother Paul and his wife at the bottom of a raised ranch. The swamp behind their house became a river and flooded the entire house. It was a nightmare. When Al got there, the couch was literally floating in three feet of water. Al used a canoe to get to the front steps of the house. Apparently, the flood from the river behind their house had also backed up sewer drains, and the whole street was underwater. It was devastating. Ma & Dad had to stay with Jeanne & her family. Deep down, I knew this would happen again. How can I stop this? Ceremony! I did a prayer Ceremony, filling the house with the White Light of Christ. The ceremony was done to put protection around the house and everyone there. I was compelled to tell the family it may happen again. With our family, I can only make suggestions; I can't force my way on them. In March of 2009, the floods came again. That morning in Prayer, I told Al it was going to flood again "today." He gathered his brothers with supplies and pumps. Then emptied the house before anything got wet. Three and a half feet of water entered the house again. Ma and Dad are safe, just as I had prayed for.

It is appropriate to convey these messages once. Free will allows everyone to pick their own path. Even though I may know something is coming, I must say it once, let go & let God.

# MESA-101

Thanksgiving weekend early 2000's, I began teaching my first of many Shaman Classes. I called them "MESA-101." There has been so much red tape about who invented the "Medicine Wheel" and its copyright I elected not to get involved. Now, I teach how I do what I do in Shamanism and my healing work. I had discussed this with my mentor, Judy. I felt it was time for me to teach, but I would not do this without my teachers' blessings. After studying with her, her teachers, and their teachers here and in Peru for many years, it is time. Judy, Alberto, Don Manuel, and Don Martin have all given me their blessings with love, so now, I'm ready.

Yes, I'm ready to teach. I Love this Sacred medicine, and I still hold it sacred to my heart. It is my Divine path. It is my life. It gives me great pleasure to pass on how I've learned to "do what I do" to those who will also *keep the medicine sacred to their hearts.*

I've finally given in to a group of girls who have been asking me to teach for years. I prepare notes weeks ahead of time about what I am going to teach; then, when I open sacred space, the ancient ones come in and take over. Some things are similar to what I have planned; other times, it isn't even close. Every class is actually taught by the ancient ones from years past, channeling through me. Each and every time, it is more beautiful than I could have ever imagined. Of course, let me clarify: I do NOT channel spirits. I connect with GOD first, then ask God to bring in the most appropriate words. Sometimes, those words come from the ancient masters who have passed. Sometimes, it is Archangel Gabriel, St. John the Beloved, or Kateri Tekakwitha. Sometimes, it's Blessed Mother Mary. But it's always, always, always God first.

The first of this four-part series of classes is the work of the **South**, the ways of *Sachamama*, the serpent. Here, we shed the past so it no longer haunts you.

We begin in the South because these teachings originate in South America.

The second set of classes is the work of the **West**, *Ottorango*, the path of the Jaguar, learning how to step beyond death and time, the ways of the warrior who has no enemies in this world or the next learning how to live with impeccability and courage.

Then the **North,** the work of *Kenti,* hummingbird, learning how to communicate with the ancient ones, those that have gone before us and those yet to be born.

And the last set of classes is **East**, the work of *Appuchine* Eagle/ Condor, the visionary where everything comes full circle, and you become the co-creator of your life, walking hand in hand with God every day in every way.

The book about shamanism & how I do what I do will be written as soon as this one goes off to publishing. God tells me the world needs healers and needs healers now!

*Update! June 21, 2023, at 5:55 am, God had me hit "Enter" and send the manuscript "MESA 101 ~ Keep the Medicine Sacred to your Heart" to the publisher. We are waiting to see the published copy. And this book continues as more chapters are written. Life is good, and God still has a sense of Humor… Wait til you hear about my sisters!*

During these Shaman classes, you will be assembling your Mesa. You will be making a Sacred portable Prayer Altar from the Q'ero woven cloth called the mestana. As you work with stones, crystals, meteorites, and other items that symbolize your life experiences, you begin to heal yourself through this system of prayers and communication with God. Once these issues are healed, they become sacred, and the symbols are carried in this Mesa (your Medicine bundle) to be used as a healing tool. The Shaman uses his Mesa for

Spiritual Healing as he works with the Creator/God to heal issues of the Mind/ Body/ Spirit of family, friends, pets situations, and more.

During these classes, we also work with Prayer—fire ceremony—soul retrieval—sand painting—power animals—crystals—Hands-on Healing—Extraction—Despacho (prayer offering to God)—meditation—egg and candle healing—100% therapeutic grade pure Essential Oils and more as God dictates.

During these ceremonies, the Rites of passage are given via our Lineage (Teachers), the Q'ero Shamans of the Andes Mountains of Peru. The Rites are similar to attunements, where the teacher plants the seeds of enlightenment, and then, by the work of the student, he is able to let those seeds blossom and grow.

The Mesa is an Ancient Tradition handed down through these rites of passage from the Q'ero of Peru, who are believed to be the direct descendants of the Inca. The Mesa cloth called a Mestana, is woven by our Andean tribe, our Lineage family, the Q'ero, from high up in the Andes Mountains of Peru. As a way of giving back to my teachers, I highly recommend each of my students respect and support the Q'ero by purchasing Mestanas and Peruvian products from them. This lineage is one of our strong points, and as we honor the elders, God continues to smile upon us. We also require a commitment to hold these ancient traditions sacred to your heart. This class is for those who are serious about Spirituality and are ready to build a strong foundation with God in their healing work.

# Peru

In March early 2000s, Don Martin Pinedo Acuna was staying with us here in the USA. He and Marco Nuñez came to teach and do healing work. It was then that Don Martin asked me what it was I wanted. I said, "Judy, my mentor can heal in an hour. You heal in an instant. I want to be a great healer like you." He put his 3^rd eye to mine, and lightning went off in my head. He held it there for a few minutes, and my entire body began to absorb the energy and wisdom he was sending me. It was amazing. It was then that he invited me to his house in Peru to study with him for a month. He said, "Then you will heal like I do." It was like a dream come true. I wondered how I was going to tell Al. When I finally got up the courage to ask, "Honey, I need to take one month out of work, and I'm going to study in Peru with Don Martin and stay with his family.

Al was so upset! He said, "Did you know they rape nuns in Peru? It was on TV last week. Have you lost your mind?" Of course, he'd say that. He doesn't miss one episode of the world news. I also knew he would support my final decision no matter what it was, and I booked my flight! *I am so blessed for the teachings over the past 26 years, studying with Don Martin and the twins here at my home and in Peru year after year. It is more amazing than I could have ever dreamed.*

After Don Manuel passed in 2004, we spent more time in Peru with Don Martin. One trip to Peru, Don Nazario Quispe (Our Elder, Don Manuel's son) met us at the airport, saying his "father told him we were coming." Marco Nuñez, who apprenticed with Don Martin for many years, is also our translator and guide. Dee has a non-profit organization to help the indigenous people of the Andes. She travels back and forth to Peru every six months, bringing medical professionals to help those who cannot afford it. She also supported a small community there and built a school for the children.

We traveled as friends, behind the scenes, and not as tourists. When I connected up about this trip, I could hear my teachers' voice saying, "It will be good as long as you take the good stuff and leave the crap behind." This is a motto that helped me a lot in my shamanic endeavors because there are some charlatans without integrity. As long as we take the good stuff, we'll always rise above.

We flew from Boston to Lima, then spent the night in Lima to get the morning flight to Cusco. Marco Nunez was waiting for us at the airport with Don Martin. They were very accommodating; we never wanted for anything. Every night, Marco would walk us to our rooms and let us know where he'd be in case we needed anything. In the morning, he would greet us with fresh water and a smile. I was never scared, not even once! He translated every Spanish and Quechua word without hesitation. (Don Martin speaks Quechua, with a bit of Spanish in between).

Don Nazario stayed with us for three days, taking us hiking up many beautiful mountains and rivers to do a ceremony. One day, he brought a bag full of textiles from his village to sell. I kept hearing my intuition say, *"Buy the poncho."* It was my spiritual guidance talking to me, what I call God. I thought, 'No, thank you, I have one; no.' I kept hearing it, and finally, I heard loud and clear, "You *MUST* buy the poncho." When I gave him the money, Don Nazario said, "My father thanks you." I questioned Marco, "*What* did he just say?" He repeated it, "My father thanks you." He said, "That was his father's ceremonial poncho." There was some talk about whether or not this was really Don Manuel's poncho or not among some of the people there. Why? Who cares if it was or not?! If it is really his, I surely will honor it. What difference does it make? It is still beautiful and was clearly made in the Q'ero village. I just sent love to those in the background who argued. None of that matters. What matters is that it is *undeniable* that this beautiful textile was indeed made from Don Manuel's village and that's close enough for me. Plus, I definitely received the message to purchase it, which to me means something *big* is about to happen.

Back in the room, I took the poncho, and it began talking to me. It had so much to say I couldn't sleep, so I asked it if it could wait to get home to talk with me. It was too much too soon. When I got home, I meditated with it, and I have an entire chapter written of the information given to me by Don Manuel. So, I ask this: whether or not it is truly Don Manuel's poncho or not. The *information* I am getting is coming from him and is absolutely amazing! God, I Love this work! Thank You, God, once again, for the amazing things you do for me.

The energy of Peru is amazing. My body, mind, spirit, and emotions continue to evolve in the daily information I'm receiving, like some sort of psychic surgery (raising my vibrations/ energy for future work). The first time I got these vibrations, I was in Boynton Canyon in Sedona, Arizona. As I sat upon the red rocks, my body began to feel this amazing energy from the base of my spine all the way up to my head, and it felt as if my crown was going to spin off my head. It was wonderful.

The very first time we had lunch in Ollantaytambo, we ate Guinea Pig. Here in the US, people have guinea pigs for pets. To see one cooked and eat it was a challenge, yet we embraced it with Love. It was actually delicious and tasted like Uncle Paul's pulled pork! Dee dared me to kiss it while she took pictures. We had lots of laughs. I'm game for anything fun. More hiking—we climbed so much I thought my legs were going to fall off. Why is it that it always seems as though we are always walking *uphill in Peru?*

Now for the serious stuff: We had a rare opportunity to participate in an Ayahuasca Ceremony. We had to prepare for this ceremony with Don Peter. He is the master of plant medicine from the jungle.

Our original trip here was to go deep in the jungle, but because of the enormous amounts of rain, the village is still underwater. We've elected to hold a ceremony here at the edge of the Amazon where we're staying. After fasting for three days in prayer to prepare for this, we're ready. Ayahuasca is known as the "vine of the dead" and must be treated with respect and honor. It must *never be taken out of the jungle.*

For the next three nights, we will have to follow strict rules in constant pray and fasting. On night one, a taste, then on the second night, a small shot glass, then on the third night, we can do a full glass in ceremony. For the first two nights, I was told by God to only put it to my lips as a taste and NOT drink the entire amount everyone else was drinking. I am glad I listened to my guidance. Everyone else seemed to be purging and puking all night long. I enjoyed the power of the medicine, seeing visions and stories Ayahuasca presented to me. They told me many things to help me on my path.

On the 3^rd^ night, I was told it was now okay for me to do the full dose of Ayahuasca. This I did in ceremony and in prayer with our group. There were many natives who stayed with all of us so that we would be safe and no one would experience this alone. There was always someone to help you if you needed it. We were all in a completely safe environment. I was the lucky one. I did not get even the least bit sick. I witnessed everyone else getting sick. My journey was that *Knowing*—that ask any question and you shall be shown. Once again, I was taken to the place where we all came from, and we're all going back. That was the first time I heard the word "Source." This is where you "Source" from, Creator/ God.

I was shown the time when Al and I were souls up in heaven, discussing our plan to come back to earth to be born. I could hear us discussing the plan of our son's birth and how he would be an intelligent man with many talents. I even saw how we planned our lives together. I saw how we designed my drinking and drugging experience and how it would help me jump to the next level in my soul's growth. I thought *I couldn't believe I agreed to that*! Now that I look back on it, I can see how it changed all of our lives. I honor that life experience and am grateful I'm on the other side of it.

*When anyone asks me about ayahuasca, my answer is simple. "Do you need to cut your arm off to know you bleed?" There are so many gentle ways to get the truth. Our group was pissing and shitting themselves all night. Most of them had Hallucinations without any control or ability to remember. Like puzzle pieces, leaving you with more questions... to figure out why you saw elephants flying with little pink skirts on. QHHT Quantum Healing Hypnosis Therapy sessions are a much better way to access the subconscious/ higher self / a safe way to enter altered states of consciousness safely with the ability to ask questions and have a completely understandable dialog with your Soul. You can see some of our sessions on our YouTube channel @ Elizabeth Rainbow Dancer.*

Everyone seemed to sleep late the next morning. I went outside to spend time with the three dogs. They were adorable but so skinny. Or is this because my dog Bull is so fat? It seemed as though they all let their dogs run free. There were no fences in Peru. Every now and then, a dog would come back with a chicken in his mouth. The oxen roam around with the pigs, goats, sheep, or horses, and they all get along. It was fascinating to see everything living in harmony with everything else. There was a peace about the people and the animals that you don't find in the USA.

I am reminded of a time I was walking my dog up the street. A new neighbor was in her doorway talking to the postman. I searched for the opportunity to wave and say "hello" when she yelled, "What the F--- are you looking at." I was appalled and silently *wished* I had the guts to say, "looking for an opportunity to meet you, guess I was wrong!"

In our travels from the South to Northern Peru, a four-hour journey through the desert, our taxi van broke down. There must have been a hundred people who not only stopped to see if we needed help, but to see if we needed water too! If you've ever been stuck on the highway in Boston, USA, it seems as if a hundred people would run you down before one person would stop to help you. I wondered: Where is that 'unconditional love for all'? Did the USA ever have it? If so, how on earth can we get it back?

I was guided to "hold the light." There was a song I remembered from elementary school, "Let Peace Begin with me…" I can hear it now. I hear, "Hold the light, be the light, be the unconditional love and light & it will rub off on others."

When you're in alignment with God, the Universe conspires on your behalf. Here in Peru, it was happening all over. I found amazing meteorites. I'd been looking for affordable meteorites at home. In Arizona, I paid $78 for a quarter-sized one! I also found heart-shaped meteorites and even male and female meteorites in tiny neighborhood stores. All over Peru, particularly in Machu Picchu, I found Feet and Heart-shaped rocks right on the ground where I walked. (Everywhere I go, I find rocks that look like footprints. It was definitely God, the Universe smiling upon me in many ways. (I know I'm doing the right thing by the many signs & symbols that are in my face daily.)

The bus ride up and down the mountain to Machu Picchu was less than desirable. Ilka, my shaman sister, was here last August. She said, "The road is so small with many hair-pin turns, the back wheels of the bus come off the ground." She wasn't kidding; it was quite a ride! There were no walkie-talkies back then; if one bus was coming toward us, one of them had to back up. Ilka was right. That was the scariest ride I had ever been on!

*Now they've upgraded, they have brand new buses, the road is wide enough for two busses, they have an up-to-date communication system and the tires stay on the road at every turn.*

I knew traveling with Dee would be good. She took us further, deeper, and higher than any tourist would be allowed to go. We were also allowed to hold special ceremonies at each of the sacred sites. At specific stone altars, we crawled underneath one at a time with

Don Martin to do prayers and ceremonies. Prayers at sacred sites are extremely powerful, especially for Mother Earth. The most intense prayer and ceremony for me was at the top of Machu Picchu. Way up top was the stone of Brunjulio, beyond the village of Machu Picchu. We walked hours past where the tourists were allowed to go. It was so far up the mountain we climbed and then stopped to catch our breath every few minutes. It *so* was amazingly beautiful. Then it began to rain, and there was rainbow after rainbow the entire day long! I had never seen such huge rainbows, Double rainbows. I was literally engulfed within the rainbow again. I can hardly stress the magnificence with mere words here; I find myself repeating how awesome it was. I was in such awe I forgot to take pictures. Finally, hours later, I pulled the camera out and got two pictures. It is wonderful. I am so blessed and honored to be working with the Divine in this world.

We also visited Lima, Cusco, Moray, the Salt Flats, Pisac, Temple of the Falcon, Salkantay, Sacsayhuaman, and the Urubamba River, then headed north and visited Chiclayo, the Temple of the Sun, Temple of the Moon in Trujillo area, Chan Chan and so many amazing villages. We met the most humble people who have nothing and yet still invite you to share at their table to eat.

Dee told us there were more pyramids in Peru than in any other country. I had no idea. The Temple of the Sun did look like the shape of a pyramid. I always wanted to see the pyramids and thought I had to go to Egypt for that! Once again, I'm amazed.

The Temple of the Moon, which was half a mile away, had been excavated by man, so we had to pay an entrance fee. This pyramid's energy was heavy and nasty; it looked like an archeological dig site. There were many rooms that had been dug away, exposing artifacts from the Moche, Pre-Inka time, Inka time, and when the Spanish conquistadors were in Peru. The artifacts, paintings, and sculptures were beautiful. The energy was not.

I couldn't get out of there fast enough. It was making me sick. The energy was so dark, almost suffocating. It felt as if the sacred burial ground had been disturbed.

Do people realize what happens to the energy of things when they disrupt them without prayer? I don't think they have a clue. Many bad things can happen. These precious things must be respected as sacred, or the price will be paid one way or another.

We left and had quite a hike in the hot weather over to the Temple of the Sun. We began climbing up the steep, narrow path to the Temple of the Sun. This pyramid was untouched by man. A guard told us we were not allowed to walk up there, so we stayed at the bottom and opened our Mesa's to do prayer. When he saw this, he *escorted* us to the top. He apologized to us that he did not realize that we were "medicine people." I was amazed once again; I love this work. On the top of this pyramid, I opened my mesa, connected up, and said a prayer to thank God for bringing me to this amazing place. We did a sacred Ceremony for Mother Earth and All her inhabitants. It was truly an experience I will never forget.

When we open our Mesa and do prayer at a sacred place, it absorbs energy, making it even more powerful than it was before. It holds the energy of the sacred places for us to connect with at any time we wish. This Temple of the Sun had wonderful, God-like energy. It was so pure you could feel its intensity. My entire body was vibrating.

The next day, Marco Nunez's birthday, we went out for a dinner celebration. Don Martin had summoned a band to come inside the restaurant to sing Happy Birthday. We moved tables and chairs and danced and laughed all night. I never danced with hiking boots on before. I can remember dancing and being *so* hot. It wasn't until I got home and saw the pictures of us dancing that I noticed the open brick oven they cooked on, right behind me with twelve-inch flames!

The next day, we returned to Machu Picchu. Don Martin did ceremony and coca leaf readings for each of us. We were sitting on the ground in a small grassy place surrounded by three-foot stone walls. There were tourists walking through the area where we were sitting. Suddenly, this huge llama came from out of nowhere. She investigated and smelled each of us and our Mesa's. Then she stuck her chest out, blocking the entrance as if to say, "No one shall cross now." We were in a private ceremony the entire time. She stayed there for hours, blocking the entrance until we were completely done. It was obvious God took over and made her do this. Things like this happen more often now; it's so blatantly obvious you couldn't even make it up to be this perfect! It would not even be in your imagination. You *know* it is from God.

Don Martin read my coca leaves. He told me, "You are in the final stages of your journey. You will break your back two more times, but you will be fine. You are at the final stages of getting what you want. Things will be easier for you. Your husband loves you. You are a powerful Healer. You have a gift, and you *MUST* use this gift. Heal with your hands. You will be a great teacher. People are jealous. Stay under the radar. 'Do protection' always."

He told me important information. The detailed meanings are truth with the depth of the ocean.

*Don Martin has been reading my coca leaves since Marco was a child. Each year, his words are precise, with pinpoint accuracy. It is such a blessing to be able to study with him all these years; he continues to challenge me. My coca leaf readings are almost as good as his when I'm connected. Coca leaves are illegal in the USA, so I can only do it in Peru. I find the fact that they are illegal to be funny because it actually would take an airplane load of coca leaves to make cocaine!*

The next day, we went horseback riding with Don Peter to Sacsayhuaman. When we were led to the stall, Betty and I looked at each other. We have not been on horses in years. I thought, "I sure hope this one is slow." As the horses arrived, I thought we should be carrying them because they seemed so skinny. I wanted to feed them my sandwich! Once again, I am so accustomed to everything at home being so plump.

We were on the horses the entire day, from sun up to sundown. Betty's horse tried to run past me, and my horse wanted to lead. Betty's horse tried to bite mine in the neck, almost getting my leg! Marco Nunez ran from out of nowhere to stop him. It was remarkable. He is truly another one of my guardian angels! Betty and I laughed so hard we almost fell off the horses!

Don Peter took five of us to a huge cave. It must have been a hundred feet high with waterfalls inside it. We had to walk upstream barefoot. It was *so* cold! By the time we got to the top, I thought my toes were going to fall off. I swear, if the stream wasn't moving, it would have been frozen! At the top, we did sacred ceremony and blessings. It was beautiful and intense.

Every time I connect with my Mesa, these moments are embedded in my mind. The intensity of the experience comes to me as if I am right there in the moment. The power of the Mesa with God is infinite!

# Don Martin

On Sunday, we went to see Don Martin at his home in Huasao, Peru. When we arrived, a small boy came out, leading a bull. An older woman led a cow and followed them to graze in the grassy fields up the side of the mountain.

The animals live on the bottom floor of these homes because the warmth of their body sends heat to the upper floors. There are so many things like this: being one with nature, understanding all of God's creation and how man should interact with them to live in balance and harmony with all. I wished we could have these animals at my home.

Don Martin led us through the courtyard to his healing room. The energy of this room is magnificent. There were many huge containers overflowing with the most beautiful, sweet-smelling fresh flowers. There were pictures of Jesus and Saints on the walls. The tools he used were off to the side on a table with a bowl of freshly lit sage burning. He is so completely connected to Spirit. Everything is Sacred to him. The sage that was burned this day is not only for cleansing but also as an offering to Bless the tools he uses. He thanks God for the healing work he helps him perform each day.

Overhead is a huge, full-size condor that hangs from the ceiling. It was breathtaking to see the whole animal. Up until now, I've only seen parts of it, the feet, head, feathers, and fluff, at the Shaman's market in the city. Don Martin's nickname is "el Condor" because the condors always come to him, and he is the keeper of Pachatusan Mountain.

What does it mean to be the keeper of a mountain? It is one of the highest honors a shaman can have to be responsible for communicating and praying every day with the Apu, the sacred mountain for the protection of Mother Earth and all her inhabitants. In turn, the mountain, the Apu, reciprocates, blesses the community with all of nature, and alerts him to any dangers beforehand.

Don Martin proceeded to bless the room and guided me to sit on the three-legged stool. I misjudged the size of my ass, and it fell over, hitting a huge staff he had standing next to the stool. The bucket of flowers went flying along with everything else. Don Martin and Marco laughed so hard as I was picking myself up off the floor. We all laughed at my clumsiness. *(And I thought I got rid of the I Love Lucy part of myself!)*

Then Don Martin got serious as he opened his Mesa, placing his rocks in specific places as if to listen to what they were saying *(the reality is that he actually can listen to the rocks talking to him).* Then he placed another mestana bundle on the table filled with coca leaves. He had me blow into the bundle three times and think about what I wanted to know. Then he opened the mestana, and the coca leaves fell into place. He began to read them… He said, "Never worry. Your husband loves you. When you cry, your husband cries." He proceeded to tell me things that there was no way on earth he would know. Looking into my past and describing things as if he was there to witness it for himself. Then he put extra protection around me, telling me to "do my healing work and worry about nothing." He also reminded me of things he told me last year. He invited me to come back and stay with him again and said, "Me casa e su casa" in Spanish, then repeated it in Quechua for Marco to translate, saying, "My house is your house. This invitation is open to you, Elizabeth, forever."

*I am so honored to have Don Martin as my teacher, my shaman brother, and my good friend. I have returned almost every year since then. Don Martin has been reading my Coca leaves since Marco was a little boy… everything he has ever predicted has been accurate. The first-year international travel have been prohibited due to covid virus was 2020. Although I'm already planning on returning again, I have been guided not to! Vilma, Wilson, Don Martin, and I talk often. This past winter, 2022, there were violent riots in Lima. God keeps us all safe as long as we adhere to his advice. I will travel when he tells me, even though I miss my shaman family and the Andes mountains of Peru.*

We feasted on corn and the most delicious guinea pig. It is a tradition to bring a token of thanks to your teacher. I always bring extra suitcases of gifts, not only for the family but for the village because Don Martin shares everything. His heart is for the entire village. He is the true meaning of unconditional love. The gifts we brought were so thankfully accepted by everyone in the village. They hugged us & thanked us so much you'd think we just gave them a million dollars. It's a dual benefit because when the suitcases are empty, we can fill them up with treasures from Peru for our loved ones here at home!

As I stated before, Don Benito was Don Martin's wife, Maria's uncle. He is known as one of the greatest Shaman who ever lived. Don Martin was his apprentice for many years, and he continues the lineage and now maintains Don Benito's Mesa. Legend has it that when Don Benito died, people stole his head, thinking it would bring them great healing powers. Don Martin had to retrieve it to bury it. Oh My! I can't even *imagine* what that was like. It is mind-boggling to think of the cultural differences in the world.

While Don Martin does his healing work with a client, I cannot speak. I can only write so as not to interfere with his healing energy. If the client does not allow me permission to stay in the room, I must wait outside until they are done. I find it very interesting, in all this time, only one American asked for me not to be in the room.

One by one, they come with gifts for the healing he performs. They give gifts of guinea pigs, chickens, eggs, flowers, or anything they can afford; the Americans bring money. Don Martin accepts them all graciously and continues on to heal the next person. He does this because this is what he was called to do by God.

It was astounding to see Don Martin heal over a hundred people a week with all things found in nature: meteorites, rocks, flowers, feathers, as well as his hands, his flute, and his voice. People were lined up around the block from sunrise to sunset for his healing powers every day of the week, all year long. His untiring dedication to these people is far superior to anything I've ever witnessed.

Don Martin's wife Maria does the Guinea pig healings. This is a most powerful healing and often used for cancer. The guinea pig is rubbed over the body, and it lets out a squeal when it sucks the illness into itself; then, if it is really bad, the guinea pig dies. If not, he is given his life back. When the guinea pig dies, he is cut open, and often, his lungs are black when the lung cancer of the client is gone.

I healed breast cancer many years ago. Just to be sure it stays away, I make sure I get this checked with Maria, and we follow through with that healing whenever she suggests it. I'll never forget the first time. She was holding the guinea pig by the feet and rubbing it over my naked body (it felt like a rolling pin my mother would use for baking). The guinea pig let out a scream as she rubbed it over my breast; I thought for sure the little guy died. I cried uncontrollably, with the thought that my illness could have taken this one's life. Maria was smiling as she comforted me, showing me he was alive, and together, we celebrated and set him free.

Don Martin's village is a simple one. The village people are peaceful and happy people. They don't ask for much. A day of sunshine is just as welcomed as a day of rain. They value everything around them and know it is all sacred. The ant has as much right to live as the spider, the condor, and the bull. They are all sacred. Everything is respected. I like to think we are getting this back in the USA. I see many people studying Spirituality & learning that everything is sacred. I really wish our children in the United States would all get to spend a week here in the mountains with these beautiful people and learn how to respect our world and everything in it.

We went to Paca to visit the village that is receiving donations from our good friend Dee's non-profit organization. They supply many tools, such as personal toiletries, knitting needles, pencils, and paper, as well as money and clothing. They even built a dormitory for the girls' school and filled it with bunk beds, linens, and more supplies. To help sustain the village, the women have been taught how to maintain their health and how to make and sell their crafts. Betty & I bought some of their hand-made sweaters and shawls from the women here to bring back home. Their workmanship was impeccable.

A few months before our trip, I applied for a citizenship grant from work. They granted me $800.00 for Dee's non-profit organization.

*Little did I know when I returned from this trip, my boss wanted a two-hour presentation given to the entire engineering group. I had to show what we did with that money. I was so nervous giving that presentation; it would have almost been worth it to NOT take that money. To my surprise, my co-workers loved the slide presentation, and many booked healing sessions with me.*

Still, on our journey in Peru, we headed north to Trujillo, up near the beach. The weather was like our autumn: too cold to go in the water, yet not cold enough to stay inside. There were booths set up on the beach where people sold their goods, much like our flea markets here in New England. Marco Nunez teased me about my soft spot for animals because I would feed them whenever I could. Back home, you don't see stray dogs like this; they all seem to have a home. After feeding one pregnant female, ten dogs followed us back to the hotel. Marco laughed with me, asking how we were going to get them all into the hotel. I wanted to take them all home with me.

The shaman's market is an interesting place. There, you can get ingredients for what they call a Despacho—a prayer offering to God. The ingredients include many items that represent things in life; for example, cotton represents the clouds, rainbow-colored yarn represents the rainbow, corn represents abundance, etc… Every rainy season, Llamas abort their fetus; it's a naturally occurring phenomenon. The medicine people send the children up the mountainside to collect them, dry them out, and use them in prayer ceremonies. The Peruvian people know of the sacredness of such things, so when they come across dead animals, they are sent to the Shaman's markets for such ceremonies.

The Despacho Ceremony can be done to petition God on our behalf. A special favor. It has been said your prayers will be answered within 30 days as long as your thoughts, words, and actions remain in alignment with God.

# Ysabel & Olinda

The next day, we went on to Chiclayo for ceremony at Dona Ysabel & Olinda's house. They are known as "the twins". They live in the "barrio" inside of the city. They are the San Pedro Masters. San Pedro is a specific cactus. This Plant medicine ceremony does not demand fasting because it is not as strong as Ayahuasca; however, we do pray continuously for the entire San Pedro Ceremony, from beginning to end.

As we entered their home, we were led to the courtyard out back. Dona Ysabel put on a white satin gown, and Dona Olinda also wore white. They looked like two angels. They spoke to us in Spanish and gave us directions about what was to take place as they each said prayer. It sounded like when I was a child, and they used to say mass in Latin. It was like a beautiful song. Each of us also said prayer, and we drank a full glass of San Pedro. Continuing with our prayer, then another glass was passed around. It was bitter, but stayed down without any problem. Each of us was given a wooden staff made out of ironwood with a specific deity carved into the staff. We were told to cleanse ourselves by scraping the (hutcha) heavy energy off of our aura (body/energy field) and throwing it into their Mesa (mestana, prayer altar cloth). This transforms the negativity and sends it to the light for healing and transformation (back to Light).

Their Mesa and traditions are set up like Oscar Miro-Quesada's (Coastal Shamanism). They had many ceremonial staffs standing up along the front of the Mesa with much larger stones and shells than the Mountain shamans. Dona Ysabel stated proudly that all of her stones were gifts, nothing was bought. Most of them were gifted to her from God. Ysabel and Olinda share one Mesa; it was set up like an altar on the ground with pictures of San Pedro (St. Peter), San Cipriano (the patron saint of shamans), Jesus, Mary and other Saints. Ysabel tells her story of how the light came to her in ceremony and hit her in the third eye, then instantly, she knew how to heal, and Olinda promised to help her. The twins were good friends, and when Olinda lost a son, Ysabel (who was pregnant with Alex and recently a single parent with a small child, Geraldo) promised to share her son with her. Together, they raised Alex.

Within twenty minutes of drinking the "Tea" the *knowing* came. It was the same knowing I got at Oscar's Ceremony. That knowing that comes in when you're in alignment with God. The knowing I get when I connect up. It was crystal clear and amazing. It was connecting up without any effort at all; simply beautiful.

We were told to walk clockwise and then counterclockwise, cleansing while scraping with the staffs. We walked, first this way, then that, as if performing a dance. We continued walking in this format for three hours around the Mesa and each other and finally led to sit on the benches.

Dona Ysabel told me she could see lightning coming out of my fingertips and the palms of my hands. Yes, I could see it also, but I really wondered if it was the San Pedro playing tricks on my imagination. She also told me I am very powerful and I have a gift, that my hands are healing hands, and to remember to cleanse myself. This is very important to remember to cleanse right after I work on a client, if not, other people's spirits will want to come into me, so I must protect myself. Thank God I know how!

When Dona Ysabel and Dona Olinda did their healing work on the others, we were allowed to sit quietly and watch. I saw entities leaving one body. I saw spirit guides, injuries and illnesses. No one needed to speak. The knowing was there. My telepathy was clear. I was able to witness each healing and know exactly what was going on and why. It was amazing and beautiful. The knowing was crystal clear, even though the language barrier of Spanish & English. No one had to translate. Dona Ysabel told me to return with the others for the flowering ceremony in the morning and she would make me a potion of healing/protection/cleansing cologne.

It was 1:00 am when we got back to the hotel. I was so awake I ran up five flights of stairs to my room. We returned for the flowering ceremony the next morning. This was a naked ceremony performed privately with Dona Ysabel. I could feel the love as well as the impeccability and integrity she brought to the healing. As she poured the flowering water over me, flower petals clung to my body and my hair. I was told not to wash them off for 24 hours. My body absorbed this beautiful energy, and I was filled with The White Light of Christ. It was a most beautiful and empowering experience.

She gave me a hug and reminded me to always protect myself. "Others are jealous of your powers," she said as she taught me how to perform this whole ceremony, including cooking the cactus. She said I must take on these teachings and hold them Sacred because San Pedro has blessed me.

I thought, "Whoa, she *must* be mistaken". This is such a big responsibility to carry on the San Pedro Lineage; am I ready for this? Shouldn't one be impeccable before taking on such a task? She assured me it was not my choice; it was San Pedro's. If I accepted this honor, San Pedro would guide and protect me.

Each day spent with Dona Ysabel & Dona Olinda was better than the first. The mental Telepathy between us became clear. Herbs were prepared without a sound as Ysabel and Olinda shared their teachings with me. I had to learn as much as I could because it would be three months before they would join me again back in America.

Something had happened to me on this journey. It was like learning something new; there was no way you could pretend you did not know it. I could never go back to the old ways. I had changed in so many ways; there was no going back. I only prayed that Al would like the new me. I Love him so very much; my fear was that he would not accept these new demands on my life. I now work for God, and my covenant with God is, 'when I call God answers… When God calls, I say YES! Without… hesitation.'

It was time to pray… Dear God, "Please make Al okay with all of this".

# Customs

The first time I was flying with Don Martin and Marco Nunez, hell broke loose when we got to customs. I was talking with Don Martin while waiting for our bags. A female security guard ran and grabbed my arm, demanding, "How do you know him?" I began to explain that we had just come in from Peru. She didn't want to hear what I had to say. She yelled, "He is in U.S. CUSTODY right now," and took him away. I was in shock. Marco, Dee, Brian & Betty were not in sight! I was not familiar with the protocol of people on a visa traveling internationally. After searching frantically, I spotted Marco Nunez as U.S. Marshall grabbed *him* and took him away with Don Martin.

When I saw them coming out of a room on the other side of the hall, I ran and asked Marco if he was okay. He was fine, yet upset. The U.S. Marshall kept asking where the 3rd Peruvian guy was. There was no third guy; Marshall just wouldn't listen. She was quite rude & forceful as she led them away again. I didn't know where they went!

I found Betty and Brian, and we were all now stuck on "stand by" while Dee's flight took off. How can this be? Our tickets are bought and paid for, (at a quite hefty price at that!) we should have a seat! Brian had traveled with Martin, Marco & Dee many times. He assured us they'd be fine. He said, "This happens all the time".

The chaos that ensued on this journey home was really unbelievable. It felt as if I was caught up in a tornado, and I just couldn't get home!

It took us twenty-eight hours to get from the Lima airport to home in Rhode Island!

In hindsight, we got caught in the chaos trap because we were all too tired to "do our medicine". This reminds me of people who say,

"I don't have time to pray" when, in fact, you can't afford NOT to take time to pray. This was a prime example.

Finally, got a call from Marco & Martin. Marco said the "police were mean" but when he explained that Martin is a very important medicine man in Peru, they stopped questioning them and let them go. They were only detained for a few hours and missed their flight, but they made another. What a relief. They are so special—in my eyes, they should be treated as Royalty! After all, they treated us like Kings & Queens in Peru. It's the least we can do for them.

A month later, we were settled at home. I was told in my morning prayers to bring my Essential oils to Dee's. I questioned "why" and was told, "You will know when it is time". Within two hours, I was at Dee's when Don Martin said, "fix my back, it hurts so much". I pulled out my oils, and they all laughed, saying, "Ah ha, you knew." It was an honor to be asked to work on Don Martin, my teacher. When I was done, Marco jumped on the table and said, fix my neck; it is sore too.

I am so honored and blessed to have met Marco Nunez and to be able to study with Don Martin. His teachings are the real deal… pure. He holds the knowledge and wisdom of the Inca, the sacred Q'ero and demands that I do the same with integrity and truth. These are the principles I must live by. Hopefully, I can do it with grace and ease.

*When I returned home, I mailed Don Martin's daughter two pairs of jeans, two dresses, and two tops. When she went to the post office to pick up the package, it had been opened. There was only one top, one pair of jeans and one dress. I am happy that some of the gifts made it to her. I know whoever took them must have needed them badly. Knowing this, I had an idea… The next time, I mailed a huge box full of Tee shirts and two rainsuits. There were enough for every postman and still some for Don Martin's family. It took three months to arrive; even though I insured and posted it "air mail", it didn't matter. What a joke. Weeks later, our postmaster said, "We can only guarantee mail in the U.S. anything shipped outside the USA, you are on your own." If this is the case, then why did they let me insure it?? Don Martin's daughter sent me an e-mail saying she only received the two rainsuits—not one of the fifty tee shirts made it to his house. Thank you, God—as you know, he only needed the rainsuits!*

# Don Manuel Speaks

On April 15th, Holy Saturday, I was sitting with my mesa and Don Manuel's Poncho.

Don Manuel began speaking to me again from the other side of the veil. I began to write as he spoke. "I miss my children. I miss my family. Nazario, the good son, don't break the connection. Stay focused. I enjoyed working with Dee.

The Q'ero will live and be remembered."

To me, he asks, "Why do you want to do this?" (Connect with me).

The conversation below—E: is me; the DM is Don Manuel

E: "Because you were a great teacher and I want to learn from you" I answered.

DM: And what will you do for me?

E: I will bring your messages to the world.

DM: It will not be easy. Do you have the passion?

E: YES, I have the passion. This is my life's purpose: to be a healer and a great teacher like you and Don Martin.

DM: I will talk to you through the Poncho.

E: Can I take this to Judy? Will you talk to her also through the Poncho?

DM: NO do not exploit me. This is for you (at this time) and then your students. The Poncho will live in your healing room and home. Do not take me out *just yet*. Later, we will talk about that.

*E: 'Cough'*

DM: STOP EATING CHEESE!

DM: OK, let's get to work.

You must respect Mother Earth. Everything, and everyone, is sacred.

See the beauty in everything and everyone.

*Giggle,* you are going to be fun. I remember your farting at the Zen Center; I was there with Don Martin, Marco Nunez, and Chico-(*we were dancing after dinner, and a little fart slipped out, truly, no one would have noticed if I didn't burst out laughing!*)

And Chico… another time… at the incarnation center… I was there with you then, also… OK, getting back to the Zen Center.

We built an Appuchetta. (A stone prayer altar), You remember?

*Interruption*—the phone rang—it was Di, my shaman sister. Di called me with a question—Don Manuel answered, and she *COULD HEAR HIM*! Don Manuel speaks with Di and me in this phone conversation. It was magnificent! She could hear what I was hearing.

He likes this, I like this, Di likes this.

I am honored to be a part of this. Di is honored.

Don Manuel told Di to STOP SMOKING.

(And a lot more personal information was said)

DM: *talking to me…* "Never mind trying to go back to write all that conversation—it was only for Di."

DM: There are no rules. You make this our way and do it how you want. You don't have to sit quietly with your eyes closed; it will work no matter how you do it.

We just had three of us here, and you still heard my words, see?

Your husband is coming; He Loves you. I will wait.

Sure enough, here comes Al… (*He asks a question & leaves*).

E: OK, Don Manuel, what can I do for you? What is it I can do for you???

DM: Go see Marco Nunez—Tell him I am talking to you through this Poncho.

Thank him for all he has done for me. Tell him: Thank You for taking care of Nazario.

Also, remember the children and my village always.

Watch Don Martin. He can be a Jokester, but his intentions are good.

DM: Elizabeth, we have only begun—we will start small.

This, I thank you. We will talk later. Go in Peace.

Of course, I wasn't done; I always wanted more…

I asked: Can we talk more?

DM: GO eat some breakfast. Happy Holy Saturday.

Easter Sunday Morning conversation with Don Manuel/ Poncho.

E: "Good Morning Don Manuel, Happy Easter."

DM: I have work for you to do today. You must plant in honor of our connection. Karen gave you a lily; go plant that in our garden next to the Eagle.

(Al and Marco gave me a huge granite eagle last Mother's Day; it is beautiful.)

I like the Inca music, Play it often.

Your Bird is loud; he is funny. (Speaking of my parrot Jose')

E: sometimes he is a pain.

DM: Ah, but he will teach you.

If someone tries to break in, he will protect you; they will not break in. They will go away. He has done this for you before. Yes, last night. Someone was on your porch; look at the footprints in the snow.

E: Yes, this is true; Al saw the footprints in the snow on our back porch!

Thank you, Don Martin, I mean Manuel.

DM: stop calling me Martin! I am Manuel. Ha ha haaaa

E: Sorry

He chuckles…

DM: Keep feeding birds; they like it here, blue jays, cardinals, starlings… they are here now. Listen to them sing. The flapping of their wings moves heavy energy away—every day, your house is protected.

E: Don Manuel, can I ask you a question?

DM: of course.

E: The amulets, talismans, and things, like the jewelry we wear for protection, do I need all that?

DM: You do not need all that. The talisman, such as the ring, is a reminder only that you are protected. It is for confidence. Not to get in fear. So is the Atlantis symbol—it is to remind you that even before this life, and then after—what you do spiritually will carry through lifetimes. You will be protected. What you put out—you get back, as you always say. Believe this is true; believe it in your core. You are protected as long as you remember not to attract the bad.

Look—the squirrel thanks you for putting out those Cheetos! *as he laughs…*

They are not healthy for him, but they are a great snack, even if they like junk food! *chuckle…*

You must eat healthy. You Americans think you can eat "crap" as you say, and feel good. Yes, you know this. What is it, how you say? You put crap in the car, car no go?

I laugh and add, "No, you put crappy gas in your car, and you get crappy gas mileage".

DM: OK, where were we? Ah, yes, the jewelry—protection—Slim Spurling… He is a special soul. He makes things using the cubit; that is the keyword here. The Cubit is the measurement in the Bible used to build Noah's Ark. Once again, a reminder of where we came from. Deep sub-conscious; really deep. UNDENIABLE –it's a reminder of our connection to God and Jesus. No, you don't have to wear *any* of these items; you can just remember *all* on a conscious level- Always—can you do this?

E: Hmmm, I think I will wear them. That is easier to look at the ring and remember all that… Thank you, Don Manuel.

*Pause* – I have so many questions I don't know where to start.

DM: No need to rush; I'm not going anywhere. I will be here as long as you want. Always.

E: *Sneeze-*

DM: God Bless You,

E: Thank You, Oh My Goodness, I'm Bleeding –

DM: Hurry! Put it in your mesa!

E: Oh My! Did I sneeze on Your Poncho!?!

DM: YES. It is OK; we are now bonded; there was blood in that sneeze; this is a good thing. YES, we have solidified our connection. Yes—we are bonded—YES, we are solid.

I am a simple man. Your life is complicated. Things here in the USA are too fast. People don't have time to pray? People don't have time. They are missing so much by rushing around. When life is simple, you enjoy the Sun, the Clouds, and the Trees. You hear them talking, they sing. Did you hear their song?

God has given us nature. Nature talks to us. When a storm is coming—notice the song of the trees and how it changes… When you see the leaves turn upside down—as your buddy Mr. Mitchell taught you—it means a storm is coming. You don't need a weatherman. LOOK! Observe the signs of nature…

The squirrels with bushy tails… will be a long, cold winter.

Elizabeth, did you like Peru?

E: Yes, it was comfortable. It felt like home at Dona Julia's. I would like to go there again.

DM: You will—in time. For now, you must concentrate on home. Stay home. Heal your friends and family. Do it, and the money will come. Brochures are OK to put on the market. Free Ads on computers are OK, too. God will bring you people to heal. People who will benefit from your healing. Don't force it; just settle into it and relax. Let's just sit and BE. Be with the trees and the birds; let's just sit… ahhhhh…

E: Thank you, Don Manuel.

4/26 –E: All day, I wrote 4/26/07. What is this?

DM: Something important to come on that date.

*(The amazing thing is, on this date in 2007, I was driving to QiGong and began channeling "El Morya," St. Paul of Tarsus, for the 1st time in my life!) Wow, that is so amazing! Are there any words that are more magnificent than the word amazing? If so, I would use it here… because this is so much more and—better than "amazing!")*

E: Hmmmm, there was a little grunt in the background—my grandfather.—Yes, I smell his presence.

DM: Your grandfather guides you also.

Once again, you have overeaten. Why do you do that to yourself?

E: Because it tastes so good, I don't want to stop. I always said, "I'm missing the mechanism that tells my body it's full!"

(In the power plant, we would call it a shut-off valve)

DM: Why? Do you think you won't eat again?

E: It's automatic; I just can't stop.

DM: Nonsense! You are in control. Use it. There will always be food for you. MODERATION! You were feeling so good today, but you are now tired; you don't have to do this now…

E: "But I want to!" I yelled!

DM: OK, now what do you want to know…

E: Tell me about when you were little…

As he began speaking, I fell fast asleep…

When I woke up, I knew the entire childhood of this wonderful man. It was beautiful; it was simply beautiful… The unconditional love poured out of this man from the day he was born. Amazing…

One Morning DM message—"Do you think of Serpent, Jaguar, Hummingbird, condor Eagle, as a metaphor? When you know they are real and live inside you; this is when they will begin to work for you." What this means to me is God is referring to the archetypes that we are given in Medicine Wheel. They are archetypes blown into our chakras in the work of the WEST and are similar to power animals. We use them just like a power animal to help us jump hurdles and overcome obstacles in life. These are extremely powerful in the life-transforming Medicine wheel, which is the ancient way of healing thy SELF. Arch-types and Power Animals are a big part of healing—think of it as Mind over Matter. Such as the time, I couldn't get up to the Grand Canyon after thinking of the Buffalo, then poof! I was up the top without any effort at all.

# Back at Home

Don Manuel: 'The beings of light of T. Parker Rd are happy here. They like it that Al put little stones around your fire pit. You think he does not understand what you do. You are underestimating him. He supports you from afar, but yet he is always there when you need him… This is perfect."

Don Manuel: "Thank you for sending knitting needles to the Woman at the Paca village in Peru. I will never forget the things you do. You and Betty did this. Neither of you asked for anything in return. You will be repaid ten-fold. God sees everything."

Elizabeth: "Okay, Don Manuel, let's discuss something. A few years ago, I was at Nicki's house and did some work on her son Sam. He lived in the basement of their house. Sam was a real bad boy. Growing up, he was always in trouble. At three years old, he pee'd in a squirt gun and sprayed it all over the kids on the school bus. At four, he was hitting bullets with a hammer in his driveway. By the time he was eight, he was lighting fires in the waste baskets in school. He has been kicked out of every school in town. Now he has quit school, smokes pot, and can't keep a job. Sam wanted my help. The energy was suffocating, so I opened a sacred space to clear it and talked to Sam. He was fascinated and wanted to learn more. He said he was going to physically clean up his space (that was very dark). I explained about Energy, Feng Shui and he was excited to get started to make changes. It looked like things were going to head in a positive direction but they didn't. As I was driving home, I got very sick. I felt like I was going to die! What happened? I thought it was good to help anyone who wanted it.

Don Manuel: "Elizabeth, years ago, your teacher told you to "stay away from Nicki. She has evil in her." "Did you ever notice true evil has a mouth so dark it looks grey and even blackish? Sometimes, their teeth are even grey. The grey is in the ones that have not totally been taken over by heavy (entities) energies, but they are very bad! The Black ones are not human. Elizabeth, you Must, You MUST protect yourself every day.

On that day, did you ask if it was in *your* best interest to do that work, at that moment in time with Sam? Did you ask if I was okay to open sacred space in the devil's house???"

Elizabeth: Oh no! I kept getting that information when I meditated, but I refused to believe it because I loved Nicki and Sam so much! They were like family to me!

Don Manuel: "See what happens and how you learn, all you now have learned, you won't make that mistake again! You must have NO opinion... when you have a belief... you can sabotage the results. Ask questions first. It's all about NOT getting yourself in that predicament in the first place. THINK, THINK, THINK— BEFORE YOU ACT. You were so busy trying to help Sam that you put yourself in harm's way.

Don Manuel: You want to fix everyone and everything; it is human nature. As Judy once told you... "You think you have to heal everyone." Some people may NOT heal in this lifetime... and that is okay. It is their path. You are to offer your help ONCE. And only ONCE." And then, you are to help *only* if they ask you for it. Most importantly, it is imperative to ask God if it is in your highest and best interest to do it before you begin.

Energetically, you may ask their higher self for permission; if not, they must humanly give it to you. Their life is for *their* lessons. If there is no permission, all you can do is hold space for them and send a prayer for their highest good. Remember, Pray first, and it's all in God's hands.

Don Manuel: "An Idol mind is the devil's workshop," you say… This is true.

I would like to address this now. If you have no purpose or direction, you will get depressed. No doubt about it. There are so many people who have NO life. They are like a fish out of water… just floundering around. They get depressed & nit-pick on the small stuff. Some get stuck on their story of 20 years ago, "no one came to see me in the hospital when I had the baby" is one phrase one of your friends has—every time she is angry at a family member… this phrase comes out. You know who I am speaking about.

It is not healthy to hold on to grudges or live in the past. This sort of thing is draining & very unhealthy for not only themselves but for the whole world. You would love to help her get over this; however, she won't come see you for a healing. Obviously, she doesn't think she has a problem. What is that phrase? 'Acknowledging you have a problem is 50% of the solution'. So here it is once again: you must wait for her to come to you. She knows you do healing work; you can NOT interfere in her life's path. She MUST come to you." Of course, you can send prayers to her higher self, but if she does not accept them, they will go to another place where they are needed. If you're worried about trying to prove that the healing works, then those are the people you don't want to prove anything to! Those are the ones that if anything will go wrong, then surely- it most certainly *will* go wrong with the ones you're trying to prove something with. And remember, NEVER—EVER work on anyone you have a problem or an Issue with. Stay away from *that* vibration!!! Just do the healing work with those who come to you & watch the miracles occur, and continue to give thanks.

Elizabeth: Oh My God, this is so big! Thank you, Don Manuel.

This morning I woke with a feeling of sadness I cannot identify. Accompanied by weakness and shortness of breath when I walk, I have Pain and Throbbing between my shoulder blades, more on the right side, and tightness in my chest. Don Manuel, come talk with me. "Hola –feelings in your chest are fear. Fear of losing Marco, your son. He is on his way to New Hampshire, to "Laconia". This is that Bike week, where lots of motorcyclists gather for a rowdy time. You will *not* lose him; he is fine. All is in divine order. Know this and trust in the Lord your God." Relief. Thank you, Don Manuel. "You know this, Elizabeth. Remember it well."

Two days later, Marco called to tell me he was home; thank you, God, for protecting my baby. He did get in a *little* accident with his motorcycle. It was just a little bump. I also know if I had obsessed with the vision of the accident, kept thinking about it, or feared the outcome… I would have called it into reality! One of the most difficult things to do is control your thoughts… however, if we don't, we will sabotage the results of the prayers. We must pray and then trust God is going to manifest those prayers. When we let go and let God, thy will be done! Thank God he is home safe.

# Deep Meditation

One night, I was thinking of Dona Ysabel & Olinda, San Pedro, and what they taught me. I did not like altered states with plant medicine. Sitting at my Mesa, I knew I could reach these altered states of consciousness **without** plant medicine if I meditated the right way. So, I Prayed, and I Prayed. Sitting here with Don Manuel's poncho. Bull is here with me. He always holds space for me, another way of 'watching my back.' He often puts his head right in my Mesa; other times, he just lies next to me on his pillow. The rains have come. Since Tuesday, it has been raining; now it is pouring. I told Al I would be here for two, maybe three hours. He says to call if I need him and asks no questions. He has come such a long way. Years ago, he didn't want any part of what I do… Now, he has total respect for me and my medicine work.

Here, as I connected in deep meditation, I saw more of the intuitive wonders that had been building up in me. I saw Lightning coming out of my fingers again. Here, now with my Mesa opened, in Prayer, the Coyote is also watching my back, the fox is here with me, and the Wolf is protecting me from behind. The Prayers worked! I felt my crown chakra spin quickly. It was as if someone had a string at the base of my neck, pulling it up to the top of my head and yanking it ever so gently.

The experience was once again amazing, comfortable, and familiar. It was that knowing of everything that ever was and ever will be. Of being one with all that is. Words cannot do justice to the things I heard and saw during this experience. It was the vision of the Eagle/Condor. Accuracy was impeccable.

I called Al into the room and had him blow his breath while thinking of a problem into a stone for me to 'read' it. He picks up my malachite stone and blows into it. As I read it, I say… "You can fix my wrists". He says, "YES". YES, that's the problem: he blew into the stone! Al has had carpel Tunnel in both wrists for a long time. Sometimes, it is very painful, sometimes tolerable. He leaves the room, and Don Manuel and I work on it. Don Manuel says, "I will fix Al's wrist, the right wrist. We begin with the fingernails; the fingers, the knuckles, thumb, palm, tendons, ligaments, cells, bones, nerves, blood vessels, carpel tunnel, done".

Thank you, Don Manuel, for healing Al's wrist and strengthening it. Okay, now time to end the prayer session.

Al and I cuddled up on the couch, watching TV. I could see the health issues of the people on TV. I could see their Auras and colors and knew what it all meant. I could see the deaf man before they identified him as being deaf. I saw a woman with a thyroid problem that, minutes later, was identified. It was great to see and then have it confirmed. This went on all night long. Connecting up to these altered states is still working. The accuracy is astonishing!

Sunday, we had more rain. The interesting thing is that yesterday, no one saw the Lightning or heard the Thunder—Just Al and me. The storm stopped over our house while I was in a Prayer ceremony and stayed until I was done.

The next morning, thunder woke me up. What a joyous sound! It's been raining every day for weeks—The flooding near the Merrimac River in MA is so bad water is up to the 2nd floor of the houses along that river. Our Electric Company sent crews to help them restore electricity. So far, so good at my in-law's house. Ma & Dad are still safe!

YES, (God's work is superb). Our backyard even has pools of water; it is the most rain we have ever had while living here.

Middle of May, another symbol came in with an extreme feeling of inner peace. As I was driving, the Lightning came into my vision again. Thankfully, I was almost home when it began. I had absolutely nothing to do when I got home, so I just cuddled up on the couch and enjoyed the downloading of another vibrational download (I really think they should call it an increase, not download, because it totally increases your Light/ your vibrations and frequency.) It was delightful. My crown was opened so wide I could see the White Light pouring in. I wondered what blessing God is preparing me for; as each previous symbol has had astounding revelations.

An important piece of wisdom is that when someone irritates you… Look at them and think, "What are they mirroring back to me"? Chances are that it is YOUR issues that need to be worked on. If you didn't have a connection to it, then it would not have irritated you! Those are easy lessons because it is shown to you very clearly.

I invited Don Manuel's Spirit to come with me to work today. I actually saw him sitting right next to me in my little yellow Narragansett electric truck. (I am a field engineer, and we are going to a new location where a house is to be built. It is my job to write the order for overhead linemen to build the job. How many poles/ wires and transformers are needed, and where to place them.) I could hear Don Manuel giggle as I drove.

Don Manuel said, "Elizabeth, you know as you talk with me, you can do this with anyone that has crossed over, (bad phrase) because it is only a thin veil—I am right here. I did not like coming to work with you today. It is too complicated and much too fast, but if you like it—it is good. But I prefer not." I chuckled, knowing exactly what he was talking about. At work, we do not have time to look at nature and notice the leaves changing to reveal a storm coming. We do not have time to watch the flower blossom or the squirrel interacting with the birds. If we could have this interactive relationship with nature, we would not need weathermen or anyone else telling us what is to come. We would know.

Don Manuel: "You must write. Start with the Christmas tree story. Write every day in your journal, later on it will be your book. For now, it is only to help you get truth out of you. Speak truth. Hold back nothing."

Don Manuel: "It is good to send healing and Reiki to those that need it in an instant—like when you are driving on the highway, like when you saw that man with road rage. I saw you send prayers to that car; the driver calmed down and went slower. See the power of this work. The power of God is within you. You must use it all the time. It can change the world to be a better place. I was taught, as a small child, to hold the vision for the future of what we wanted it to be. 'Alberto says, "Dreaming the world into being," he learned this from me. Picture what you want your earth to look like, feel like, smell like, and see, then hold that in your mind every time you pray; add that prayer every day, and soon it will be so.

I shared my little story about "life is like a cup of water, when you do good things for yourself you fill the cup, when you give to others, whether they demand or not—holes come in the bottom of the cup… the best thing to do is to keep a healthy balance—so the cup does not go empty or overflow. Don Manuel smiled. "You are getting it, my child."

I now have another phrase… Life is like driving a car—ONE wheel represents MIND, ONE wheel represents BODY, ONE wheel represents SPIRIT (or Soul), and ONE wheel represents EMOTION—if you don't balance each of these four aspects, you'll go out of balance, in other words, this is where illness or Dis-ease begins. Don Manuel smiles and states how proud he is, "You are a teachers' dream; a blessing; one who never stops learning."

# Prayer Altars

After finding the prayer stones on T. Parker Road, I prayed with the beings of Light of T. Parker Rd. to get more information about these prayer altars. They told me that I also have prayer altars here on our property. When I asked them to show me, they led me out back into the woods. Within 10 feet of entering the wooded section that was very thick, I uncovered huge rocks. One of them is over three feet in diameter and shaped like a giant pyramid. Another is like a park bench, absolutely perfect to sit on.

Tuesday after work, Bull and I went over to the Sacred Rock; as I held myself against this rock to align myself with the Universe and God, I got my period. How sacred! YES, I know this—it is thundering, and here comes the lightning. My spirit is dancing. Ahhhh; my Spirit name is "Rainbow Dancer".

*Now I'm wondering, as I proofread these stories if I have to keep this book in chronological order. Obviously, that is nearly impossible because as the thoughts flow, the information just keeps coming each and every time I edit... If I have to write it—date by date... It would be quite boring... So here it is, as it is... My thoughts, as they come in... one after the other, in no specific order... I really hope you like it.*

# Vibrations

While sound asleep one night, I was hit with a "tone" like a chime that reverberated throughout my entire being. I know this is an adjustment to raise me to another level in my Mind, Body, and Spiritual growth because it has happened so many times before. The first time it happened, I wondered if I was getting Parkinson's or some grave disease. After I connected to God, it was explained to me that this was happening to raise my vibrations to prepare me for future work.

I LOVE IT! God, what are you preparing me for? Is it the time to come? Is it what everyone is talking about? Ascension?

On one occasion, the house was vibrating so much I thought it was just me again, but the dog jumped up, and Jose' our Parrot, fell off his perch! Al slept through the entire thing! That certainly was more than the entire house; it included our property, and trees were down in our woods. New England *rarely* gets earthquakes; this was my first one.

In prayer this morning, I was told to "command to work only with those of 100% pure White Light of Christ/ God". I also asked God to raise my vibration & tone to that of the proper vibration & tone that is compatible with 100% pure White Light of Christ/ GOD.

My son, Marco, called to see if I wanted to take a ride with him; he had errands to run. We went to Staples in the plaza up the road. I stayed in the car so I could watch the lightning. The entire parking lot was empty. With so much open area, it seemed as if there was so much of the sky we could see. It was so beautiful without any obstructions in the way. I watched as Symbols from Heaven came down… the lightning would strike *three* times in the same spot. It resembled a light—on again, off again, on again three times! The exact design (symbol), in the exact same location each time, then it went in a semi-circle with the center down towards earth, and then ends up towards heaven. Like a giant U. Each strike of lightning would happen three times. This was amazing and perfect! I have been told that lightning never strikes the same place twice. Not so, for I have just witnessed it. It was so magnificent as if God was giving me Morse code.

When we returned home, cloud formations seemed to be bellowing from the heavens down, towards me as I stood at the side of my house. I was watching them in awe. Ray was on his porch next door, commenting on the "cool" clouds. I went inside to get Slim's rings to point them at the green-grey clouds and watched them dissipate (In Slim Spurling's book *Slim's Universe*, he talks about cloudbusting—the green-grey clouds of tornadoes).—There was a low thunder in the background; with Slim's rings in hand, I watched them dissipate. Slim's tools are amazing, and if you can get your hands on the specific ones he made himself before he passed, you'll see how powerful they are. They emit God's infinite White Light!

# Healing Examples:

Thursday, Sally Called; apparently, Janet was to perform a healing on her daughter and canceled. Sally said, "Janet has had 50% Kidney failure; she is very sick & asked me to call you. Would you please do a healing on her"? I immediately called upon God and Janet's guides as I continued distant healing & called in all my Angels, Saints, Spirits, and guides to pray for Janet's highest good. Don Manuel came in and took over; he knew Janet personally. He had me remove anyone or anything sucking or draining—any demons or entities of any kind that could be harmful to Janet & replace them with Love and White light. He summoned me to see the year 2045 with Janet's free will and that she will have a healthy body until then if she so desires. (She may leave at any time. It is her free choice.) "Make sure anyone working on Janet has pure intent in case she ends up in the hospital" he said as he guided me to pray with him. Then I watched as Don Manuel, Don Benito & Don Martin worked on her, beginning on her toes and moving up her body, commanding healing with Father God of all that is. I literally saw their fingers on her feet, and as they moved up her legs, her skin moved as if the thumb was pressing on her leg! They worked on every part of her physical body, then moved on to the emotional, mental, and spiritual layers. They worked with vibrations/energy and even changed the colors of her organs. Her complete Aura changed color. It became the rainbow body many speak of when each chakra spins with the beautiful colors of the rainbow. The work was intricate and detailed. It took over three hours & then they explained that she would feel much better within twenty-four hours. It was a blessing to hold space for Janet and be able to witness this healing. Within 24 hours, Janet was up doing her normal chores.

The Sun is finally out. It's been cold and rainy for too long. I'm doing prayers out on the porch with my Mesa. The raven flew so closely overhead to come and see; he landed in a tree right here until seven Blue Jays chased him away. The dragonfly came and circled me, Bull, and the whole porch twelve times. The hawk is soaring overhead. I know this will be a magical day.

Karla came to visit; she brought me flowers.

She said, "Thank you, I can see again," as she gave me a big hug. It was just a week ago, she came to me for a healing. She couldn't see out of her right eye & was in total panic. I performed sacred healing on her. While listening to God's information, I was also guided to add a certain type of healing. This is a specific healing for a body part that has gone astray. I told her the healing would take at least three days for the physical body to catch up to the energetic body. She began to see shadows in black and white before she left the house. I advised her to be patient and pray. Then, I honestly forgot about it… until today. Thank you, God, for Karla's healing. I am so blessed to be a witness to God's miracles.

Once again, I thought, "Many years ago, I would have called my friend with excitement to tell her Karla can see!" I probably would have said something like "OH MY God" as I elaborated on & on. Today, I was thankful and grateful for being able to be the conduit for this healing energy from God. It is such a sincere, humbling feeling. As I hold it inside, I feel humbled, and this feeling is far superior to my ego flying.

My buddy Ilka once told me it is different when you obtain a state of mastery. You no longer think it's a "big deal". She is an opera singer. She said when people relish the thought of being on stage for many years, wishing and wanting to be the star… Then, when it finally happens, you're not so excited. You're puking and nervous, and—well, there is a responsibility to doing it 'right.' Yes, this is exactly it.

It is more of a humbling experience, where the excitement is gone, Replaced by a feeling of responsibility. A feeling of 'Can I fill these shoes?' 'Can I step up to the plate?'

Will I be good enough to walk this path of impeccability? God, please guide me!

One Friday night, we had a house full of people over for dinner. Diane called. She didn't give me much time to talk; she was in a panic; she bit her tooth & felt like she broke the bone. I was able to sneak away without anyone noticing. This time, the healing was done in slow motion; I saw God fixing the bone structure under the tooth. Her jaw & gum area were repaired like meshwork. Then I told her she should still call the dentist. She said, 'No, I feel great. I wanted you to do the work". I gave thanks once again to God for this amazing work. I am so blessed to be a part of this.

*MY MESSAGES FOR TODAY: You have the knowing of everything that ever was & will be. You can bring it to the surface whenever you need it.*

*LISTEN LOTS—SPEAK LITTLE.*

*There is a lot of information about what is going on & for my ears only. I am not even allowed to write it in my journal. It is between me and God.*

Paula called; she is in Falmouth staying at a cousin's house, & there was something in the basement. She said, "Haunted things have been happening in this house. Could I please put protection around her & her husband?". They have been drinking & she can't do it. I sent prayer and sacred protection & when I removed heavy energy, it was nasty! It was way worse than what she said. I continued a more thorough analysis of all parties involved. I found very heavy energy on Paula's husband's left foot, so I removed it. Cleaned up the rest of their surrounding areas. It was the next day when Paula and I shared a story that she explained was the foot her husband had had problems with and now no longer has pain.

# Betty the Elephant

There was a program on TV called "Not to be forgotten"; stories about Rhode Island throughout the years. One story was about an elephant, "Betty" who was killed. She was shot in the eye on Route 44 in the center of Chepachet. I know the exact place. Every time I'm working in the area, I could feel the heavy energy. I always thought it was because of the old antique shops that are so dark and dingy. Now I know—it was Betty. She was a twelve-year-old elephant who was in all the circus shows & they very often paraded her through town. One man owed another a substantial amount of money. He asked, "How can I repay you?" The other replied, "Shoot that elephant & we'll call it even". After she was shot in front of everyone watching the parade, she was dragged across the street down a dirt road to a tannery. Betty's soul must be lifted up to heaven. I went to my Mesa and prayed. I connected with Betty and saw the entire scenario as if I was right there. I could even smell the dung and the pipes of men smoking as they were watching nearby. Without emotion, I prayed to be a clear, clean, pure channel of love and light to bring Betty's soul up to Heaven. A white cloud surrounded Betty's body as it rose up to heaven. Thank you, God, another day's work is done.

Before walking into a bookstore, I like to say a prayer, asking God to bring me the books I need at this time. The last time I did this, six of them jumped right off the shelves, flying right out at me. God, I love this work! I always get excited when I have a new book to sink my teeth into! My thirst for knowledge is a blessed thing.

# Greyhound

My neighbor Tom called me about his dog, a small Italian greyhound. The Dog had been shaking so much he spent two nights in the animal hospital. The vet didn't know what else to do, so they sent him home. When I went to take a look at this dog, I knew it was critical. He had not had anything to drink or eat in over two days. It is important to mention here there was a picture of Satan on the wall in the boy's room. This boy was Tom's son. This picture invited the dark side into not only the room but also his life & was a big part of this problem.

I ran home to mix a brew I knew would help. It was my special mix of organic unheated raw butter/honey & then organic/fertilized/raw eggs. I held the dog and got into Prayer to calm him down. I put a bit of the mixture on his gums, which made him lick his lips… I continued this, and within one hour, the dog stopped shaking & began to eat the egg on his own. I told Tom what to do through the night… when the dog can eat solid foods, put him on a specific diet. Before I left, I had a talk with the boy, explaining the horror he was inviting by having that picture on the wall.

The next day, the dog was doing fine. Tom was so grateful. A few days later, when Tom's wife came home, she took the dog to a Vet. They put the dog on steroids. Once again, the dog started shaking and having problems. A few months later, I saw the dog; he looked awful. A 15 lb. dog was now over 35lbs. His belly and head were shaved. Tom said he had a liver biopsy because the steroids were messing him up. I was shocked. Why wouldn't they continue what helped this dog so much?

*Why couldn't they see what worked? Yes, I know I must respect people & their FREE WILL… However, it does upset me when a dog must pay the price.*

# Dowsing

I've been involved with Dowsing ever since my first Shaman class. I can be found at the American Society of Dowsers Convention each year, giving talks and teaching. Dowsers are some of the most down-to-earth people with advanced consciousness that I have ever met.

Dowsing is a way to get accurate answers. Most people know this word in relation to finding water underground, but there is so much more…

Here's a mini-lesson we teach at our local library throughout the year:

**Dowsing**: You can use a pendulum, a necklace with something hanging from it, or even the pull chain from your ceiling fan.

Anything with a little weight hanging from a single chain will work. It needs to swing freely without anything in the way.

Hold the pendulum in your hands. *Connect with the creator that gave you the breath of life, fill yourself with White Light (on the day God created Earth, there was a spark of light… when we tell you to connect with the white light, it comes from the center of the spark of light… the exact moment life was created, the brightest light is in the center of that spark… the origin of creation) when you connect with God and tell God to fill you with the White Light, it comes like a garden hose of energy into the top of your head, filling every morsel of your being, feeding your soul with the Light of the Holy Spirit. Anchor this light into the center of Earth where there is a light as bright as it is in the Heavens.*

Hold your pendulum and blow with a bit of your breath on it to it to connect with it, then, "Thank it for giving you the best answers for your highest good". Or you may get interference from the last person who used it… Hold the pendulum in your dominant hand with your thumb, index finger, and middle finger touching the chain. These three fingers complete your energy field to the chain; the pendulum is now an extension of your electrical field. Pull the chain up about two inches and let the heavy part of the pendulum swing free. Hold this over your non-dominant hand and ask, "Father/ Mother God, creator of all that is, please show me YES". And watch the direction of the swing of the pendulum. Picture the face of the clock in the palm of your hand so you can decide if the pendulum is swinging from 12:00 to 6:00 or 3:00 to 9:00. Sometimes, it will be in a clockwise or counterclockwise direction.

Take note of this, for this direction is your 'YES'.

Say "Thank you" to God/ your higher self and to your pendulum for the answer. Again, hold the pendulum the same way and then ask, "Father / Mother God, please show me NO". Then, watch to see what direction it swings. This is your 'NO'.

After you have identified the way the pendulum swings for your Yes and No answers,

Then, you may begin to ask questions.

Always begin with **Can I, May I, Should I?**

**Can I;** meaning, do I have the capability to do this?

**May I**: meaning do I have permission from the God to ask this?

**Should I**; meaning, is it in my highest and best interest to do this?

*If and only if* you get YES For all three of those questions, should you proceed to ask questions? If you get NO for any of them, stop right there. You can begin again tomorrow.

When you first begin to ask questions, keep them short and simple at first. Respect is absolutely needed for this to work. Always say 'Thank You' when you receive answers. Gratitude is also a must and will result in good, clear communication.

Do *not* rephrase the question several different ways because you did not like or 'believe' your first answer. This is a sure way to sabotage the work.

It's as if you're saying you don't believe the answer you got. You might as well slap God in the face… Don't bother asking if you don't trust your answer.

Go do something else.

Dowsing goes back thousands of years; encyclopedias have it listed as the 15th century in Germany when it was used to find Metals underground. Commonly known for using Y-shaped branches of a tree or L-shaped metal rods to find water. According to *www. Wikipedia.org,* in the Vietnam War, the United States Marines used dowsing in an attempt to locate weapons and tunnels. Today, there are many different variations of rods as well as items to dowse with. Many think that dowsing is limited to finding material things. Not so. Dowsing is another form of finding answers to any questions you have. It is another way of getting confirmation for the information you are receiving when you connect with the Creator/ God.

Sandee Mac, President of the American Society of Dowsers, called me to see if I would be interested in going to Bosnia to dowse the entrance to a pyramid recently discovered by Dr. Sam Osmanagich. I had read about this gentleman and would love to meet him. However, I already had a group scheduled to come with me to Peru on those exact same dates, so unfortunately, I missed Bosnia and meeting Dr. Sam.

Once again, when God wants something to happen, it happens… Months later, I was at the Earth-Keepers venue in Arkansas, setting up a table to display my book "Ancient Wisdom" when the gentleman next to me introduced himself. "Hello Elizabeth, my name is Dr. Sam Osmanagich," he said. Delighted beyond belief, I was able to converse with him and his lovely wife the entire weekend.

# 2nd Broken Back

I'm still working as a field engineer for an electric company. My job is to write the work orders for Overhead Line Guys to build. On this day, I have a customer way out in the woods who needs a pole line extended on the dirt road and all the way up the driveway to his house. It will take 11 poles with 150 ft. of wire between each of them to get electricity up to his house. The work order for the job ends in #666. I met the phone company engineer there because the telephone company actually installs the poles for us in this town. We need to measure the distance between poles, hammer stakes in the ground marking where the poles will be installed, as well as draw a sketch & itemize the supplies needed for Overhead Line guys to build the job.

My colleague for the phone company arrived & we discussed the job in detail. It had rained for weeks, and there must have been over a foot of mud. I grabbed a stake from Hank and climbed up the 4-foot muddy embankment to hammer it in when my foot began to sink. It all seemed to happen in slow motion. Just as I was beginning to fall, I could feel my body twist as I leaned back to try to prevent my fall. WHAMMO! I heard a snap pop and felt severe pain and burning down my leg as I came crashing down on a huge rock! I was a mess, not only physically, but I also looked like I'd been dragged miles through the mud! If the pain wasn't so bad, I'd have laughed at the mud. Hank ran to check on me. He asked if I wanted him to call 911. He was sincerely trying to help. I was really frightened and thought if I stopped moving, I might never move again; the pain was excruciating. Calling 911 would have meant putting my health in someone else's hands. Crazy as it seems, I knew I had to do everything from my wisdom first before going to the hospital. Hank called Al, and they got me home.

When I got home, I immediately began all of my remedies. Nothing helped; the pain kept me up all night. In the morning, the company nurse called and insisted I go to an urgent care therapist immediately. The therapist put a girdle on me and hooked me up to traction with sixty pounds on my hips! When she let the sandbags of weight go, it was as if she dropped it over a cliff! The jerking sensation sent such a sharp pain through my spine that it was so severe I couldn't move. Childbirth was not this painful! I was terrified and crying, hoping this woman would help me. After all, she was an expert… or so I thought. I was devastated, and I knew something was drastically wrong.

When I got home, and Al saw me crawling to the bathroom, he convinced me to see our Doctor at Urgent Care. After a bunch of X-rays and MRI that showed an annular tear, a broken sacrum, L4 & L5 hairline fractures, a broken tailbone, and four bulging discs. Doc gave me pain pills and a note to stay out of work. He said the "OXY Cotton" should help relieve the pain. He told me to go home and do ABSOLUTELY NOTHING and come back to see him in two weeks.

Lying in bed, I couldn't help but remember the sequence of events leading up to this accident. The fact is that this job number ended in 666. That number has a history of negativity with it. This was just too weird.

Okay, so what is it with that job number??? I also remember working with this job, trying to put it on the computer. Several times, as I would type, boom, it locked me out, erasing everything! Later, I found out when the job finally went through to be built in the field—the Overhead Lines guys also had many problems. The wrong equipment was loaded onto the trailer, trees were not cut, and it rained so much the overhead line trucks had to get towed out to the main road street… Wow, this was really weird.

Being home from work day after day, I spent more time in bed than out. The rest of my days were spent on the couch or lying on the floor. I've gotten to the point where I can prop pillows up & read. That's a blessing. Marco has bought me a laptop and wired it to my bedroom; I can surf the web now & then. It breaks up the day. Thank God for our dog, Bull. He's here with me & has such patience. Thank God he waits for Al to let him out because I can't even do that.

I know this is big, and I must get the message before this back pain will go. Dear God,

Please help me get this message soon! My life is on hold because I cannot do what I want, nor what I need to… I spend lots of time looking out the window, watching the deer, fox, raccoon, squirrels, and birds. Is this why I am hurt? To watch nature? To read books?

On Saturday, Al insisted I get out of the house, so he took me to his sisters for the family reunion. I couldn't do anything because of my back pain. I basically sat around. I tried to hide the pain so much. I didn't want anyone to know how bad the pain was, or they would think, "What kind of healer is she if she can't fix herself!" Then I heard Don Manuel say, "The best healer in the world is one who KNOWS pain!"

Now, this was really something to think about!

I spent all the time at home resting and trying to figure out why I was in so much pain. I wrote in my journal daily; sometimes, I wrote pages and others, just a couple of words. I totally understand how people can get into the victim role and ask why me? It is easy to do. Some days are depressing. I am used to living life in the fast lane with lots of friends and co-workers calling all the time. Now, that pain limits me, and I don't go out like I used to; I'm not getting the calls that I used to. Maybe no one wants to bother me because they think I may be lying down and resting. It's really too quiet.

It seemed to take forever for me to manage the severe pain I had on a daily basis. But I finally built my body and mind up to where I thought I could control it enough to return to work. As the thought "*I'm going back to work*" was in my mind, I fell down the stairs, banging my spine on each step all the way to the bottom. I had regressed back into the most unbearable pain, and I could hardly walk. Months of bedrest only made it worse, and I had gained 40 lbs. This time, I was determined to get stronger. I knew if I could heal it once, I could certainly heal it again! With hard work and determination, I did it! I could manage the pain enough to go back to work.

I learned to listen to my body. If I wanted to clean the house on a Saturday, I could only do one room at a time… if I did two, then I'd be in pain in bed the next day. So, I learned how to work smarter, not harder. I hired people to help me clean.

I cooked in stages. First, I'd prep the food, then sit… then cook, then lay flat, then we would eat, and dishes sat in the sink until I had rested enough to wash them.

When I could literally hear my body say enough, I learned to change position or stop what I was doing; I was finally gaining strength. Within six months, I was back at work! I did it and continued following my intuition because God was talking loud and clear, managing every day with God's medicine and Essential Oils.

# Deer

We've had deer in our backyard since 1986. They are precious to watch & I am blessed to witness their lives.

Last year, a baby deer would come right into the yard; he had so much white on his back that it looked like a figure eight. His legs were white, up to his thighs. He was so beautiful. My brother-in-law told me the fireman on the next street wants to get him—a trophy for his wall! I was furious at the thought of this. This baby deer has been coming here all year. I prayed with all my might for the protection of this beautiful animal.

One of the larger deer that comes has a tumor on its right shoulder. I nicknamed this one Tuma-guy. This deer is not laboring in any way and has been coming for over thirteen years. In the middle of May, I noticed a sack under "Tuma-guy's" belly with nipples. Oh My! Tuma-guy is a girl! I had never seen a pregnant deer before, so I searched the computer for pictures. What I found was that she is nursing. Every day, I would watch her with two other females, also with nursing sacks. The last week of May I was watching Tuma-guy with binoculars from my upstairs window. There is a spot in the woods behind our house that is very thick with pricker bushes and shrubs. One cannot walk into this area because it is so dense. I watched Tuma-guy approach this area not 200ft from my back door and saw two tiny baby deer come running out to greet her. I was ecstatic with happiness. I called Al, screaming with excitement, "We have babies!" It's as if my own child gave birth!

Each day, I watch Tuma-guy in the woods with the babies. At the end of August, she brought them out into my yard. Then, one day, I'd see the other females out with the two babies; it seemed as if they were taking turns with the babies… Finally, one day, the three mothers came out with five babies! Oh My God, what an event this was! It was so exciting to witness the babies with their spots and the mothers tending to them.

I put birdseed into our bird bath when the squirrels won the battle and destroyed my bird feeders. Now the Deer come to the bird bath to eat the seed. They're destroying our grass and have eaten all the shrubs, but I don't care. It's a small price to pay for the beauty I get to behold each and every day. As November rolled around, we could hear shotguns out back. The man across the street called DEM. I am grateful for him, as I really don't want to be the one to complain about everything; he did it for me. DEM told him there is NO hunting on this side of Route 295. It's the Law. DEM went out back and took a tree stand down from deep within the woods near the cemetery.

Bless you, DEM, and thank you for protecting our deer.

One Sunday morning, Al spotted the buck. Not one, but four of them came to visit. They came one at a time. First, there was a little buck with an antler and a half, then the big buck came with 10 points on his antlers, and then the 6 points and another with 8 points came. They very seldom come out of the woods, so it is very difficult to get pictures. As a special treat for them, we always place bruised or older fruit and vegetables deep in the woods so the deer stay safe, deep among the trees. Christmas Eve, I went to place some apples out there and found a tiny antler waiting for me. I knew immediately this was a gift from them. That evening, I saw the baby buck come in the yard. Looking through the binoculars, I could see a spot of blood from his missing antler; thank you, lil' buck. I will treasure your present.

# St. Theresa

Stella called me, and she was hysterical. Her best friend Pat had just committed suicide. This dead woman was a very strong spirit & is creating havoc for Stella, her husband & family. The chaos has already begun. Stella asked if I would help. Of course, I would. Stella is one of my students.

In prayer, I received a lot of information: "the pain is gone", Pat said as she asked that I respect her privacy—She said what she had to do. This was her soul's plan before birth. As I was getting this, Stella called to tell me what happened. Her friend killed herself in a park downtown right along the riverbank. I saw the statue of St. Theresa and all of the details in my prayers just moments before Stella said it. How could I ever question the authenticity of this work? I saw the entire scenario of what happened & why the woman did this. This is all I can say here; I must keep the rest of the details confidential. I performed Death rites for Pat & she is now at peace with God in the Light. The chaos stops; Stella and her family are back to normal. When Stella came for a session, we made contact with Pat and set it up so they could communicate together without me.

*Important revelation to remember here:*

*Think about this for a moment… God was the beginning; God made all, everyone & everything… That is indisputable. Therefore, if God was the one that made all…. Then even that which turned evil was originally made from God… Whouaaaaaaaa, this is big.*

*That which strays must be returned to God…*

*This is the message I received while in prayer today: Before I study with someone, I connect in prayer to ask what percent they are working in the Light. When I began studying, I could not work with anyone less than 50% Light. And I was reminded to "take the good stuff and leave the crap behind". This is because one must remember that Shamans are not God… They can have powers, but remember always they are human and come with human faults as well. Ego is one fault that flies around the shamanic world just as any other. You will see many great Healers who once had amazing healing powers, only to 'get a big head' and have those powers stripped from them. One must remember to stay humble, such as the Dali Lama. Amma. Mother Meera and Sai Baba aim for impeccability and unconditional Love to keep the powers bestowed upon us by God. Especially for the healing work; we are not doing the healing— it is all God's work. Now that I am teaching, I must only study only with humans of 98% Light or Higher. You will see how this works in your own life. As your Spiritual Connection grows and your Light becomes stronger, you will see how you no longer need lessons from humans. That is when the Masters of Pure Light and Love channel the information right to you. These Masters are now talking to me from Beyond the Veil. Be true to yourself.*

# Blessed Virgin Mother Mary

The room began to smell like roses, then a dozen, then more. Everywhere I turned, I could smell roses. The calmest voice came into my right ear. It was deeper than I had imagined. My intuition knew who it was. Somehow, in my dreams, I always thought her voice was higher pitched than this. Not so. This voice was deeper, still feminine, yet soothing to the ears. The sound was something I wanted more of. The feeling was so comforting as if I had longed for a home for years and finally got there.

The orb began to spin, sort of like heat waves, as they rose from a hot tar paved road as it entered the room. Once it began to materialize, my heart began to pound. My brow began to sweat, and my breathing intensified. As my heart pounded in my chest, I wondered what lay ahead. Little by little, I could hear this voice as if she was sitting right here on my shoulder, yet I still felt her presence with a tingle up my spine. On some level, I knew who it was, yet I was scared nonetheless. This was my first encounter with the full manifestation of the Spirit World. I couldn't help but think, 'Why does she come to me?'

The orb spun slower and began to take solid form. Still hearing the voice, I was guided to "breathe, remember to breathe, my child; I will not harm you. We come with joy in our hearts to guide you for such a project of the greatest magnitude. "I am the Blessed Mother Mary," she said.

And here she was, the Blessed Virgin Mother Mary, standing right here. My very first *thought* was, "Oh no, you must have made a mistake; you want my sister-in-law, Annette; she's the Saint in the family. I still swear". Her verbal reply was, "Oh yes, I've been meaning to talk with you about that… It's got to stop!" Oh My, Oh My, Oh My! *I said that in my head, and she heard it!* It took two hours for my breathing to get back to normal and for me to know I was not hallucinating or having a stroke.

I couldn't take my eyes off her. She grinned as I scanned every inch of her. As a child I wanted details that I never got. I wasn't going to let this opportunity pass me by without analyzing her. She appeared to be twenty-seven years old. Her skin was perfect, soft like a baby's. She was no taller than me, but she had a slender frame about 5'3". Her hair was much darker than I imagined; it was light ash brown with a slight wave to it. Her ears were tiny with perfect lobes. Her eyes were hazel like my mother's because when she turned in the light, at times, they were blue, and other times were brown or green. I thought, 'Why is she always portrayed with blue eyes?' Again, she answered aloud, "My eye color is all colors the eye can be, enhanced by the environment". Ah, yes! I remember when my mom wore blue, her eyes looked blue. She appeared to me this day wearing a white scarf (it was much thicker than a veil that a bride would but not as thick as her dress or shawl) it draped over her head much like the one that appears in pictures at church. Her dress was light blue, with a white sash tied in the front. The material was made of something I'd never seen here on Earth before. It had a soft feeling sort of like fine Egyptian linen that had been washed so many times it had a beautiful transparent sheen. I felt this as she brushed past me; I wanted to touch it, and she again heard my thoughts. "Of course, my child", she stated as soon as the thought entered my mind; she held out her arm. She was barefoot, and her toes were symmetrical… you know what I'm talking about here, where the big toe is largest, and they range in size from large to tiny… not like some human feet where the big one is the second toe. She seemed to glide when she moved, almost as if she was hovering one inch over the floor. In my amazement, I could not tell if she was standing on the floor or not. She was here for real. It was so clear; I was looking at Mother Mary.

Since that day, I can't begin to tell you how many times she moved me out of my comfort zone. I mean, my husband has been raised strict

French Catholic. He has a prominent job in society and sports a suit & tie more often than not. Where we come from, people usually end up in the "nut house" when they hear voices. Can you imagine me telling him, 'Honey, I'm talking with Mother Mary?'; Gulp! I didn't think it would go over so well. Mother Mary continued: *"This information must get out there, and one day, your very own son will search for this wisdom. It will be here for him. Write with Love in your heart for your Son. All of humanity will reap the benefits of this mother's love for her child."*

But wait! I had so many questions. I wanted to know about all those who've passed away: my father, my mother, and all of my relatives. I wanted to talk with her about so many things. I wanted to know about UFOs and other Planets. The colonies on mars they're talking about and everything that has been hidden from society. I wanted truth in so many things! She promised me I would have all that information and more when the time was right. She repeated, "For now, just type what you hear". Each day, I would type, and each evening, I would be rewarded with more information for the many questions I had. I was shown many things in detail, and my thirst for wisdom was satisfied day after day.

When I finally relaxed into the realization of the situation, I then wanted to obey. Mother Mary began with, "Remember those days, so long ago, when you were in Business School? Like a video screen in my eyes, I saw myself typing, writing short-hand, and taking dictation… I answered, "Yes". She replied, "Type exactly what you hear. Begin now…"

This was my first encounter with the passing of Souls up to Heaven:

I was raised Catholic, and I must admit, I never knew much about the Blessed Mother. Not that I didn't respect her; I only said the "Hail Mary" as part of my daily prayers. In reality, I never gave her much thought, not like some people who have her statue on their front lawn with children kneeling before her. My thing was Jesus. He was my guide. I talked to him every day. He was a big part of my life, and even at church on Sundays, I'd pray directly to him. God was something bigger than Jesus and something I couldn't touch, never mind imagine. So, my connection to the Spirit was Jesus. Growing up, that was it. Pretty much cut in stone: Jesus, Church, Catechism, Prayers. That was my spirituality. I got on my knees and prayed, but I never listened. That was many years ago, so much has changed. I would have never imagined my life would be like this. Obviously, by the way, things have played out; I must have agreed to work with Mother Mary. YES; The Blessed Mother Mary came to me one August many years ago.

*That book **Ancient Wisdom by Elizabeth Rainbow Dancer** is the result of those typed sessions with Mother Mary sitting right here by my side. She guided me to use a 'Pen Name' so I could remain anonymous and still get the information out there. I could tell Al when I was more comfortable. That book was published and went live on Amazon on December 24, 2010, at 5:55 pm. Christmas Eve, as I was making meatballs in the kitchen, I heard loud and clear, "Go to the computer". I went into my office, and the computer was on, and it was already on the webpage for Amazon without me doing a thing; I didn't even move the mouse. (I still don't know how it got on that page)!*

*When I got up the nerve to tell Al, I asked, "Are you okay with this?" He replied, "are YOU ok with this?" Yes, oh yes, I am so okay with all of this; it is my life, finally comfortable in my own skin and more amazing than I could ever imagine.*

*I work for God.*

*For this book to be live on Christmas Eve at 5:55 pm is a miracle in itself. Anyone who knows me knows how much I love Christmas. Once again, confirmation for the work is truly coming from a source more powerful than I could imagine. It comes from God.*

Now, keep in mind, at this point in time, I was already doing healing work with great results. I thought I was pretty much on my path and receiving Divine Guidance. I actually thought I had seen it all…

Then something happened out of the Heavens and blew me away…

I was visiting my friend Phyllis when we called the Ascended Masters to bring us their message for the day. Within seconds, my entire body began to shiver. A very loud tone came above my left ear. It was so loud that it was physically painful; I could hardly stand it. Then, it felt as if someone had a sledgehammer on my chest, crashing it onto me. Bang! Bang! Bang! My chest was crushed with pain. As I began to cry, I felt one child after another coming through me. One at a time, I saw each face come into my chest, passing through my heart to my crown and following up to the white light up above me. There were literally so many tears in my eyes; I could not see Phyllis sitting right in front of me. She stayed calm and guided me to stay with it, reminding me to BREATHE. She reminded me to repeat out loud, "I am a divine being of Love and Light," over and over again. I could hardly speak as I stuttered the words out loud. She knew what was happening; it was my 'I AM' presence coming into me (waking up), an aspect of Mother Mary.

I had no idea what was happening; I literally thought I was having a stroke! Fear had engulfed me into such a panic I could not control myself. Shaking and tears continued through this process as Phyllis reminded me to breathe.

I realized that every child that had crossed over in the 2003 tsunami was passing through me. I stayed with this process and watched them, all traveling up to the White Light of Christ. There were so many faces: infants, toddlers, adolescents, teenagers, so many faces. I couldn't stop crying—it seemed to take hours. Each child was passing through me with a thunderous impact that shook my bones to the core. It was a traumatizing and physically painful experience.

I struggled so much with words to write this incident here to explain what happened. There are really no words on this earth that can give it the credence it truly deserves.

After more hours of meditation and connecting with the Blessed Mother Mary, I received answers. She explained to me that the physical pain was due to my fear blocking the process. She also explained that I was Mother Mary in a previous life. She told me that she has reincarnated into many souls in this lifetime. An aspect of her is in many people. It will be my job to find all of these aspects of Mother Mary and help them to integrate as I have. She will guide me accordingly.

Now, each day, as I meditate with Mother Mary, we pass souls up to heaven without pain. I am just a machine, a conduit, a clear vessel for them to go directly to the White Light of Christ. Mother Mary told me if my emotions got in the way, it would make me physically sick. I still see faces, but now I have no emotions involved. It is just as if I was watching someone's slide projector show. I would have never imagined this would be happening to me.

I am so sincerely humbled by this. I thought, oh my, these are some really big shoes to fill. Just as I had that thought, she said to me, "You, my child, have already filled them. You have more work to do. Now, you must pass the children, past, present, and future, through your heart to the light. It is your job. This was borderline overwhelming. I say borderline because I don't want it to stop. I am honored to be a part of this, and I thank God for making me a part of his world.

*As the years have gone by, I learned so much more. Many people claim to be this one or that in past lives; how could twenty people all be Jesus in a past life? It's all about the word 'aspect.' You see, our soul is limitless, so when someone goes into a past life regression, and they experience the life of Jesus, it is because their soul is actually sitting side by side with Jesus. The soul can actually experience everything exactly as Jesus did. Therefore, there is no difference in the past life... they did tap into that past life as Jesus.*

*So, is this what happened to me? I tapped into the past life as Mother Mary. There is so much information coming in, and our mere words cannot describe it in enough detail to paint an accurate picture. We will take the 'aspect' and understand it here. All is well.*

# Dr. Ed

Exactly one week after my experience with Blessed Mother Mary channeling the book to me, Dr. Ed's father died. Talking with Dr. Ed's wife, I asked when the funeral was. I heard, "Sunday at noon; see the guy at the gate, and he'll tell you where to go." (Little did I know, the funeral was on Monday) When I arrived at the cemetery, there was no one at the gate. After driving around for a half-hour, I spotted a security guard. He informed me that there were no funerals today, "it must be tomorrow," he said as he drove off in his little golf cart. I immediately knew there was another reason for me to be there. I attempted to drive away; my car was stuck. It just wouldn't go. I stopped to connect up in prayer to see what was going on. At this time, I realized I was parked right in front of Dr. Ed's family headstone. There were five small stones representing others that had previously passed. A large hole in the ground covered by planks was obviously prepared for his father's burial. As I prayed, I felt the comforting peace and pink light with the smell of roses as Blessed Mother Mary came in. We passed Dr. Ed's father as I watched him follow the golden White Light thread up to the sky into the heavens. When I felt it was complete, I said thank you and attempted to drive off again.

I was unable to. My car wouldn't move. Once again, I connected up to see what on earth was going on again. Blessed Mother Mary came into me again. She had me pray to be a pure, clean, clear vessel of Love and Light then we passed souls through my body once again. All of these souls whose bodies were buried here had been stuck on this third-dimensional earth plane. One by one, I saw their faces as they entered my chest. They traveled through my heart, up to my head, through my crown to follow the golden thread of the White Light. I watched them as they traveled all the way up to the White light of Christ. I saw babies, toddlers, adolescents, teenagers, adults, and elderly people. One man was in a wheelchair, another on crutches, and one even had half of her face missing.

When I felt complete, I held the Light for an additional ten minutes, giving thanks to God for all. As I looked down, I realized my emergency brake was on. Who on earth did this? I certainly did not consciously put the brake on… I was on flat ground.

Al & Aunty Irene were waiting for me at Maria's house. When I walked in, Aunty Irene said, "How was the funeral?" I said, "It's tomorrow". Al yelled from across the room, "then where have you been all this time?" (It was now 4 pm). I said, "Doing Prayer." No further questions were asked; it was as if no one even heard me speak. The room was full of people talking sharing stories & jokes. How could I tell where I'd just been & what just occurred? They would think I was nuts.

# Hilarion

One Thursday, traveling to Qi-Gong, I thought of "Hilarion". He was St. Paul of Tarsus in a previous life. After he ascended, he became known as Hilarion. Many of the Ascended Masters take on different names after the ascension. As I was driving, he came in and began speaking *through* me. I could hear my voice change & get very slow. I had to look in the rear-view mirror to see that my lips were actually moving. There were no thoughts in my mind, yet the sound was coming out of my mouth; my lips were moving. It was similar to my voice, yet lower & slower… It was really wild. Immediately, I asked Hilarion to make sure I drove carefully & not hit anyone. "Please Keep me safe," I asked. His words were profound and for my ears only. His message was accurate & clear as to what I needed to do to prepare me for the future. He told me I would be taken out of the "workforce" because my Spiritual work needed to be 'ramped up'. I would be a catalyst for changes to come. I was not to fear this new role because I would be guided every moment of each and every day.

*Up until now, I have had communication with God, Angels, Saints, Ascended Masters, and Guides. None of them came through my physical body or took over my voice like this.*

*I had always been taught that it was not necessary to get information to give your physical body over to them. When your Light is pure, the information will be pure. When I questioned why this happened, it was to show me what happens when we let go and give our voice to the masters. It is fine if I choose to do this or keep communication the way I have been. There will be clients who wish to hear a different voice; it will help them know that the Master is talking through me. This is for them, not me. It does not make the information more-pure, one way or another.*

*Either is fine, as long as my Light is pure and my* **connection to God is Clear and Solid and first.**

I parked right in front of the plaza and had to sit for a few minutes because, once again, I was in awe. My mind could not concentrate on the class in front of me. Qi-Gong? Or should I sit for a bit, gain composure then go home? Hilarion said I "would be fine, go inside now". Reluctantly, I obeyed, thinking, 'Okay, if I can't do it, I'll leave.'

In class, Master Wu taught us meditation while sitting in a chair. For the entire class, we focused on the "golden light" as he called it, coming in through your crown charka, filling you up & down through the "balls of your feet, three feet into the Earth".

It was absolutely Amazing. How appropriate to do that type of meditation right after Hilarion's channeling? Somehow, I felt Master Wu knew.

Since that day, I have been discussing things with Hilarion—Ascended Master, Master of the White Brotherhood Medical team, and Healer of the Universe. Then I connected with Kuthumi, El Morya & Sananda. I could not speak with Jesus Christ until I called him Yeshua, Sananda then, the connection was crystal clear! Of course! I knew Jesus as Yeshua, Sananda! That is what I called him back in the day! Yes, I walked the earth with Yeshua. I was there then, and now, I am in contact with all of these masters today. I relish in the truth that this is all coming together. It all makes complete sense to me. I see the past lives that I have had as clear as what I did last week here on this earth. I recognize brothers and sisters who have lived with me in past lives. First, the energy is recognized, then when you look in their eyes, the connection is made, right to their soul; it is my soul talking to their soul. It is a kinship that is also acknowledged by them. It is that knowing—that we've done this before; thicker than blood, Family, and friends. A love for each other that cannot be denied. This is our Sisterhood, our Brotherhood, and Our Tribe.

Just when I think things can't get any better than this—they do! They just keep getting more amazing than I could have ever imagined!

# Mary Hardy

I was invited to give a talk about my Shaman class for the American Society of Dowsers in Vermont for their annual convention. I packed the car, and off I went. The drive through the mountains was spectacular; I'd chosen the path that brought me through Franconia Notch and Cannon Mountain, New Hampshire. I couldn't go any further; I just had to stop! It was a perfect June day, and the "Old Man in the Mountain" was still there, it had not fallen as yet. I did prayer at the base of the mountain, thanking God for bringing me back this way. It was a 4-hour drive one way, so I wanted to be sure to arrive before dark. Lyndonville Vermont College was a huge campus, but the Dowsers always had plenty of signs to guide you around.

After registering and getting the necessary tags, I was escorted to the auditorium, where the opening ceremony was about to begin. I was 2nd in line to be on stage. On stage, I had one minute to introduce myself, say where I was teaching, what I was teaching and what time. The first woman standing in front of me was an older lady, nicely dressed with her hair up in a twist. We didn't chat; we only had time for a smile and a nod. When she took the mic in her hand, she said, "Hi, my name is Mary Hardy". Wide-eyed in shock, I knew that name! Everyone in the healing world knew that if you got sick, you sent a "witness" to Mary Hardy, and she would use her radionics machine to see what was going on. She was a doctor of naturopathy, and once she identified what was out of balance, she could guide you with appropriate herbs/oils/homeopathic remedies. For over twelve years, I had been sending my spit on a napkin to this woman! I have spoken to her many times on the phone but we never met in person. So here she was, handing me the microphone because it was my turn, and I had a split-second decision to make. I *really* wanted to yell—'*don't go anywhere! I want to talk with you!*' but I couldn't... so I watched her walk right out of the auditorium as I gave my little introduction! I spent the rest of the evening asking everyone where I could find Mary Hardy.

On Saturday afternoon, Susanne grabbed my wrist and dragged me through the crowd to the cafeteria. We stopped at a table of women, and she said, "Mary Hardy, this is Elizabeth; Elizabeth, this is Mary Hardy". Mary Hardy said, "Well, Elizabeth, about forty-five people told me you were looking for me; what can I do for you?" we all chuckled. She invited me to sit, and we had the most amazing conversation. I left as I accepted her invitation to teach shamanism to her group in Allegan, Michigan.

The morning of my flight to teach shamanism for Mary Hardy's group of 23 women and one man… I called Judy. "Hey! I think I'm going to die". Judy said, "What?!" I said, "I keep hearing *we are taking you to meet your family*. Judy, my family is all dead. I've only got a couple of cousins left. I keep hearing *we are taking you to your family*."

Judy said, "Well, what are you worried about? You know there is no such thing as death; I'll see you on the other side". We both chuckled, and I got on the plane.

# Holy Grail Vortex

I sat on the airplane and looked at the paper Mary had given me. She said this was her Holy Grail Vortex. As I looked at this paper, I said a prayer and asked God, "What is this prayer Mary talks about?" I immediately heard God—"say the prayer, get your camera and look out the window".

As I looked at the paper in front of me, I repeated the words in my head:

From the point of Light within the Mind of God,

Let light stream forth into the minds of men.

Let Light descend on Earth. (I saw a circle rotating counterclockwise in my mind.)

From the point of Love within the Heart of God,

Let love stream forth into the hearts of men.

May Christ return to Earth. (I saw a circle rotating counterclockwise in my mind.)

From the center where the Will of God is known,

Let purpose guide the little wills of men,

The purpose which the Masters know and serve. (I saw a circle rotating clockwise in my mind.)

From the center, which we call the race of men,

Let the Plan of Love and Light work out

And may it seal the door where evil dwells.

Let Light and Love **in** Power restore the Plan on Earth. (I saw a circle rotating clockwise in my mind.)

(This is the Great Invocation by Alice Bailey). When I prayed with this prayer, I was told emphatically that the correct words were Light and Love **in** Power. NOT light and love and power. The word

***And*** is a mistake! When the author originally wrote this, she confused the words **in** and **AND**... the world does not need power; it needs light and love **in** power!!!)

As soon as I was done saying this prayer, I looked out the window and saw my very first rainbow circle spinning in the clouds. It was a rainbow in a circle on the clouds outside the window of the aircraft. It followed me from the Cincinnati airport all the way to Grand Rapids, Michigan. I have many videos and pictures of it. When I asked God what this was, I was shown a vortex of God's infinite Love and Light, God's energy-spinning Rainbow.

This Holy Grail Vortex is used to spin energy back up to Creator God so God can fix it!

Use it wisely with Love in your heart. Use it for Tornado, Hurricanes, Chemtrails and any anomalies that wreak havoc on Earth. God created all, and when it is out of balance, return it to God for Healing and Transmutation.

# Sisterhood of the Emerald Fire

When the plane landed, I grabbed my suitcase and headed to get the rental car. As I handed the gentleman behind the counter my license, he grunted and said, do you have another form of I.D.? I said, "What?!" He explained, "Your license expired two years ago. I can't rent you a car." Oh my God, this is crazy. I said, "I'm old; I don't get stopped anymore! I never use my license!" He was not laughing. He said, "Well I'd be worried if I were you, how are you going to get back on that plane?" Standing there in disbelief, so many thoughts running through my head, what am I going to do now! Here I am in Michigan; I met Mary once; I don't know anyone here! The more I explained, the more obstacles the man identified. The hotel is one hour away; I can get a taxi to the hotel, but there are no taxis in Allegan, so how will I be able to get to Mary's and buy food for the weekend?

At that exact moment in time, my cell phone rang. It was Mary Hardy. "Elizabeth, where are you? We had to run errands in town. You don't need a car. Come outside; we're right in front of the Car Rental!" In disbelief, God again answered my cry for help. When I approached the van, Sandy jumped out with arms stretched wide open and said, "Welcome home". We both cried like old-school friends who have been apart for fifty years! God surely brought me to my Soul Family, my tribe.

Mary and her Husband Dean introduced me to Sandy, "She's one of our sisters".

Mary has a group, "the Sisterhood of the Emerald Fire". This is a group of ordained women from the lineage of Mary Magdalene who work with Young Living Essential Oils and Healing. The men in the group are called the Nights' Templar. St. John the Beloved is the head of the Knights Templar; they protected Mary Magdalene as she taught healing in the caves after Jesus died.

In 1968, Mary and her husband, Dean, were traveling with their two young sons when they had 4 hours of missing time and were instructed by the Elders of the Planet to build a pyramid for their youngest son, John. The Pyramid was built in 1975. You can read details about that in one of her books "Pyramid Energy: The Philosophy of God and the Science of Man. Mary, her husband Dean, and their friends built that pyramid at their home in Allegan, Michigan. *(I will say, it is a most magnificent place to meditate!)* Mary tells us this pyramid is used "as an antenna system to restore Mother Earth's grid to her original harmonious love-based energy patterns by putting heart energy back into the grid". In 1996, Mary was guided by St. John the Beloved in the field of Essential Oils and the etheric Knights Templar to heal the planet using the Holy Grail Vortex. You can read more about this in her most recent book, "The Alchemist's Handbook to the Glia Brain and Higher Consciousness".

# Hurricane Sandy

After God showed me the circular rainbow, I knew then this (HGV) Holy Grail Vortex could spin energy to create healing and like Mary said, to also disperse hurricanes or other natural disasters.

I would soon find out for myself just how powerful this (HGV) Holy Grail Vortex Prayer was when Hurricane Sandy was coming to destroy New England. Wikipedia says: Hurricane Sandy (unofficially referred to as Superstorm Sandy) was the deadliest and most destructive, as well as the strongest hurricane of the 2012 Atlantic hurricane season. The storm inflicted nearly $70 billion (2012 USD) in damage and killed 233 people across eight countries from the Caribbean to Canada.

I had been hosting Ysabel and Olinda, two female Medicine women often called "the twins" from Northern Peru at my home for the past fifteen years. They were the experts in the famous Egg/Candle healing. They have also opened their arms to teach me all they know. When they are staying with me here in the USA, the three of us work together on every client that comes for healing.

During this egg/candle healing, we repeat the rosary continuously, over and over, while working on the client. The rosary helps us focus because we cannot have one un-pure thought in our minds while the healing is happening. If I were to think about cooking dinner or what's for lunch, even for a moment, it would sabotage the healing. The rosary keeps all thoughts on God so his infinite Love and Light can do the healing. The most fulfilling moments are when clients return to us to tell us how we changed their lives. One of my favorites is when a lady returned and said, "Remember me? I was given 4 months to live and my Cancer is gone over a year now! I came back to say Thank you!" God does create miracles. We just have to do the work and hold space to allow his miracles to take place.

In the Autumn of 2012, Hurricane Sandy was coming up the coast. I was to drive Ysabel and Olinda to New York City so Kathryn and Michael could host them for the weekend, and then they were due to return with me for another week before going to Pierre in New Brunswick, Canada. We all worked together, and one would drive them up, and the other would drive them back. I meditated several times, asking God if it was even appropriate to have them go to New York; the news and weather forecasts were scary. Most especially because Hurricane Katrina and the devastation of Louisiana were still fresh in our minds, I kept getting "Yes." they need to be there, and you will all be safe.

Dennis and I drove the twins, stopping many times off Route 95 to go to the edge of the ocean to do HGV and Prayers to STOP Hurricane Sandy's destruction, balancing the weather and energy of Mother Earth to keep everyone safe. We held prayer steady, met Kathryn and Michael, and hugged the twins, Ysabel & Olinda, goodbye, and then drove back to RI. The next day, Hurricane Sandy hit. New York was frozen in time. People were unable to get gas or drive in or out of New York City. The Gas stations literally had no gas. Power was out all over New England. News stations were showing cars parked all over the roadways that had run out of gas. Kathryn called; she, Michael, and the twins were safe, staying put. I was preparing to cancel clients for the rest of the week when God said, "Wait". I never expected to see them at my front door at 10:00 the next morning! Michael, a pilot for our local airlines, was a smart guy; he gassed up when they predicted issues. Typically, people in Rhode Island run to the market for milk, bread, and eggs! Luckily, Michael thought of Gas! HGV was certainly in my mind; everything worked out better than I could have dreamed.

# The Marys

When I began holistic training so many years ago, I also became an ordained minister and then a Doctor of Divinity. After working with Mary Hardy, I knew she and her group were indeed my soul family. I am honored to also be ordained into Mary's group, The Sisterhood of the Emerald Fire. This is a group of healers working with Young Living Essential Oils (God's medicine and the purest oils on planet Earth) from the lineage of Mary Magdalene, guided by St. John the Beloved.

Over the years, I've traveled back to Allegan, Michigan, many times a year, doing healings, teaching, sharing, and helping to raise the consciousness of humanity.

Back in Rhode Island, I was holding monthly meetings for the American Society of Dowsers ASD, teaching introduction to dowsing at each meeting. It was a fun and inspirational group of advanced healers from all over Rhode Island. One day in 2014, I asked if they were interested in an experiment. I was traveling again to Peru and wondered what it would be like to send and receive prayers from Machu Picchu, Peru, to and from all over New England. From the top of Machu Picchu, Wilson and I prayed "the Our Father" and "Hail Mary" in English, Spanish, and Quechua while twelve women from all over New England sent prayers to us. This was a most powerful experience. When I returned home, I called the women and invited them to my home to see pictures and watch the videos. (You can view these prayers on our YouTube channel @ Elizabeth Rainbow Dancer). Each woman came with a dish to share, and we had a delightful gathering as they asked if we could do this again! Since that time, we have been meeting monthly, and God calls our group "The

Sisterhood of the Marys". The phrase "the Marys" is often referred to as "the Healers" because, during the time when Jesus walked the Earth, all the women named Mary were, in fact, the greatest Healers. St. John the Beloved guarded Mary Magdalene as she healed people in the cave using oils.

One morning in prayer, God said, "You must get your girls ordained." I thought, oh no! That is a 501c3 nonprofit, and so much paperwork! Ok, I will do whatever you wish.

Right then, my phone rang. It was Mary Hardy. She said, "Hey, Elizabeth, do you have anyone there who wants to be ordained"? Unbelievable! Within a few months, Pat and Mel from the Sisterhood of the Emerald Fire Ordination Committee flew into Rhode Island.

The house was decorated with huge bouquets of flowers, lace and bows. There was a banquet of food. The women wore elegant gowns of Emerald flowing like angel wings. It was the most elegant ceremony and nine women became ordained. Our group became the first leg of The Sisterhood of the Emerald Fire here in Rhode Island. Since that time, our Sisterhood has grown, and we also have many legs across the United States. It is a network of highly conscious men and women who emanate pure Unconditional Love with the focus on healing Mother Earth and all her inhabitants.

# NDE

In March of 2015, I went to Peru with my friend Joanna. We left Boston, flew to Lima, then jumped on the little twenty-seat plane to Cusco. The plane took off, and just before landing, we were told we had to turn around and go back to Lima. Our landing in Cusco was interrupted by weather. For many years, airplanes did not have the ability to fly into Cusco when the clouds came in or the weather was raining. This was one of those times. When we landed back in Lima, they would not let us get off the plane. They opened the exit door at the front of the aircraft; it was so hot, over 97 degrees F! We sat there without any air circulation for over 3 hours. Our last meal was in Boston, and we have been on this journey for over 30 hours. Anyone who knows me knows I always packed food. This time, all of our snacks were gone, even the little chocolate-covered acai berry candy! My head began to pound. By the time Wilson picked us up in Cusco, I could hardly keep my head up. It was the worst migraine ever, and I never, ever get headaches.

Wilson informed us that we couldn't stay at Vilma's as planned because a pipe broke and there was a big problem. Last minute is very difficult to find lodging in Cusco but he found us a cheap hotel. When we got to the hotel, I asked for an hour to lay down (Never, ever, do I need a nap; something was drastically wrong. When Wilson and Joanna came to wake me an hour later, I opened my eyes to see directly in front of my face was a wall covered in black mold. I could barely hold consciousness. Wilson and Joanna dragged me to the little tuk-tuk taxi, and we drove to his father's house. It was an hour ride, I don't even remember. I was later told that Don Martin met us at the door and helped me to the couch, sending Wilson to town to buy Oxygen. Don Martin worked on me, then left me to sleep. There was a small child, about eighteen months old, who came into the room; he banged his forehead to mine over and over again; each time he banged my forehead, his body illuminated like a spark of golden light that surrounded him. Then he left the room, and a huge Angel came in; his wings were so huge, they dragged behind him on the dirt floor; he had long, curly, silky, very dark hair, almost like black hair, but it was the darkest brown. He said, "I'm looking for someone from the Fidi family". I said, "Take me, I'm a Fidi" (my grandfather was Adolfo Fidi). He said, "No, you have more work to do" and he left. Disappearing right through the door. Then I sat up, feeling fine, completely healed, as my cell phone was ringing. Here in the Andes Mountains of Peru, where there is never any cell service, my phone was ringing. It was my cousin Michael telling me my cousin Maria just died.

When my aunt Irene passed away in 2012, she had COPD. Aunty Irene was very close to me. She was like my second mother. When she got sick, I went to every appointment with her. We lived a few streets away, so it was easy for me to help her out. After Aunty passed, our 'Fidi' family fell apart. Some family members were angry she selected me to be the executrix of her estate. She had a tiny house and very little money that was to be divided between 9 nieces, nephews, and one brother. My uncle Sal was upset because, at one time, she did tell him he would be her sole heir, but then she changed her mind, and her will was explicit. There were more than hard feelings; the family had not spoken since.

Now, here I am, March 19, 2015. Maria passed away, and I spoke with Michael, then one at a time. I talked with Danny (Maria's brother), my cousin Michele and all of Maria's children. I talked for hours with all of them on my cell phone from Don Martin's house in the high Andes Mountains of Peru. (And my cell phone kept its charge too)!

Our whole family was together for the funeral; it was as if nothing happened. We hugged, talked, and shared stories once again. Uncle Sal didn't come in; he's still living away, and as I understand, he still won't talk with me. In 2020, I found out he had given his whole paycheck to Grandpa to pay for that house and help his family when he was in the military. Of course, he thought that house should be his. I'm sure if he had voiced that to the family, all of the cousins would have refused their tiny share! What a sad situation for lack of communication.

*Fast forward to 2022, I called Uncle Sal on his birthday & we both cried and made peace. Six months later, I went with Michele & Todd to visit him on his deathbed. No one knew he was sick. I can't tell you how relieved I was to be able to make peace and have many conversations during those six months. Listen, Listen, Listen to your deepest intuition. Had Michele not mentioned it to me and told me to "do your thing", I would not be at peace.*

A few months later, Alexandra and I were going to meet Brenda and Rozlynn for lunch in Salem. We walked by a store with a brass angel figurine in the window. I ran inside, my heart was pounding! "Who is THAT!!!?" I asked. The woman brought me the angel and the tag with it… that said "Archangel Gabriel". Since that event in Peru, I have been wondering who that Angel was that came to me, and here was the statue that looked EXACTLY like him! Oh My God, that was really Archangel Gabriel! I knew that face as if he was my own flesh and blood!

# Aura Photos

Saturday morning, I was compelled to drive over to my friend's shop. She has a beautiful collection of books, crystals, candles, jewelry, etc. I arrived with iced coffees for everyone & realized that she was hosting a friend who took Aura photographs. This friend traveled the world and brought beautiful wares to sell. After a brief conversation, he took my Aura photo. The room gasped when they viewed the photo. I ran over to see what the reaction was for. The Photograph showed a huge white circle with the very tip outlined in Purple and Gold. It was then explained to me that the "white photo" was extremely rare and showed one "Enlightened". I almost wished no one else saw this. This is one of those times where I could understand God saying not to speak of it for 120 days. Just like when Mother Mary came to me, I was told to hold it in for 120 days. I could not tell anyone for 120 days… that way, the 'WOW' stayed in every cell of my DNA.

You know when you have something fantastic happen to you, then you tell one person, and they share your excitement. By the time you tell the story 20 times… the excitement is not half as high as it was the first time you told the story… by holding it in for 120 days… the story excitement and those high vibrations never leave your Soul!

Driving home, I was guided to pull over onto a beautiful lot that was for sale.

I was relishing the fact that so many beautiful things have been happening to me.

Then, the morning doves surrounded my car. Maybe 20 of them. I couldn't turn around or even back up… they were everywhere. In a minute, I knew why… they wanted me to plant my feet on the property—to connect with Pachamama (Mother Earth) and give thanks. Wow… amazing. After I got out of the car and said prayers, they coo'd and surrounded me. When I was done praying, they left.

Months later while doing my morning prayers, Mother Mary channeled the ingredients for me to make a line of Sacred Sprays. Specific Prayers, Specific Essential Oils, Specific ground crystals, and Specific Frequencies with other Specific ingredients are put together in a Specific way with a bit of grain alcohol to preserve them. I was even guided on where to go to purchase the specific bottles to house these Sacred ingredients. I followed directions explicitly, and the first batch of Ancient Wisdom Sacred Sprays was born. You are to spray them as you would an air freshener. There are five different types. Clearing, Abundance, Vitality, Transformation, and Protection. I passed them around to family and friends for their opinions. Everyone said they 'smelled' good. I knew something was missing… Proof: I must get proof. I heard this message loud and clear.

Amma came to Boston. She is likened to be like Mother Theresa. Some call her the Indian 'hugging' Buddha. While meditating at her venue, I heard my guidance tell me to "Go buy a white outfit". I thought I didn't look good in white, no. Then I heard it again: go buy a white outfit! So, I walked to the back of the room, and right there was a rack of white outfits on sale, all in my size. I purchased the outfit for $25.00 and knew I'd get further directions regarding the outfit soon.

The very next morning, while doing my prayers, I heard, put the white outfit on, take the sacred sprays, and drive. I got in the car and literally heard; take a left, take a right,… and followed these directions directly to the bank, where I withdrew the exact funds that I would need for the rest of the day. (Of course, not knowing that at the time.) Leaving the bank, I followed more directions: take a left, take a right all the way into Wickford, Rhode Island, where I found myself parked on the side of the road in front of a bookstore. I was guided to take my sprays up the stairs into the shop. Standing inside, a woman introduced herself to me; she was Katherine, the owner. She asked if she could help me. I said, I don't know; I was guided to come here today, and I'm not sure why. She asked, "What's in the bag?". I explained sacred sprays. She said, "Wouldn't it be nice to prove they work?" She just so happened to have a Kirlian Camera. This camera is one of the most expensive because it is documented as the most accurate in photographing the Aura (electrical field) of a person. This is when it all began to make sense. I had been asking God for Proof that the sprays work.

The first photo we took was in the neutral state—that is, just walking off the street.

Then the person got up, walked to the opposite side of the room, & was sprayed with Clearing over their head as they turned around in a circle (to let the spray fall onto their aura). Each spray was sprayed in the same format, away from the camera and on the opposite side of the room. Below are the findings.

Katherine took a photo each time we sprayed an Aura spray; we got colors that were perfect for the spray that was sprayed! For example, if you were healthy and wealthy, your aura colors would be violet and Green, so after spraying the Abundance spray, these colors were active in the Aura.

When the "protection" Aura Spray was used, the photo actually showed a huge cross of Jesus right in front of the person sitting there, you can see in the photo, A huge cross right in front of the person; it looks like the person is holding it, and it is over three feet high! I'm so excited; we finally have proof for each Spray that the colors are accurate for each desired outcome!

When I got home, I ran to tell Al. He told me to hide this and not tell anyone as I was reminded... "You know, they killed Jesus!" Hmmm, guess I'll just keep it in the drawer for now; I never wanted to be a guru. I know God will let me know what and when to do something with these sprays.

There are nine photographs; here are the details:

#1 is the Neutral State—coming right off the street, sitting in the chair with small talk with the photographer without any spray being used.

Here is the analysis of the colors of the Aura: the blue on the *left* side of the person is CLEAR light blue, reflecting active imagination & good intuition. Color of communication, calm & quietness. It can indicate the ability for Telepathy. The bright bluish-green on the right side closest to the person indicates the healing ability & love of the Mother. Ah, Mother Mary. Golden glow on *the right* side from the waist to mid-headline indicates dynamic spiritual energy and coming into one's own power as well as devotion & harmony. It indicates strong enthusiasm, inspiration, and a time of revitalizing and unlimited potential. Associated with wisdom, sometimes looks like a halo. The Green is a color of sensitivity & growing compassion. Balance Sharing & devotion & healing. All matters of the heart. The color of Abundance & new Beginnings it can reflect that a person is open-minded & reliable. The yellow in this green area is the color of mental activity, new opportunities, lightness & wisdom & intellect, the power of ideas, and awakening psychic abilities. The light column coming from the golden halo on the *right* side is the connection to God because it is also on the left side, visible from the top of the *left* head.

#2 is after the person is sprayed with "Clearing Spray". The majority of color over the head is not orange, yellow, or red; it's gold! Is this the halo? Yes, this is the Halo of God from mid-ear level all around the head with a tinge of red on the outer tip—this is strong passion, indicating strong physical energy and power. Bluish-green on the right side & bright clear blue on the left side. Pale violet reflects spirituality & humility in the left neck area.

#3 is a person in an "anger" state of mind. She was asked to think of something that made her angry. Which actually caused a hot flash in this woman as the picture was being taken. The Dark Red color on the right side shows deep anger—(this woman stated she got very angry when she thought of her neighbor shooting his dog because it was sick; the interesting thing here is that the man actually lives on the right side of her house). It is also interesting that the left side is still very clear yellow indicating wisdom. I find that even though she was as angry as she could get, the yellow still peeks through most of the top & her left side, indicating that wisdom has a clear path in coming to her.

#4 is after spraying the Clearing Spray on the previous #3 (angry) client. This one is clearly golden-yellowish. It is definitely not yellow; it is the golden halo, and her right side, which is her giving side, still gives the greenish-blue, which indicates the healing ability and love of the mother. All of the dark red is gone from the Aura after spraying the Clearing Spray.

#5 is after spraying the PROTECTION SPRAY– notice the cross of Jesus right in front of the face, about 3 feet tall in a red color beginning at the solar plexus (the soul), lightly across the face, above the head and extending the arms to the left & Right sides like a huge cross of Jesus. This cross is seen among the yellow on the sides and the golden color around the halo. The Red is the color of strong energy, fire & primal creative force—what better way to say the creative force that gave the spark of life, Creator! God! Represented by Jesus! Clear Green coming in from the left side: Compassion, devotion, matters of the heart, abundance & new beginnings. With Bluish-green, meaning healing ability and love of the Mother—Mother Mary.

#6 is after spraying the Clearing spray—was actually when I sprayed with Clearing spray—a good dose. It shows clear all the way! You can see a complete golden halo around the whole picture with a bit of bluish-green on the right side: Healing & love of a mother (divine mother Mary). Gold reflects dynamic spiritual energy and coming into one's own power as well as devotion and harmony. It indicates strong enthusiasm, inspiration, and a time of revitalizing and unlimited potential. It is associated with wisdom & a Halo.

#7 photo was taken after spraying the Vitality spray—starting on the left side, violet, the color of inner vision. A blending of heart & mind, physical & spiritual. It reflects independence and intuition. Ability to be practical & worldly. Pale shades reflect humility & spirituality. Across the midsection, good intuition, royal blue indicates honesty and good judgment, and the person has found her chosen work. Deep blue's devotion to Divine. Light blue going up to the top reflects active imagination & good intuition. Green compassion, balance, devotion, healing, matters of heart, abundance, new beginnings, open-mindedness. Bright bluish green indicates the healing ability & love of Mother—Divine Mother Mary.

#8 After spraying the Transformation spray—Royal blue, indicates honesty and good judgment and also indicates the person has found her chosen work. Blue-green on the right side healing ability and love of the Divine. Bright Yellow wisdom, power of ideas & awakening psychic abilities. Gold reflects dynamic spiritual energy and coming into one's own power as well as devotion & harmony. Strong enthusiasm, inspiration & a time of revitalizing & unlimited potential. Associated with wisdom & the HALO. A tinge of green in the upper left side of the aura indicates open-mindedness. Magenta in the right neck area indicates great passion & unconditional love.

#9 was taken after spraying the Abundance spray—violet, the color of inner vision. A blending of heart & mind, physical & spiritual. It reflects independence and intuition. Ability to be practical & worldly. Pale shades reflect humility & spirituality. Magenta indicates great passion & unconditional love. Between violet & green is a hint of golden halo. Deep blue's devotion to Divine. Light blue going up to the top reflects active imagination & good intuition. Green compassion, balance, devotion, healing, matters of heart, abundance, new beginnings, open-mindedness. Bright bluish green indicates the healing ability & love of Mother—Divine Mother Mary. Green compassion, balance, devotion, healing, matters of heart, abundance, new beginnings, open-mindedness.

So here it is, Proof, I actually have PROOF that the Sprays work!

One friend reported a $400 daily income in a store she has, and after spraying the Abundance spray, her income went up to $1000 a day. Everyone who has used the sprays to date has declared immediate changes in emotion and delightful outcomes upon daily use. I program prayers into each and every batch with my Soul Family: Jesus, Mother Mary, The Legion of Angels, Archangels, Saints, Spirits, and Guides, all under the guidance of God.

When I am working at the Electric Company, I can actually pray & have the phone become silent until I am done typing my work into the computer. If an irate customer calls, I can calm them within a minute to where they are so happy they send thank you gifts (which is pretty rare for the Electric Company). The sequence of events that unfolds each day is uncanny. Everything is in alignment, and doors continue to open that I never thought possible. People call upon my healing services, and I tend to their needs. It's all come to a beautiful blend, no longer the life as a Shaman separate from working as an Engineer for the Electric Company. It's all just me; it's become a way of life, walking hand in hand with Creator God every day in every way.

# New Brunswick

Pierre & Janice hosted me at their place in New Brunswick, Canada, in January. I immediately accepted with excitement. We often travel to Peru, and we always have fun when we are together. They already had eleven clients scheduled to see me before we even picked the date! I was to fly from Boston to Nova Scotia, then land in Moncton, New Brunswick. When I got to the airport in Nova Scotia, I couldn't believe how small it was. Thinking I had a few hours to spare… I began talking to Judy on Skype on my iPad, walking around showing her how cute, when I heard "last call for Moncton" over the loudspeaker. Quickly, I gathered my stuff and ran to the counter, where a young woman led me to a door and said, that's your plane right there. This tiny plane was outside, quite a bit away, just sitting on the tar pavement. I looked back at her to question, "That little plane?" but she was gone! Out the door I go, dragging my wheeled bag, backpack, and pocketbook stuffed full to the brim. A young man yelled, "Hurry up!" from the door of the plane as I fumbled to get my luggage up a dozen metal stairs. I had on my favorite cowboy boots and winter jacket, scarf, hat, and mittens! After all, I needed to be prepared because I heard New Brunswick gets enormous amounts of snow, and it's really, really cold! As I entered the plane, I realized I could not stand straight up. The ceiling of the plane was very low. So, hunched over, I dragged my wheel bag behind me (which didn't exactly fit; the width of the aisle was smaller than my bag!) and the backpack on my right shoulder. When my bag got caught, I went flying…

Ok, let me paint the picture here… picture this.

After my bag got stuck and wouldn't go further, my right foot (with my pointy-toe cowboy boot) got stuck in the metal apparatus underneath a seat behind me to my right. (which was behind me now because my body went like a projectile) as I was pushed forward by the weight and momentum of my bags and my rushing… right into this lady's lap on my left. My left hand landed on her thigh, my right hand on the arm of her chair with my face two inches from her nose as she screamed, "Get off of me". I tried with all my might but could only say, "I caaaaannnnnnnnnt, I'm stuuuuuuk! She repeated, "Get OFF ME!" by now, I was laughing hysterically and could barely speak as I muttered the words again, "I caaaaaannnnnnnt, I'm STUUUUUCK"—Finally I catch a breath and say "I can't, I'm stuck!"

I was literally two inches from her face. She was pushing her head back so much to try to get away from me, but she couldn't because the back of her chair prevented her from going back any farther. But she still pushed her head back; so far, it looked like she didn't have a neck; her chin was literally digging into her chest.

I could hear the pilot over the loudspeaker saying, "PLEASE TAKE YOUR SEAT," and then finally, he came out to see what the commotion was, and he and the man in the seat where my foot was stuck had to twist my boot & ankle to unhook it from the metal frame under the seat. As I was helped up, I apologized to the terrified woman in the tan Nanook jacket and took my seat. The only seat left open on the plane. As I looked up, I noticed I was the only one laughing, and yet most of the people had their cell phones pointed at me. Oh, dear God, this must be on YouTube. If you find it, please send it to me.

I love a good laugh.

There were 30 people waiting for me at the Introduction to QHHT Quantum Healing. And each one signed up for private QHHT sessions with me. Pierre and Janice are gracious hosts and showed me the greatest hospitality of New Brunswick. Again, I felt like God brought me more family. This group was so loving; my heart is still overflowing with joy.

# North Carolina

Kathy called to say she was friends with Pierre and Janice, and she wanted to host me in North Carolina.

Within a month, I was back on an airplane flying to Chapel Hill, North Carolina. Kathy was gracious and delightful to be around. We had a list of clients so long she had snacks in between, so I was able to focus on three clients a day.

We worked until 11 pm each night. There will certainly be a QHHT Book written soon; with each client, God awakens me more and more. I am so humbled when the client's higher self-trusts me enough to speak with me.

I actually fall in Love with that Soul piece of every client. Each session is like putting in another Netflix movie with on-the-edge-of-your-seat adventures.

# Retirement

For the past week, I kept hearing "Retire" when I did my morning prayers. Our company had a policy where you could retire if your age plus your years of service added up to 85. I was 55 years old, and I had 34 years of service; that was plenty of points needed for me to qualify for early retirement. My first thought was, "No! I'm not that old!" I'm not ready for retirement!"

This was not an option! No way! I truly loved my job. I loved my life. This was **NOT** an option. Or so I thought… until I went into meditation. God assured me that this is my divine path. It was time for me to devote my life to my passion, working with God healing Mother Earth and all her inhabitants. Humbled, I've come to respect God's messages because *I know I must.* And thankfully, they are always better than I could have dreamed. I submitted the paperwork to retire from the Electric Company as I heard loud and clear, "Get up and begin your new life, you work for God".

*The routine is still the same: get up, greet the sun, pray/ meditate (now sometimes for an hour, sometimes for five. It depends on what God has to say) breakfast, clients, phone calls… travel, teaching, ceremony and whatever God has in store for me, it is always better than I could have dreamed.*

# UFO Stone

February of 2012, Vilma, Don Martin's daughter, called me. She said, "My father said you need to come to do a ceremony with the UFO Stone." I answered, "Vilma, I mean no disrespect, but tell your father I have no interest in UFOs, Past Lives, or Orbs". I could hear Vilma talking Quechua to her father; then she came back to the phone. "Elizabeth, my father, he says… You can NOT deny YOU FLY At night".

Well, I had just woken up from a good night's sleep when I had *THAT Dream*. It's a recurring dream where I am flying, and I arch my back to go around a corner to avoid hitting a pole, electric wires, and a huge pine tree on Cherry Hill Road. Oh God!

**How could I deny that!**

"Vilma, tell your father I'd be happy to join him in the ceremony with the UFO stone". Within a month, Pierre and I were in a van with David, our driver, and Don Martin. It was a six-hour drive up the switchback roads with camping equipment and snacks for several days. Don Martin helped set up our tents, built a fire, and began the ceremony. We stayed in Prayer and ceremony the entire time we were up there. We were so high up, on the cliffs, looking down to the roads looked like the cars were smaller than ants.

The UFO stone was approximately 3 ½–4 ft in diameter, and the holes around the center line looked like they were drilled, so precisely only the finest machine could have done this. But there was no way any machine could have done this as there was no electricity anywhere, and this stone has been like this for many, many years. Only the ancestors knew and told stories about it. One side of the UFO stone was broken off and burned because it had been hit by lightning. At about 3:00 am the next morning, Don Martin woke us up; he said the Ceremony must begin now, before sunrise. I dressed in my ceremonial poncho with Condor and Eagle feathered headband, rattle, and Mesa in my hands as I sat on the UFO Stone while Don Martin did sacred Prayer and performed the rites of passage the way his ancestors taught him all through the deepest darkness and into the sunrise through the afternoon. It was such an honor to be blessed in such a way. I surrendered to the process because I know God brought me here, and there is no doubt I work for God.

## Quantum Healing

Shortly after visiting the UFO Stone, I was in Prayer, and I heard God say, "You must work with Dolores Cannon". Now, after all these years, I'm talking to God just like I'm talking to you. I said, "OK, but I'm really busy this year, teaching all over; I am on a plane at least once a month; I'll do it NEXT year". I heard, loud and clear, "NO! YOU MUST DO IT NOW! SHE'S NOT GOING TO BE HERE MUCH LONGER!!" Immediately, I booked flights to Arkansas for Dolores Cannon's QHHT Quantum Healing Hypnosis Therapy class. I find it amazing that I said NO to Vilma when she said Don Martin wanted me to work on the UFO stone, and my answer was that "I had no interest in UFOs, past lives, or orbs". Now, here I am in a class with Dolores Cannon, learning Past Life Regression QHHT technique after witnessing orbs and ceremonies on the UFO stone!

Dolores was 80 years old. Her husband was the hypnosis guy for the military when he got in a head-on collision with a drunk driver. She took on doing hypnosis with him and eventually became very good at it because she was very curious. She tells the story about how they were helping typical clients who wanted to stop smoking and lose weight. And she thought, what happens if we go deeper? That was in the 60's. Dolores was one of the first to realize people were dropping into past lives when they went deeper! Then she thought, what happens if we go deeper than THAT? And that's where the client was able to contact their Higher Self, the Soul part of themselves. Dolores Cannon called it the subconscious.

Once the Subconscious is contacted, you can have a conversation with it. It actually talks about the client as if they're a third person in the room. This QHHT session is far beyond anything I have ever witnessed, and I have been doing successful sessions with clients since that very day. Another book will surely be written about those sessions because the world needs to know… *we are so much more than our physical bodies! Until then, I urge you to have your own session.*

Dolores passed away three years after I got the message to study with her. I'm eternally grateful I listened to God's message; it changed my life again, in a good way, exponentially. I audio record every session and, for the past few years, have also been video recording them. Clients allow me to put parts of their sessions on our YouTube channel @ Elizabeth Rainbow Dancer. Here you can see the client talking about their past life, and also, when the higher self/soul/sub-conscious is talking through them, messages for humanity and words of advice come through. Be sure to watch the four videos with "Moses".

So, it looks like this: When the client comes for a session, we talk about their life in the interview. I need to know what's important and who is important to them. And we comprise questions to ask the higher self-based on the issues the client has. Then, they are relaxed into a guided meditation. *At no point in time are they ever unconscious. They are always fully in control at all times.* I wish Dolores didn't call it hypnosis because it's more like tapping into your deepest intuition. Sometimes, the client drifts into a past life; some go to a future life experience, and others visit a parallel life experience. Wherever they go, they describe what they see, hear, and feel in detail. They visit an important place and time that has information for them that will help them based on the issues they currently have. After that, we contact the Higher self/ Soul/ Sub-conscious and ask it the questions the client and I have prepared. One by one, the questions are answered. With each question, I ask more and go deeper. My aim is to get the client the most information I can so the information is clear. We also ask to strengthen the connection so the client can contact the higher self on his/her own. Then, we ask for a body scan and healing with instructions on how the client can do this for him/ herself at any time she/he wishes. These sessions average four hours, and our website for this work is www.QHHT-Elizabeth.com  Feel free to contact us at any time. We'd be delighted to answer any questions you may have.

Dolores passed away in October 2014. In March 2015, I was invited with two other students who were also in her "recommended dedicated practitioner" program. There was no level 3 when Dolores was alive. There was level one, two, and "Recommended Dedicated Practitioner". I flew to Arkansas to meet with Julia, Dolores' Daughter. Candace Craw-Goldman was Dolores' right-hand person, she helped with all the training, and her husband did all the computer work; they were also at this meeting. Julia viewed sample videos we brought and was watching one from Stu, who also practiced shamanism. In Stu's video, he attended to the client using some shamanic techniques. Julia stopped the video and expressed how much it was against the rules to mix modalities. I could hear Dolores speaking to me, loud and clear. I also heard Dolores say to me, "Tell Julia she can't make this up as she goes along; she has got to decide what she wants to do before she tells the people". The last thing I wanted to do was start telling Julia what to do. Especially because Dolores always said ***she would never channel through another person when she died***. Everybody knew that! And here she was talking to me!

Julia was still clearly distraught about her mom's death. But Dolores was very strong when she said, "Tell her now!" So, I opened my mouth and spoke, "Julia, I may never be invited back here again, and I don't know if you're going to like what I'm about to say, but I can hear your mother loud and clear. She's saying, "you can't make this up as you go along, you've got to decide what you want before you tell people." Well, you could tell by her face that it went over like a lead balloon. Sue joined Julia, and they left the room. That weekend was the last time I saw Julia, and that was many years ago. She did change rules many times when she first took over the business, and I've sent prayers every time Dolores asks. She told me to work on my own and not with Julia at this time. Dolores continues to pop in on my sessions now and then with words of wisdom for the client and sometimes for me too. She continues to say things are so different there. **"She can't stop talking to all of her students. She is Channeling through anyone who will listen".**

In my Shamanic training, we take care of business before telling the client. Never, ever do we tell the client they have a demonic attachment or entity… they will go into an emotional tailspin, and it becomes extremely difficult to work with them. We remove it first. Rarely do we say what they had… because they will often get caught up in the drama telling everyone they know about it… all that gossip can, in fact, call the entity or issue back. It is best not to say anything; just remove it and be done. It's often called clearing or healing.

Because I cannot leave an entity or heavy energy in a person… if it's there and it needs to go, I *must* mix shamanism and QHHT. So, when a client comes for a QHHT Session, if God tells me they will need more, I do my Divine Guidance Quantum Healing. This is my session similar to QHHT; I allow God to dictate whatever is needed to get the client to a healthy state of mind/body/spirit and emotion. QHHT and Divine Guidance Quantum Healing can help in four hours, which takes months in Shamanism and years in psychology.

*At 66 years of age, I'm so blessed to have traveled the world; people continue to host me for this healing work and my teachings. It's an honor to be called to help my teachers; my ego would be flying high if it wasn't for God reminding me to remain humble. I am happy to be able to share it here on paper. Remember always, these words are truth, from my perception. I Love you.*

# Reddish Orange Balls of Light

In July 2014, I was teaching a shaman class with 23 people in Allegan, Michigan. We had just finished the Despacho Ceremony (a prayer offering to God). (You'll have to see our book for more details; "MESA 101 ~ Keep the Medicine Sacred to Your Heart by Elizabeth Rainbow Dancer, published in September 2023). At the end of building Despacho, we bring it to a Fire Ceremony and burn it as we sing and petition God on our behalf to come take our prayers up to Heaven for manifestation. It was a beautiful ceremony, and I had clients in the morning, so I headed back to the Hotel around 10 pm.

As I drove down 36th Street onto Lincoln Road, I noticed a bunch of reddish-orange lights in the sky on a huge mountain. At a glance, it was comforting because it reminded me of the mountains in Cuzco, Peru. Then I realized there are no mountains in Allegan, Michigan! I pulled over to get a better look and called friends, who arrived five minutes later. Sandy, Roxanne, Carla, and I witnessed these reddish-orange balls of light popping in and out, zooming around towards each other, on top of each other, and just a second before they popped out of the round shape and turned into a White backward letter C, (like a comma or exhaust from a vehicle) and disappeared... one by one they disappeared, and then what appeared to be the mountain behind them slowly faded from sight.

Just to get an idea of the size… With my arm stretched out in front of me, they were the size of my pinky fingernail. As if a helicopter was flying about five miles away but helicopters don't behave like that. These lights were zooming around like hairpin turns in the sky, popping in and out, on top of each other, zooming all around really fast all over the place at the same time.

Since 1997, I have continued my holistic healing practice. My expertise is the work of the late Dolores Cannon since 2012, the QHHT Quantum Healing Hypnosis Therapy session. This session is where the client is guided deep into meditation to contact their higher self, the spiritual aspect that guides them. Some call it Source. In that state of consciousness, it then has a voice and answers all our questions. It is very much like channeling accurate information from God.

The morning after we saw these reddish-orange balls of light, I had a client. Typically, at the end of each session, I ask, "Is there anything we forgot to discuss today?" This client had no idea what I saw and yet she proceeded to give detailed descriptions of what I saw the previous night.

She said the reddish-orange balls of light, which I called them, were "not HUNDREDS" as you have spoken, there were only 88". The reddish-orange balls of light were the

*Beings* and what I perceived to be the mountain was, in fact, the *vehicle.*

I stored that info away for future reference because I'm always searching for truth, and I want facts.

Ysabel and Olinda, the twin shamans from Northern Peru came to work with me again in Dec of 2014. We had just dropped off the translator and were driving home with my friend Roxanne when we pulled over to take videos of an interesting light show in the sky. At that time, I called my cousin, who is in the military; he said, "Get as many pictures as you can because there is nothing in the sky our government tonight". This was not anything like the reddish-orange balls of light; this was a bunch of lights flashing across the sky.

In July 2015, at our campground in Narragansett, Rhode Island, Al and I were sitting around a campfire with two friends. We saw one ball of reddish-orange light come across the water, towards us and go right overhead and up the road before taking a right-hand turn (exactly where the dirt road turned right) and continue up the hill...

there were NO trees obstructing our view... and this was about twelve to fifteen feet above our heads.

I have been praying for Truth since the first reddish-orange light anomaly I saw, praying to see it up close, praying to see it again, and this time it was absolutely Clear.

If I were to paint a picture about 12 feet over my head, I would say it was the size of a basketball. One and one-half inches of the outer circumference was the solid color of reddish-orange; the center was like plasma, like a kaleidoscope of colors changing from red/orange/yellow. This center area was also slightly transparent, like looking through a flame as if you could put your hand right through it. Yet, I knew if I touched it, I would get burned.

After the first reddish-orange ball of light went up the road, I turned back to the water to look in the direction where it came from & a second reddish-orange ball of light came up towards us, moving in the same exact pattern, making the right hand turn exactly at the same place where the first one turned.

Then, a third one did the same thing, and finally, a fourth did the same exact thing. All four of us witnessed this.

Of course, one is in complete denial and says it was a Chinese lantern, as he was totally freaked out and only gave it a two-second glance while the rest of us stared until they were completely out of site. No way was this Chinese lantern. Chinese lanterns do not have movements like that. This seemed alive, as if it had consciousness. And, they were so close, we got a real good look. We were staring at them for the entire time! They were definitely NOT Chinese lanterns.

I am a certified welder by trade; I know fire, I know the different types of flame, I know the welders' arc from the torch, and I know plasma from the plasma cutters at work. This reddish-orange ball of light had plasma in the center!!! I don't know exactly what their purpose is, but they are definitely some sort of PLASMA energy.

Since the very first site of these balls of light, I have found many pictures online. www.mufon.com has people from all over the world posting videos similar to what I witnessed. No one has yet to say exactly what they are. We're still looking. Military? Drones? Out of this world?

This is the best video I could find on YouTube to show you exactly what I saw when they were far away, high up in the sky.

https://m.youtube.com/watch?v=FBKBs2QMzzM

In this video, I wish he didn't zoom in and out so much, but when it's clear, you can see the center pulsating. Be sure to watch this on a large computer screen; you can see the pulsing in the center. It is almost exactly what I saw in Allegan, Michigan. Only there are six here and I saw 88!

In July 2018, I was back in Allegan, Michigan, for the Sisterhood of the Emerald Fire Conference. Dotty and I had just left the school house (at Mary Hardy's) and were driving to the hotel to meet Pam, her sister, and Mom. It was about 10:15 pm. As I was heading down 36th Street, I began telling Dotty the story: "Hey Dotty, in 2014, this is where I saw those reddish orange balls of light, I was driving down the road just like this and OH MY GOD THERE THEY ARE!!!" Right up there in front of us were these balls of light, coming like a train right at us! I pulled over, put the car flashers on, and began videoing them. There must have been 15 of them, one by one, coming over the trees heading to us, and when they saw us, they turned black and changed direction… descending behind the big red house to our right, and it looked like a black balloon falling out of the sky. You can see these videos on our YouTube channel @ Elizabeth Rainbow Dancer. You can hear our voices and chuckle when you hear me say, "I still see you! I got you on video!" when it turns black. https://youtu.be/vSBGLakntiQ

# Paracas Skulls

One morning, I saw a news article in the paper in Rhode Island talking about 125 skulls found in Paracas, Peru. There was a picture of one Elongated skull with red hair. Something happened when I saw this picture... I had to find them! I sent word to Wilson, Vilma, and Don Martin to help me find them. Within a month, I was back in the Mountains of Cusco. Wilson picked me up at the airport with a huge thermos of coca tea. (You can't breathe at 12,000 ft. elevation without it!) He apologized for not being able to arrange for us to see the Paracas skulls. He said, "They are really far away; it will take a plane ride to Lima, then another four-hour drive to Paracas. By the time we get there, the museum will be closed. Even if we want to do all that traveling, we will have to find a place to stay the night, which will also be difficult because there are no hotels in that area. It sounded like this would be next to impossible. However, I am used to God's miracles, and surely God has brought them to my attention for a good reason. I put my prayers out there and *Let go to Let God*...

We continued our journey through the Andes Mountains, visiting all the sacred sites in Prayer and ceremony with Don Martin. Sacsayhuaman, Moray, Pachatusan, Salcantay, Ausangate, Ollantaytambo, Pisac, Urubamba River, and, of course, Machu Picchu. Thoroughly exhausted from too many high elevations and very little sleep, Wilson boarded the plane with us back to Lima. We had one more sacred site to pray on before heading home.

Peru really does seem to have more pyramids than Egypt. Pachacamac is one that is most magnificent and the view of the ocean from the top is most exquisite! They have since developed a website: http://www.pachacamac.net/, but the pictures do not do it justice; you need to see it in person and experience the energy to get the full effect.

The next day, we were back at the hotel in Miraflores, packing for the trip home, when we decided to head out for lunch. Once again, I asked the taxi driver… "Do you know anything about the Paracas skulls"? I had been asking everyone we came in contact with during this entire trip. I was holding on to hope when he answered, "Why, yes, there are about seven of the skulls now at the archeological museum up the street".

In disbelief, I screamed, "WHAT!!! Take me there"!!!

At the entrance, I asked the first person I saw where the Paracas skulls were. They pointed, and I ran up the stairs so fast I think I took two steps at a time! I was so excited! (Wilson laughed as he reminded me that I ran right past the person I was supposed to pay to enter!) As I came around the corner, I saw the skulls, each on its own three-foot pedestal enclosed in plexiglass so you could see complete 360 degrees around the skull. There were seven of them with ample space so you could embrace each one, its aura, and the energy it emitted. Walking to each one was like an invitation to meet a person I had not seen in a hundred years. Tears rolled down my face; emotions welled up inside me that I could not contain. Sniffling… with an enormous amount of unconditional love overflowing from my heart, I fell to my knees and visited with each one. Praying and then telepathically listening to their story. They are precious. Absolutely precious. I knew they were from out of this world. They have a divine connection to Heaven, God, where we come from.

Even though it has been stated in many news articles that their heads were banded to be shaped in that elongated way, I know this is nonsense!

NO WAY! YOU WOULD NOT GAIN VOLUME BY BANDING THE SKULLS.

The museum seemed empty except for the security guard who came up the stairs, and as he turned the corner and saw me on the floor with my Mesa, praying, he immediately turned around and left; he respected this sacred moment and gave me privacy.

When I saw the Elongated Skull with the Red Hair and the wooden hair stick, I knew him as royalty. He had the most to say. He explained where they came from so very long ago. I sat on the floor with him in Prayer, communicating and embracing this ever-so-sacred moment. He reminded me that we walked together at another place and time and that we agreed to meet here at this exact moment in time. He also reminded me of promises I've made so very long ago.

Hours later, Wilson had to almost drag me out of there. I didn't want to leave! They were closing, and we had to catch our flights back to the States.

Back at home, only a few months after visiting with the Paracas Skulls, I read another article about the baby skeletons found in Paracas. It stated one baby was about eighteen months old, and the other was an infant. Again, I called Wilson and sent him on a mission to find them. The following April, we were back in Peru when Wilson's smile could be seen all across the airport parking lot… Yelling, "Elizabeth! We found them! We found them!" referring to the baby skeletons.

We headed directly to Don Martin's house and were greeted by Maria, Vilma, and the children. Vilma now has two adorable little girls. Their birth dates and knowing they carry the blood of Don Benito, Dona Maria, and Don Martin… Oh my God, I can hardly imagine what kind of healing powers they will have, being raised in that family.

Don Martin gave us his blessings, but he could not come with us; there was already a line of clients around the block waiting for his healing. Wilson, David, and I headed out to see the baby skeletons. It was an hour's drive from Don Martin's house. We arrived in what looked like a plaza with a little church decorated for Easter celebration. Next to the church was a small dilapidated house with a small wooden sign nailed to the side of the front door. The sign had hand-painted letters scribbling the word "Museum $10." in Spanish. I rang the bell, and a tiny gentleman answered, took my money, and pointed to the courtyard out back. There was a small overhang from the building on all sides to protect the skeletons from the weather; other than that, they were totally outside in the weather. There were no pedestals, no plexiglass, no climate control, and nothing preventing anyone from touching these skeletons. There were several skulls just lying on Mestana cloths, sitting on top of "pallets" out in the open. (Pallets are what my husband has in his warehouse to hold many hardware products). The courtyard was small, maybe thirty by thirty feet square. The ground was dirt, and there were a few trees, more for fruit than shade. There were no guards; you were allowed to touch anything you wanted. Out of respect, I prayed and followed God's guidance. Surely, he brought me here for a reason. There were several skulls. Some were misshaped, sort of elongated, but not as big as the first ones I saw, the Paracas skulls in the Miraflores museum.

Then I saw the babies. The infant was still completely wrapped up like a mummy in cloth that looked like it might be thin linen. The eighteen-month-old was fully displayed in one piece, leaning up against a piece of wood to prop it up. My immediate reaction was the floodgate of tears pouring down my face. This toddler's head was almost one-third the size of his body. They were definitely part of the Elongated Paracas skull family. They were precious!

These skeletons were recently discovered, and it was obvious that I was there way before scientists. It was such a blessing and an honor to be able to pray for these babies. I am forever grateful to God for the many blessings he has bestowed upon me.

On the ride back to Don Martin's, I was thinking about the time I met Dr. Sam Osmanagich, the gentleman who discovered the

Bosnia pyramid. I asked him what exactly led him to dig in that area. He said, "I was just driving by and had the thought. I wonder what's in there". Now we're driving (I can't say where just yet), and as I look over to my right… I see a small mountain, and I'm thinking, "I wonder what's inside there"? As soon as I have that thought, God tells me "NO"! Wait until the right people will respect the sacredness of the ancient ones and their artifacts. Until that time comes, I cannot tell anyone where this pyramid is… I await further instructions. Of course, from God!

# Global Leadership Cruise

Right about this time, life sped up so much that I didn't have time to write. I was seeing clients daily as well as, nights and weekends. Oils were a big part of the healing process. Young Living has added supplements and now has over 700 products.

We must maintain compliance when we speak about them because our government has rules against claiming God's medicine can heal. So, in order to remain compliant, I can say these products maintain and support health and wellness, passion and abundance.

The products speak for themselves, and you will hear my testament of how they brought my life back exponentially better in the chapter on "Tremors". With every client, we are focusing on the lifestyle, healing the entire person, mind/body/spirit, and emotion. It works when they are ready to make changes that have been harming them. Then, it can be miraculous. And we have witnessed the miracles, life changing improvements in so many ways with so many clients. Young Living has a referral program that is very generous. They actually reward you for referring another person. It is a direct sales marketing company. Many years ago, pyramid companies took advantage of people with terrible scams. That is illegal! Young Living is not that! Young Living allows us to be independent distributors, totally legit.

Young Living is a company that puts integrity and God first. Their Seed to Seal promise is a first-hand promise of excellence, making sure the product is pure right from the beginning, where it was created the way God intended it to be. Their oils are known to be 100% therapeutic grade, non-GMO, pure. They even hand weed the farms. I trust the purity of excellence in all of their products because they have improved my life many, many times. Can you tell how passionate I am about young living? NONE compare; not one company even comes close.

One day, the phone rang, it was Mary Hardy. She said, "Well, congratulations, Elizabeth, you just made 'Executive', you qualify to come on the Global Leadership Cruise; would you like to come with us?" I answered, "Oh my God, YES!"

When I got off the phone, I had to tell Al. Now you see, I never ever wanted to go on a cruise; Al and Marco have asked me many times. My answer was always the same. "No, they're nothing but an eating/drinking frenzy!" I always preferred flying to a place where we could go behind the scenes and meditate up on the mountains or down on the beach. The thought of a cruise ship party boat docking for half a day when I didn't have time to see anything behind the scenes that was inspiring appalled me. So now I have to tell him I'm going on a cruise. Yet, the word 'NO' was NOT an option.

I went downstairs; he was sitting in front of the TV. I said, "Al, I just hit a milestone with Young Living, and Mary Hardy has invited me on the cruise". He shut the TV, looked right at me, and said, "Now, let me get this straight: you never, ever, wanted to go on a cruise, and *this lady* Mary calls, and now you're going?" Crazy as it seems, I'm going. Then he continued on to remind me... "Now, Elizabeth, remember, these people are all professionals; you want to make a good impression; you probably don't want to tell those power plant stories and jokes on the cruise". Of course, I have learned a lot, become a classy lady, and know when and where to be polite and ladylike.

(I've even learned to walk and talk without spilling wine all over someone.)

Within a few minutes, the phone rang again; it was Marco. He said, "Dad tells me you're going on a cruise! I'm not going to give you a hard time if you promise me, as soon as you get off that ship, call me. If you like it, we're booking one for me, you & Dad." "That's a deal", I said.

Within a month, I met Mary and her son Mark in Florida. They flew in from Michigan, I came in from RI and my suitcase broke during the flight. I wasn't scared because I knew everything happens for a reason. On our walk over to a restaurant for dinner, Mark noticed a TJ Max with suitcases in the window. Perfect! I'd grab it on our way back! We had plenty of time before boarding the cruise tomorrow morning.

At dinner, I said to Mark, well, I've seen you many times at conventions, sisterhood meetings, and the schoolhouse, yet we have never really had a conversation. Since we're going to be spending the next week together, tell me about yourself. Mark is typically very shy. He blushed and said, "What do you want to know?" I said, "Everything".

As he continued, he said, "Well, I worked in a plant". Oh my God, did I hear that correctly? A plant? A manufacturing Plant? This was too crazy; all my funny plant stories came out in that conversation, and we laughed and laughed and laughed, and Mary blushed and laughed, too! We were like two schoolkids! Then I told Mark and Mary how I'd promised Al I wouldn't be telling the "Plant" stories and jokes on the cruise… they all laughed when Mark said, "Well, You're NOT on the cruise YET"!

The cruise ship held 4500 people, and because Young Living bought the entire ship, there were only 2500 of us. The crew treated us like royalty. I had a room all to myself with a huge window on the 8th floor. The first night, we had just left Belize and were headed to Honduras.

I was woken up from a sound sleep when I heard some *clanking* noise from the closet. The hangers were banging together, and it felt like the boat was rocking. I looked out the window. First, I saw splashing from rain; then I saw all sky and no water; then the next minute, I saw all water looking directly at the ocean and no sky. The boat was literally rocking side to side. Because I have never been on a cruise before I didn't know what to think. I opened the door to my room and looked into the hall. Hector came running: Miss Elizabeth, are you okay? I said, "Yes, Hector, is this normal? For the boat to move like this?" Hector said, "It is okay". Then we heard glasses come crashing down from the lounge just ten feet from us. I said again, "Hector, is this normal? I'm not scared, but is this normal?" Hector said, "OK, Miss Elizabeth, because you are not scared, I can tell you, this is NOT normal". We had 20 ft waves and 60 mph winds. It was a bad storm, and we could not get out of its way because we were in the small, narrow waterway between coral reefs.

Back in the room, my phone was ringing. It was Mary & Mark checking on me.

Young Living had an app where everyone could communicate with each other. Everyone was in prayer. What an amazing company this is; they far exceed my expectations day after day.

We went to Belize, the Mayan Temple, and Honduras, the oldest church in Honduras. It was absolutely sacred in so many ways. God had instructed me to bring sacred stones that I have prayed with in my Mesa on my altar for many years and bury them in sacred places around the world. At the Mayan temple, I opened sacred space, prayed in ceremony, and buried sacred stones from other sacred places. God was clear exactly when and where this had to be done. I was to tell no one at the time. He was balancing the grid, the ley lines of Mother Earth.

When we returned, as soon as the boat landed in port, I called Marco and said, "I Love it!" He said, okay, I'm booking a cruise for me, you and dad"!

The following years have been amazing beyond belief. God brought me all over, returning sacred stones to sacred places all over the world. Places I never thought I would ever see.

On the cruise to the Bahamas with Al, Marco & Harry, I was woken up at 3:00 am. The boat was floating through the open seas and it looked pitch black out. Al was sound asleep. God told me to get up and go outside. We did have a balcony so I grabbed my Mesa and went to sit on the balcony. In my pajamas, a light breeze was blowing my hair; it was perfect. Once again, this was on the 8th floor. The moon was full, and there was enough light to shine on the waters below. We had just left the Bahamas that day and were heading to a tiny island. A big deal this little island, its Norwegian's privately owned island. There is nothing in sight, nothing, not another boat, no land or buoy in sight. I began prayers to open a sacred ceremony; I could feel the presence of God as the Holy Spirit filled me with his infinite love and light. There is nothing quite like it when you're filled with the unconditional love of God. I was guided to do the Holy Grail Vortex, then toss the sacred stones right into the water at a specific point in time. I was told this was directly over the city of Atlantis. Tears ran down my face as I realized how sacred this was. The sequence of events leading up to this moment has been perfectly aligned. I could never have planned it with such precision. And yet, here I am as I surrender to the process, and everything is in Divine order, just as it should be. I was merely a humble servant of God.

Back home I go, working on clients and with every Quantum Healing Session, each one is more amazing than the last. I'm told that book and the Mesa book must be written! Every month, I was once again on an airplane to another sacred place. I've been invited to do my healing work and teach all over. It seems as though everywhere I go, I return with another amazing story. Some make me laugh so hard; others humble me to my knees. This is my life.

# Make-up

Young Living came out with toxic-free makeup. It is wonderful, as all their products continue to be far superior to all the rest. My friend Idania is a senior makeup artist for Sephora. She came to show me what colors are best for me, and we did a video to show people how to put makeup on to look their best. My next trip was to Las Vegas with our team for the GoPro training event. Of course, I packed my new makeup and I was confident because I wrote directions down and how to use it!

The next morning, Lorrie and I were getting ready; I was seated in front of the mirror at the end of the bed. Lorrie was in the shower. I pulled out my notes and saw 'Step 1' lotion, Step 2 concealer, and Step 3. I grabbed the right brush and applied the foundation; by the time Lorrie came into the room, I was putting eyeliner on when my elbow slipped, and I had black paint covering my whole left eye/cheek and into my forehead… we laughed so hard when I said: "I don't think this is what Idania had in mind when she was teaching me!!!" I wish we had taken a picture of that mistake! Lorrie and I laughed so hard our sides ached the whole day!

On a serious note, toxic-free makeup is precious. If people only realize everything they put in and on the body affects their DNA, they would fall in love with Young Living. All of their products are easy to use, and you don't need notes! It really does make your face feel fresh and clean.

# Why Young Living Essential Oils

Many years ago, Dr. Norma Milanovich introduced me to Young Living essential oils and homeopathic expert Mary Hardy. This was the beginning of a beautiful friendship and the introduction to the wisdom of essential oils. I fell in love with these oils, and my love became my passion. I wanted to know everything about them. My guides directed me to study everything I could about Essential oils. My studies fed my soul and ignited my desire to learn even more.

During this time, we went to every convention, read every book, and met everyone who had anything to do with the entire process, including Chief Science Officer Dr. Mike Buch and the founders of Young Living Oils, D. Gary Young and Mary Young. I have become five times certified in the famous Raindrop technique, Vitaflex technique, Emotional Release, Biblical Oils, and the Chemistry of Oils with Dr. David Stewart CARE, the Center of Aromatherapy Research and Education.

The Mona Farm is one of the most beautiful places on earth. Surrounded by snow-capped mountains, with the sun shining across the land and the smell of the plants, it is a garden of pure love and peace. While walking around the farm, I found myself in the middle of the Melissa plants. With the sun in my face, I was taken to my knees. I felt the brightest white light come into my crown chakra as I was guided to "put my feet into the dirt". This light extended through my body and came out of my feet; as it surrounded me, it anchored deep into the light of the earth. I sat on the ground, removed my shoes, and dug my feet into the dirt. During this moment, I drifted deep into meditation. It felt as though I were the only human on earth, having a conversation with God. I have meditated before, and yet, at that moment in time, I felt one with God. I knew immediately that I was one with these plants and that they were directly from the Creator God. I was literally shown how these plants are alive with God's life force, the same life force that resides within each one of us. The oils are the blood in the veins of the plants. These oils are alive. They have the ability to raise our consciousness and our vibrations. When our vibration is high, we maintain wellness. Each of these oils has the ability to raise our frequency higher, supporting our life force in every way: mind, body, spirit, and emotion. I was shown why Young Living essential oils are far superior to others. I was shown how D. Gary Young and Mary Young continue to support the Creator God in all that they do. This God Force Gene is the key in all of Young Living products. This is the magic key to how and why Young Living works. It is a partnership with the Creator and Mother Nature's creation. When we connect with the Creator God and ask via muscle testing, we can be sure to always select the proper oil.

Breathe it in, soak it up, ingest… the oils are here for you.

It has been an amazing journey with Young Living through the years, watching their legacy and integrity stand the test of time. They continue to enhance our lives in so many ways with essential oils and now over 600 products enhancing our wellness, passion, and abundance.

My original intent was to use these awesome oils; my passion for helping others enhance their lives turned into a rewarding business opportunity.

Where else can you go, building your business while someone else tends to making the product, testing the product, stocking the warehouse, boxing, and shipping directly to your client while you receive monthly rewards and income at the beach?

There are many factors that make therapeutic-grade essential oils: environmental factors, including where the plant is grown, type of soil, fertilizer (organic), altitude, etc… and physical factors, including how and when the plant is harvested (what time of year as well as what day or night), how it is distilled and how it is bottled. All of these factors have equal importance, and Young Living's "Seed to Seal" promise assures everything is done with integrity for the benefit of Mother Earth and all its inhabitants.

Once the oil has been distilled, it is very important to test its composition. Without testing, we really don't know what the chemistry is. Many companies do not test oils because it is time-consuming and expensive. Young Living goes above and beyond to test several times, from the seed all the way through the process to sealing it in the jar.

Wouldn't you prefer knowing the science indicating which oil is best for aromatherapy or perfume and which one will support your liver?

And, when you learn that one drop of synthetic oil is harmful to our DNA, you'll know why it is imperative to use only **therapeutic grade, NON-GMO, Young Living essential oils.**

One of the most valuable experiences I can share is the training I received from the best of the best to show you what our oils can do for you and your family and why Young Living is the Leader in Essential Oils.

**Young Living stands by its Seed to Seal commitment to excellence. And, as guided by Creator God, I stand by Young Living essential oils.** www.youngliving.com use our referral code 1001744 Elizabeth Desrochers as your sponsor and enroller. You'll be glad you did!

# Tremors

By 2018, My body was breaking down. I'd preferred sitting over standing and lying down more often than not! By September 2018, I came down with internal tremors. This was much different than the enlightened download vibrations I had previously enjoyed!

My body was shaking on the inside, but I *could* hold a paper steady in my hand. The shaking seemed to move from hip to knee, to arm to head. It was like a patch of movement in different parts of my body at different times. Because I taught shamanism and often brought groups to Peru, I thought for sure it was parasites.

I went through 3 primary care physicians, a neurologist, CAT, EKG, EEG & all kinds of scans, specialists, and tests. No one could help me figure this out. One rude, arrogant doctor said it was my imagination; needless to say, I won't work with him again!

When I went to Illinois for a Live Blood Analysis, Pam showed me heavy metal toxicity in my blood through the microscope. I also had apoptosis; my blood was literally dying before my eyes. Instead of normal blood running around on the screen, mine looked like a balloon blowing up and then popping! You can also see my blood analysis in our YouTube videos @ Elizabeth Rainbow Dancer.

Here's what we did… first, we tested my pH.

Testing your pH will show how acidic you are; this is the first sign of the body being out of balance. I was so acidic it did not even register on the pH strip. You can get these strips at your local pharmacy or online.

I found a laboratory to test for heavy metals, and I sent my hair in for hair analysis. My results were horrific ~ My levels of toxicity were so high they were off the charts.

You can test for Candida yourself: upon waking, spit your saliva into a clear glass of water and look at it within 15 minutes to 1 hour; if the saliva looks like it has grown tentacles dropping into the water like a jellyfish, then you have Candida.

The first time I did this, my test looked like a dozen jellyfish floating in the glass! Remember when I was welding, I'd send the guys out for a Dunkin Donuts coffee with seven sugars… yes, seven! My diet was pure sugar for many years. I would eat dessert before a meal, not after! My diet was horrible.

Because I had been teaching essential oils for many years, I knew Young Living was the BEST on the planet. I have been to their farms; I knew their work ethics firsthand; they even pray over their oils and insist they are 100% therapeutic grade, NON-GMO, and PURE— They are so pure, to this day, they still hand weed the farms. They test, test, and retest many times to make sure the best constituents are in each batch, and on top of that, they also have 3rd party testing. They never use harmful chemicals or pesticides in or around any of their products.

I knew this was the company that could help get me toxic-free!

I targeted five things that I knew were in my body: Parasites, Heavy Metals, Candida, Brown Recluse Spider Bite (on the back of my knee in 2012), and Lyme Disease, which was first diagnosed in 2006.

I went to my dentist and had my mercury filling removed. Thank God I only had one. (If you have more… It is recommended that one quadrant of fillings be done at a time; if not, it may be too shocking to your system).

Carbs and sugar made my tremors worse, so I tried to cut them out, only to find out I was severely addicted to carbs. I would wake up at 2 am and had to have those little fishy crackers and peanut butter, or I couldn't sleep. So, I decided to do the "SLIQUE" Gum from Young Living. SLIQUE is their dietary program (oil, tea, shakes, gum). I decided to chew Slique gum every time I wanted carbs… and within three weeks, the addiction was gone. Now, it was a choice, not an addiction, and I can easily say NO!

**I cut the following out of my diet:**

-Everything white: white bread, pasta, rice and white potatoes.

-All carbs (except vegetable carbs)

-All grains (because I feel grains are not being cleaned and processed properly, and they are coming through with toxic roundup and pesticides to our plate. I feel H-Pylore bacteria is the problem we have that makes every American look like they are pregnant, men and women!)

-All sugar, crackers, cakes, chips, junk food and fruit and nuts (especially peanut butter).

-All condiments containing sugar of any kind, especially high fructose corn syrup.

**I added to my diet:**

-Young Living Master Formula Vitamins (One a day vitamin packet)

-Young Living Essentialzymes (digestive enzymes)

-Young Living Life 9 (Probiotics before bed)

I added the following to help *detox my issues*:

-Zeolite

-Young Living ParaFREE

-Young Living fish oil: Omegagize

-Fresh Cilantro with every lunch and dinner

**I added all Young Living Supplements to *build up my body*:**

Agilease, Powergize, Multigreens, Super Cal, Super C, Super B, Super vitamin D, BLM, Omegagize, illumeyes…

Every day, I would dowse out (kinesiology/muscle test) which oils to take.

Check out the book "Ancient Wisdom" by Elizabeth Rainbow Dancer and read the chapter on dowsing if you don't know how.

Dowsing is another way to get answers; you can also use muscle testing or Kinesiology. Every day, I would dowse and find my body needed a recipe; one of my favorites is 12 drops of Thieves, 6 Oregano, and 2 Sacred Frankincense. This is a strong recipe, so I put it in capsules and drink a full 8 oz of water with it, just to be sure it makes its way all the way down to my tummy before it dissolved!

Once a week, I put my feet in the Ionic foot bath.

Daily, I put 4-5 drops of Thieves oil in a diffuser and run it for 4 to 8 hours in the living room and kitchen. (Now I still continue to run Thieves in our diffusers to keep the air clean, and now we have a diffuser in every room of the house).

The book "Supplements Desk Reference" by Jen O'Sullivan is a great book to read about the best supplements on planet Earth!

The Essential Oils Integrative Medical Guide by D. Gary Young is one of the best books about essential oils. Also, look for the App so you'll have the information at hand.

I swapped out all toxic household cleaners, personal products, and makeup for non-toxic Young Living products: I now use Thieves household cleaner, Thieves laundry detergent, Thieves hand soap, Thieves dish soap, mountain mist deodorant, copaiba/vanilla shampoo & conditioner.

Heavy metals can come in from what we breathe and what is in our body and on the skin. Everything in our environment must be looked at because toxins hide everywhere. Think about it: the pillowcase you have on your face every night can seep toxins into you as you breathe. Laundry detergent is so very important.

I also did the Hannah Kroeger Wormwood kit to be doubly sure I had no parasites.

After four months, I dropped 40 lbs. After six months, I went back to Pam for another Live Blood Analysis, and my blood was healthy, running around the screen. And my hair sample for heavy metals results showed everything was in the normal range.

After one year, my heavy metal toxicity was still so low it was not even registering on the chart. I feel healthier than ever, and I hope telling my story can help someone investigate all areas that can help them. Remember always that anger will hold on to an illness, so be sure to remove all emotional issues first and pray.

Connection with the creator God that gave you the breath of life will ensure you always have good intuition and guidance.

I know this looks like a lot of work, but seriously, I saw results after four months; after six months, my problems were gone, and after one year, my problems stayed away, and I'm better than ever.

To learn more about Young Living and their Seed to Seal promise, visit www.youngliving.com. Be sure to use Elizabeth Desrochers, member number 1001744, as your Sponsor and Enroller. We are delighted to train you, your friends, and your family to help you build a business too! When you Love the products, you can't help sharing. Sharing is caring, and Young Living rewards you for sharing too! We are so passionate about YL. Call us; we'd be happy to talk with you too!

Would you believe a friend said to me: "You'll never keep the weight off, you can't maintain that diet"! Well, that was five years this past September, and I'm still not eating carbs or sugar. I am 138 lbs., and I feel better than ever.

So, here's the recipe to have a great day:

When you wake up, GET UP. Make your bed, Pray, shower & wash your hair (*Every day*)

Eat when you're hungry, not by the clock. Plan ahead so that when you are hungry, you have something that is nutritious and delicious.

Take vitamins, pure food & water (only what God designed to be eaten by humans) (we love our Berkey water filter).

If you need to strengthen your physical health, add appropriate supplements; if you need to strengthen your physical body, add appropriate exercise, strengthen your mind with appropriate reading and videos, treat yourself to a session, and strengthen your heart by loving people wherever you go and whatever you do.

You have many choices; make them with Love in your heart.

Every day, call a friend you haven't seen in a long while, stay connected, build your community ♡♡♡♡ know this is your Best Life Ever.

# Corona/ Covid/ Hip

On March 18, 2019, Al was scheduled for hip surgery. The doctor called the night before to tell us it was on as scheduled. "Be there at 5:30 am tomorrow," Dr. Marchand said. Al replied, "As long as you didn't celebrate St. Patty's Day, Doc, I'll be there!" Al probably should have had this surgery a year ago. He always works through the pain. When he finally decided to have it done, there was a four-month wait.

Actually, waiting four months for surgery worked out in our favor. I put him on a four-month **Joint and Mobility** protocol to build up his body so it would be stronger than ever in preparation for surgery. We Oiled his body every night with Young Living's **Cool Azul** for pain over the hip area. Of course, dowsing out (what I call muscle testing) which oil to put where… **Copaiba** on his spine and added to his nightly green tea a drop or two of **Lemongrass, Peppermint, Copaiba, Goldenrod**, and occasionally, **Sacred Frankincense**.

Here are the supplements he took: **Master Formula** vitamin pack, **Life 9**, **Omegagize**, **Sulfurzyme**, **Agilease** (supports the body's natural response to acute inflammation), **powergize** (great for anyone trying to boost their game), **Multigreens** (supports healthy cell function), and 2 oz of **Ningxia Red** juice. **Aminowise** and our favorite Greens First drink were added to his morning workouts as he strengthened all the muscles of his body.

Dr. Marchand's group had us watch 14 videos to prepare. I was supposed to be Al's coach, sleeping at the hospital to help him for up to three nights. We were physically as well as emotionally prepared for this surgery.

The Covid virus just hit America, and there were reports on the news of a "Lock Down". We have never had anything like this before and people were really scared. We arrived at South County Hospital, where four people were blocking the entrance. Two nurses and two police officers. One nurse said, "We need to screen you before you enter". She asked, "Do you have a cough, a cold, or a fever? Have you traveled outside the USA within the past 14 days?" We both answered "no" to all the questions and proceeded to the waiting room, which was empty. The entire hospital seemed to be deserted.

At 7:00 am, a nurse came to take us to another room. They would begin preparing Al for surgery. Dr. Marchand came in and explained that I could wait in the waiting room and he would return to talk with me as soon as the surgery was over. I sat and waited. The waiting room was deserted; not a nurse, receptionist, or janitor. Nobody else was around. Fifty-seven minutes later, Dr. Marchand came out of the operating room to tell me surgery was successful; Al would be in recovery for about an hour, and then a nurse would let me in to see him.

A man came to sit at the desk where the computer was and asked what I was doing there. He told me the hospital was closing because of Covid, and I had to leave. I told him what the doctor said, and he said the rules had changed: "This virus is bad; you must leave; we are closing the hospital". I was unsure of what exactly was going on, confused because I had watched all those videos and was supposed to stay overnight with Al. I have never, ever heard of a hospital closing. This was insane. I was threatened; I could leave on my own, or the police would be called to escort me out.

As I was walking to the parking lot, my phone rang; it was Al saying they already got him up to walk. He said, "I'm a little dizzy, but I got up. I Love you, go home and don't worry". Something didn't feel right, and I didn't have clarity, so I prayed!

When I was leaving the parking lot, I should have gone left, but God took the wheel and made me turn right. I was only a few miles from our favorite beach. So, I went there. It was deserted. The restaurants on either side of the beach were closed, and no one was in sight. I went to the water's edge and said prayers. I heard, "This is the battle between good and evil; trust in God, and you'll be fine". Tears ran down my face; it was overwhelming as I sat on the sand sobbing. There was a dread that came over me, feeling like the world was coming to an end. I prayed for strength, clarity, and the courage to do what God brought me to Earth to do. When I caught my breath, the sobbing subsided, and I could hear the seagulls. Three of them landed right in front of me as I heard "Trinity"

The Father, Son, and Holy Spirit. This was bigger than anything I've ever known and I would only get through it with God and trusting with his infinite Love and Light. I walked to the beach and headed back to the car.

When I sat in the car, watching the inlet to Galilee, I was still praying when my friend Lynn called. She said she had a strong urge to call me and see if I was okay. Lynn knows the bible inside and out. We prayed together. Although we both knew we were safe, we also knew many people were terrified of this Covid virus. We prayed together for over two hours, and then she said, I'll stay on the phone with you while you drive home. We talked the whole way home. When I pulled into the garage, I knew it was going to be okay; we were all safe. We would weather the storm because God is in charge.

It was a nice sunny day, so I went out to get the mail and sat on the chair outside. Our cousin Richard drove by and saw me sitting outside, so he pulled into the driveway. He wanted to see how Al made out. As we were talking, my phone rang, it was Al saying "Come get me". I said, "Richard, he must be drugged; he wants me to go get him, Al, put the nurse on the phone". He insisted, "Come get me" & I could then hear the nurse saying, "Mrs. D, he did the stairs so he's good to go and they're closing the hospital, you've got to come get him".

When I arrived at South County Hospital, they wouldn't let me in; they pushed Al to the sidewalk in a wheelchair and put him in my car. The next morning, the physical therapist came to our house to check on Al. She was fully masked up with something that looked like a hazmat suit and a face shield. That was the only time a nurse came to the house. No one ever came back again because of the COVID lockdown. Nurses would call to see how he was doing, go over exercises, and guide us by phone.

Basically, we did it all ourselves (Thankfully, with the guidance of God)!

# Elks

October 10, 2020

Morning meditation, I hear, "Today is **10 10 20 20** we have a gift for you.

As I went through my day, A beautiful Sunday morning. Al wants me to go for a ride in his 64 Vette. 1964 Corvette Stingray. Originally, we were going to go to the beach with Mark & his wife, but she canceled to help her son study for his test. Then Mark called & said his friend Ross had tickets for an Italian dinner at the Elk's Club in Bristol. I told Al, "You go with the guys; I can't eat pasta and breaded cutlets anyway, so you go with the guys". Every so often, he'd return and say, "I really want you to come. I was getting pissed off because the thought of wearing a mask in a restaurant, taking it off at the table to eat, and wearing it again to exit really, really, really, got me angry. (We were still in the middle of the Covid virus scare) All I can think about is this mask-wearing in a restaurant is bullshit. It goes against everything, I believe. I refuse to wear a mask in a restaurant! It's like having a pissing section in a swimming pool! He explained this place is right on the water and he really, really wanted me to come. So, we compromised, I made a deal with him and say, "Ok, I'll go as long as I can sit outside near the water, maybe in the car with a book, you go inside, drink & eat with the guys.

It was a beautiful day and a nice drive, so we had the top down. When we arrived, there were many Ravens and Seagulls circling around… I chuckled when I said, "Al, they're going to shit on your head." We both laughed. This Elks club was a brick building right on the water with a deck overlooking the water; on the right side, there was another building that looked like a castle; on the 2nd floor was another outside deck. The day was absolutely perfect. Mark drove up in his 72 vette & parked next to us. He introduced me to Ross, and I don't remember much after that until I was inside, sitting at the table, taking my mask off. I seriously don't even remember putting it on, walking inside, waiting in line, and walking to the table. In the blink of an eye… It was like a time-lapse.

Mark began talking about how he became an Elk. I said, "My father was an Elk. In fact, he was a tool-maker pre-1959 and made the rings for the Elks. Actually, I have his ring right here. I pulled my Mesa (portable prayer altar) medicine bundle out of my pocketbook, placed it on the table, opened it, and pulled out my father's ring. Mark took it, showed Ross, and, as they looked at it, called Fred over to the table. Fred was one of the oldest guys there. Fred took the ring and described every detail of the Benevolent and Protective Order of Elks, the letters on each side of the ring. B. P. O. E. There is a black onyx square in the center with a tiny metal elk that is held in place with the tiny screw in the back.

Then Fred says, "Come with me," and he takes me upstairs to unlock a door to a room that was as big as it was downstairs, but because of "Covid" it's been locked. There was a table-like altar in the center of the room with a huge book; on either side of the book were these sashes, dark purple with metal triangles and other emblems on them. There were two on the left and four on the right. They looked like our Sisterhood of the Emerald Fire sashes we received at ordination into the sisterhood. The book was very old and warned; it was so, so, old with a warn leather covering and a huge cross embedded into it. I asked Fred, "Can I touch it?" He ran over to me because by now, Al & Mark were in the corner of the room talking with him… He came to me & did the sign of the cross like a priest would bless someone on the altar as he said, "ok, now you can".

I touched the book with my left hand, and the light came through the ceiling surrounding me as I was surrounded by this ball of light;

it was as if it was the sun shining through 8 ft diameter, only it was moving quickly… like rays of sunshine moving over me through the floor below. I knew it was the Light of God from the Heavens, and coming straight through without restrictions through me into the center of Earth. I could feel the vibrations and knew God was Anchoring the Light right then and there. As I opened the book and looked at the words, I was getting downloaded with information. I immediately began praying the "Our Father," and I heard, "Surrender and allow. Anchor the Light, Anchor the Light. That prayer is not sacred enough for this. This is before the man has created those words, this is pure, this is pure, Source". No words could have done it justice. Tears just rolled down my face. I surrendered and allowed.

I realized it was older than anything I had ever touched before. It was a 1609 Bible. The pages were like parchment papers… or what they called papyrus paper. A long while back, when I was a child, one of my teachers had one from Egypt for us to touch. It was very thin and soft, like that.

When the vibrations calmed down, I could hear slight mumbling in the back of the room. Al, Mark & Fred were talking there. I went to the window to look at the water from the upper deck, and I heard my father say, "You wanted a place on the water; this is for you."

Mark walked over to me to comment on how beautiful the view was; with tears in my eyes, I could only say, "This is amazing". I knew he & Ross were part of the templars back in the day when Jesus walked the earth, along with Al; these are our guardians who protected "The Marys" after Jesus died. Mary Magdalene, Blessed Mother Mary, and Mary Jacobe.

We returned downstairs; the waitress came to ask me if I wanted Sausage and Peppers. I was shocked because I thought the meal was chicken cutlet and pasta. I was absolutely delighted that I could eat! It was absolutely delicious. Fred came out of the kitchen with two applications and handed one to me, saying, "You need to be an Elk".

Al jumps up and says, "I always wanted to be an Elk." This shocked me. I had no idea. So, we pay the fees and submit both forms. I absolutely wanted to be an Elk, but back in the day, they didn't allow women; I was even more shocked to know now women are a big part of the Elk. Within a month, all the approvals were in place, and we attended the ceremony. The most amazing thing here is the fact that I was actually initiated into the Benevolent and Protective Order of Elks on my father's birthday.

Thank you, Dad, I humbly accept.

A few years ago, Al & his brothers went boar hunting in Maine and found a huge Elk skull with a giant rack. They brought it home for me. When I got home, Al said, where do you want it? I said put it on the bed. It barely fit. I had to meditate with it to make sure it was not killed, and if it was killed, then I'd do a ceremony to bring his soul to heaven. I laid on the bed and meditated with this enormous elk skull with antlers for 2 hours. God showed me he died in battle with another, and of course, now I see his forehead has a big crack in it. We honored him with feathers, and he lives on the main wall in our Great room.

# CDL

Marco is all grown up now. He has his own electric company. It amazes me that his very first word was "Light," and he was fascinated with lights and electricity from that very first word. He became the youngest person to obtain his Master's electrical license in Local 99 and now has a crew of 20 people working for him. As his business grew, he and Al bought a building. Part of this building is rented, and RSM Electric has 5500 sq. ft.

My clients come first. When I have a free day, I'll go to the shop with Al and offer my help. Some days, I paint off the scissor lift; some days, I place plugs on the end of wires, and other days I help pull wires through walls & pipes. It reminds me so much of my happy days at the Power Plant. And sometimes I'm so silly, I crack myself up!

One day, I was sitting on the little creeper; it looked like a mechanics stool with four wheels on the bottom. After I completed a little task while sitting on this stool, I pushed off to ride the creeper to the other end of the building… It was so much fun!

Then one of the wheels caught the rug & the creeper stopped while I kept going!

Marco yelled from his office, "Mom, are you alright?" He got to see the entire episode because he had surveillance camera videos on his computer that showed me flying across the floor! I think I giggled all day after that. I couldn't stop laughing.

Al has had his CDL License since 1974. He used to take me for a ride when we were dating. He would let me drive when we got to the high school parking lot. I have always loved big trucks ever since my cousin Danny played with them in the sandbox! Now, Marco has two bucket trucks. It didn't take long to convince Al to teach me how to drive them, and at 65 years old, I got my CDL. Another milestone: I am the first female welder in all of New England Electric System and the oldest woman to get her CDL in Rhode Island. Not many women can say that!

*You may have noticed I didn't write a lot about Marco. That is because it is his life, his story, and not for me to write. He continues to amaze me day after day. His intelligence is far superior to anyone I know. His unending love for Lights and Electricity shows in his work ethic and creativity. (I would love to do a past life regression with him; surely, he was someone of great importance) God Bless you, Marco.*

# Sisters

Because I have studied many years with Medicine Men and Women from all over the world, I thought, surely, I must have some Native American in me. Previously, I refused to send my DNA in because I thought they'd use it for something negative! Well, this one particular day, I thought differently; I thought, I'm 66 years old; who cares what they do with it? So I prayed, filled out the forms, spit in the tube, and tossed it in the mail.

On March 28, 2023, I received my DNA results from AncestoryDNA.com, and it showed 100% Match to Noreen Cxxx. Dxxxxxx. I prayed and asked God to show me what to do. I certainly do not want to be the one to create problems for a family. Imagine, this news could be devastating.

God showed me the vision to look up Noreen on Facebook. When I saw her picture, it was the same picture on Ancestry, I knew we had a connection. She seemed very familiar. I prayed for God's guidance as I typed a message to her. I said, "Hi Noreen, we have not met. I just got my DNA results, and it looks like you know about Ancestry. Your family tree is awesome. Can you help me? (I attached the screenshot that shows her picture, my picture, and the words 100% match.) Blessings Elizabeth.

She replied, "Hello, yes, I would love to meet with you for coffee. That is so interesting. Where did you want to meet? I live in West Warwick on the Cranston line."

I replied, "Awesome! You probably can't see my DNA results because I have not allowed them to be shared as yet. This is scary as much as exciting. I live in Johnston; we're so close.

She said, "Wow. I grew up in Johnston. We could meet at Brewed Awakenings in Johnston.

I answered, "Yes, Brewed Awakening is good."

On Friday, Noreen typed, "Can I bring my sister?" I said, "Sure! I love meeting new people".

Saturday, April 1, 2023, Al and I spoke about how nervous I was; he did his best to calm me down. After all, my main concern was not to hurt anyone. Who am I to crush their image of their perfect daddy? Al & I wondered if they would be upset or angry at me.

He suggested I walk in at 9:59 as I was preparing to leave the house a half hour early… too funny, huh? (I was praying all the way to the coffee shop!)

As I pulled into the tiny parking lot driving my SUV, another SUV pulled in the same way that I did. We both pulled forward and backed into parking spaces (now facing each other). My intuition felt it was "Her". I heard, "She's just like you". I thought, "WHAT!?!?!? I heard again loud and clear, "SHE'S JUST LIKE YOU!"

It was raining out. I waited until 9:59 am. Threw my keys in my purse, locked the doors, and got out as I saw she was doing the same… at the same time. I could see she tossed her keys in her bag, grabbed her bag, and got out of the car at the same time I did.

Then we walked on the sidewalk and into the coffee shop together.

As we looked at each other, she said, "Elizabeth?" I said, "Noreen?" She said, "This is my sister Lucia. Would you like a coffee?" I couldn't speak; I was so choked up with tears. Words came out of my mouth that were totally unidentifiable! Noreen took charge and said, "Lucia, get her a coffee and a tea". She looked at me and said, "Come, sit down." I was literally shaking. She took my arm and said, "I'm going to make this easy for you. You are either my grandfather's daughter or my father's daughter." I heard loud and clear, "We don't care which, we love you anyway"!

Her words couldn't have been more perfect.

Surely, it was God's guidance reassuring me all would be okay.

We talked a lot and identified that we have the same biological father. Norman Cxxx, and he used to drive Teresa Pxxx to work at Speidel every day until they were very old.

(https://en.wikipedia.org/wiki/Speidel)

I was born in February. Noreen was born in August of 1957. Yes, that's correct; our biological mothers were pregnant at the same time!

Lucia is 4 ½ years older than us. Noreen and I were in the same High School graduation class of 1975. We have the same high school friends! As we continued to explore our background, we found ourselves finishing each other's sentences. I heard again, "She's just like you." When I said English class, Mr. Ascenzi… both of us said at the same time, "He was so cute!"

Noreen has four children. Lucia has three grandchildren and great-grandchildren.

My DNA paternal side has over 17, 403 matches. My maternal side has only 1701.

This is truly fascinating! Noreen helped me understand my DNA Results. She has completed her family tree all the way back to the 1500s! I must say I was completely shocked. All these years, when I would get up on stage to introduce myself, I always began with, "I was raised Catholic, Italian…" I thought for sure I had olive oil running in my veins! Nope! My DNA results show I am only 40% Italian! 30% Irish, Greek, and French! Ancestry shows our ancestors coming from those countries to the St. Lawrence River. The Bear Clan of Lake Huron Natives entered in 1590. Then they came to Vermont, and in the 1900's, they came to Rhode Island.

That was day one, April 1, 2023… I can say God certainly has a sense of humor. Noreen and I have been meeting every chance we get, text messages, phone calls…

We are so alike it is uncanny!

Friday night, we met at the Tiki bar @ Georges of Galilee. Noreen, her husband Guy, their daughter Danielle, Guy's sisters Debbie and Michele with her husband, the neighbors, friends, and their husbands… Al handed me a glass of wine; I spilled it all over his shoulder, dripping down his shirt all the way to his elbow as Guy laughed and said, "Danielle! Look! I told you! She is just like your mother!" Noreen had the clumsy gene, just like me!

We are having so much fun; what a gift from God. The more we talk, the more we find out we are alike in so many ways.

Noreen has introduced me as her "**Twin from another mother**".

We are having so much fun—God is good, God is great & always makes things better than I could have ever imagined.

*8.23.2023, Lucia is having a gathering for me to meet Uncle Ed and Aunty Pat, who flew in from Florida. Uncle Ed is my Biological Father's brother and best friend. He is the only one of that generation who was close to my Bio father. The first time we spoke on Zoom, he cried, "You look just like your father." I asked him, "Do you think he knew about me?" He said "I can say without a doubt, NO! He would have never let you go. He would have taken you under his wing and protected you forever!" (That makes sense since Teresa told everyone I was a tumor when she was pregnant with me.)*

*We met Uncle Ed and Aunty Pat last night, Uncle Ed took my hands in his, and his eyes filled up; of course, we were all crying. Emotions are strong, and my heart is full.*

*Noreen, Lucia, and all the family I have met make me feel so loved; it is as if we are trying to make up for 66 lost years. We continue meeting more family and just met Uncle Ed's son Michael & his partner Ernie at a dinner last night, 8/25/2023. My sides still ache from laughing so much. Of course, I realized this all began on April 1 (April Fool's Day). I laugh to think God surely has a sense of humor!*

*The fun continues, and I feel loved beyond measure.*

# Boat Fire

On Memorial Day, 2023, Danny and Diane invited us on the boat. We met at the marina. The big boat is a 44 feet Azimut, docked right next to their speed boat, "Sonic". It was a beautiful, sunny day. We relaxed, had snacks, sat on the big boat, and shared stories. Danny said, "Who wants to go for a ride on the Sonic?" I jumped up like an excited little kid. "Me! Me!"

Danny was driving the Sonic. Al was in the front seat. Andy (Danny's son-in-law) and, his daughter Lily and I were seated in the back. We were going slow through the marina to keep our wake at a minimum. As we exited the marina, Danny started to accelerate the boat. It shut off.

Sonic is 36 feet long and has two inboard motors. To see what happened, he lifted the back seat, exposing the engines. Andy then said, "There is smoke coming from the cabin (underneath). Al ran and grabbed the fire extinguisher. Smoke started billowing out of the dashboard instruments. Danny grabbed a knife & popped a switch on the dashboard where 6-inch flames poured out. They immediately extinguished the flames when we noticed a 45 ft sailboat was heading right towards us. The lady on the sailboat yelled, "We have no steering! We can't steer!" We were all yelling, "We can't move", "we're stuck", and "We're dead in the water". Then the big sailboat hit us.

The front to the middle of their sailboat hit the middle back all the way to the left side. It was like slow motion. Thank God, no one fell out of the boat, no one was hurt, and the boat did not sustain enormous damage. What could have happened is so scary. They could have hit us straight on; their boat would have climbed right up the back of our boat. Had they hit us sideways, it would have cut our boat in half. Had the fire not been extinguished so quickly, fiberglass would have caught fire, and we would have all had to jump in the water. God was surely with us, keeping us all safe.

As the boat hit us, I heard God loud and clear, "There's a portal here if you want to take it". I thought, NO! I'm not ready to die; I have so much more to do! NO! NO! No! (Had I died that day, it would have been with my favorite people, in my favorite place, doing my favorite thing. It would have been perfect) NO! It's not my time; I am not ready!

Lily said, "Papa, I was praying. I was praying to God." Her words rang in my heart like a symphony of angels letting us know this child knows!

# Tornado

At approximately 8:45 am on Friday, August 18, 2023, my phone alert started ringing. It said, "Take cover! Tornado in the area! Get to lower ground ASAP! Get to the basement or middle of the house for a safe place." I went to the basement, sat on the bottom step, and heard, "What are you doing?!! Go Upstairs to your Mesa (Prayer Altar) and pray now!"

While running up the stairs, I thought, 'Oh well, if this is the way you want me to die, so be it.' I ran to my bedroom; my Mesa/Altar sat on the floor directly in front of a big window. I sat on the floor in front of my Mesa and Prayed for the "Our Father". When I looked out the window, I saw the Maple and Oak trees bending like they were rubber palm trees! (Oak and Maple don't bend!) All the leaves were flying in one direction as if the wind was so strong coming from the left. The noise was so loud! It sounded like a freight train coming through the woods. I stood up, held Slim Spurling's ring, and screamed the Our Father and the Holy Grail Vortex prayers with the emotion, commanding "thy will be done"! It seemed to calm down, and my phone rang. It was Claudia; I yelled, "Pray with me now!" We both prayed the Our Father and Holy Grail Vortex. As soon as we were done, it stopped. I told Claudia we needed to hold that high vibration for the next 10 minutes and that I would call her back.

The rain seemed to stop, and everything was calm. Al ran into the house. "are you okay? Ray (who lives next door) called me; he was on the toilet & heard a freight train coming through the woods. He said something happened; go check!" Al had been at the garage for an oil change. When Ray called him, he was heading home, so he swung by the plat behind our house. Directly behind our house is approximately

200 yards of woods then a small neighborhood of enormous million-dollar houses. Parasol Ct. and Carriage Way are directly behind us. The tornado landed right there! We got in the car to assess the damage. From our street, there are a few branches and leaves on the roads. When you turn into Carriage Way, you can see everyone has their trash in front of their houses. It was trash pick-up day. On one side of the road, not a paper out of place; on the other, it looks like a war zone. The closer we got to Parasol Ct, the more damage we could see. Trees uprooted, broken, leaning on houses. Patio furniture in swimming pools, everything looks as if it was tossed around violently. We chatted with neighbors. Everyone was outside in disbelief. No one was hurt. Outside of a few shingles off the roof and trees leaning on houses, not one tree had punctured through a house.

After reading Facebook (which I love because it has real people, real-time, telling their side of the story) and the news stories, we could see the Tornado's path.

The tornado touched down on Byron Randall Rd in Scituate, where it took out hundreds of trees. Then it came down Route 295, where it picked up a car with a woman in it and spun it around to where it landed back on Route 295. After that, it came through the Greenville Ave exit off Route 295 and landed briefly in the woods on Pine Hill Ave (Crushing huge trees). Then landed on Parasol Ct (Approximately 300 yards from our back door) and carriage way before heading directly north of that, and then it landed on Highland Memorial Cemetery and Rhode Island Ave. The trees that were snapped like toothpicks through this path were over a foot in diameter and over 35 to 45 feet tall.

This tornado was an EF 2—111-135mph. It is extremely rare for Rhode Island to have a tornado. This is only the third tornado we have ever had in my lifetime.

Rhode Island had a tornado when I was 12 years old. My cousin Maria was 16 years old and took us for a ride to see the damage. A three-family house in the Silver Lake area was picked up and moved one foot; the whole house was turned. The only indication anything was wrong was the foundation sticking out one foot kitty-corner to the house, and the electric wires had disconnected from the pole. The second tornado was in 1986, but no one could remember those details.

***** Looking back on my life...*

*To this day, I have recurring dreams of Aunty Theresa and Uncle Dan's beach, the house, and the neighborhood. In my dream, the road curves to the right and goes around, approaching the house from the right, when in reality, the road is actually straight, and you take a left turn and then a right approaching the house from the left side. After meditating on this, I was shown these are parallel lives we visit during our dream time. How interesting! I also have another recurring dream when I'm in the powerplant, and the stairs are over there on the left, and the overhead garage door is different... in reality, the stairs are over there on the right... another parallel life? I was just reading this to Danny, and he remarked, "Did you know the road did come around that way before the 1938 hurricane"? Now I'm on a mission to find those old maps! If that is true, it must have been a past life. It is my favorite dream... I always wake up fulfilled and joyous after having that "dream". Time will tell the truth in detail of parallel and past lives. Of that, I'm sure.*

*I completed Chemistry after my passion for Essential Oils became an obsession to learn all I could about these little bottles of God's medicine!!! I continue to live in a place of "seeking truth" in all that I do, and my thirst for knowledge is alive and well. I am five times certified in CARE, the Center for Aromatherapy, Research and Education. Vitaflex, Raindrop, Emotional Release, Biblical oils, and Chemistry. I also studied CBD oils with Dr. Oli Wenker. Young Living has a CBD oil without THC; they use a blend of essential oils that give better results without the "high". We are so very blessed to have Young Living Essential oils and all their pure products that enhance our lives in so many ways.*

The visions I receive now are clear and accurate. My life has changed so much. Just as the Shamans told me years ago, what I thought was real, isn't... and what I thought wasn't real—is.

It took me many years of study and twenty Masters before I even *thought* of teaching. Now, I've got 26 Master's teachings and hundreds of classes on my resume. I've taken the good stuff and left the nonsense behind, of course, after learning why it was there and what it had to teach me!

These are my wise words of wisdom for you:

NEVER STOP LEARNING; this is how Knowledge turns into Wisdom.

Study with as many Masters with Integrity as you can every day of your life.

Walk your talk with integrity and aim for impeccability at all times.

Take criticism with Love because it is an easy lesson.

NEVER—EVER—Get offended by criticism because that will stop you from learning the easy lesson.

Use your "Wisdom" for the highest good—Trust in God—and Pray.

We all think that we're on the right track, so when a problem arises, we hardly see 'it can be me'. When we have an issue, turn it to the center, turn it around, look in the mirror, and face yourself. YES, it is always about you. But when you see it is always about you, it can be the most powerful of all healings… Pay attention to details… Look within… This is how you heal yourself…

When someone does something you do not like, use this as a mirror to correct yourself.

What is it in you that needs correcting? If it wasn't upsetting you, it wouldn't be about you. If it is under your skin, it's definitely about you! Fix you; everything else falls into place.

I digested all that is, into the knowing of all that is, and the power surged through me—One with lightning, One with rainbow, One with all of Humanity, all of Mother Earth and all her inhabitants. I am here on earth to be of service to Humanity, a liaison between the worlds, those seen and unseen. I work for God.

**See our websites:**

www.ancientwiz.com

www.qhht-elizabeth.com

www.essentialoilsri.com

www.elizabethrainbowdancer.com

*Email:* info@ancientwiz.com

www.youngliving.com *Be sure to use our #1001744 as your Sponsor & Enroller when you join. You can receive discounts and commission checks for referring friends when you are on their auto-ship program.*

**Look for our books:**

*"Ancient Wisdom" by Elizabeth Rainbow Dancer*
*"MESA 101 ~ Keep the Medicine Sacred to Your Heart"*
*by Elizabeth Rainbow Dancer*

# Photo Album

*Ysabel, Elizabeth, Marco Nunez, Olinda,*
*Don Martin Pinedo Acuna Providence Zen Center,*
*Cumberland, Rhode Island, USA*

*Elizabeth High up in the mountains at the*
*UFO stone Araypallpa, Peru*

*Elizabeth and Don Francisco,
Cusco, Peru*

*Don Martin Pinedo Acuna,
Moray, Peru*

*Don Martin Pinedo Acuna & Elizabeth (Joking around!)
Pachatusan, Peru*

*Elizabeth in Machu Picchu*

*Machu Picchu*

*Elizabeth & Dona
Julia at Humpi Tika
Center for Healers
Ollantaytambo, Peru*

*Marco Nunez, Elizabeth, Don Martin Pinedo Acuna, Ivoryton, Connecticut USA*

*Elizabeth, Marco Nunez, Don Martin Pinedo Acuna, Smithfield Rhode Island USA*

*Marco Nunez, Don Martin Pinedo Acuna, Elizabeth at the Providence Zen Center, Cumberland, Rhode Island, USA*

*Elizabeth with children of the community of Sacsayhuman, Peru*

*Elizabeth with Llama,*
*Animal rescue center Peru*

*Elizabeth, Machu Pichu (again!)*

*Ysabel, Elizabeth, Olinda at the "TWINS" home in Chiclayo Peru*

*Humpi Tika Ceremonial Hut at Dona Julia's healer's retreat center, Ollantaytambo Peru*

*Elizabeth, Maria, Vilma, Wilson (Don Martin's family) in Don Martin Pinedo Acuna's home healing room, Huasao, Peru*

*Elizabeth, Mondor, Peru waterfalls*

*Elizabeth, Prayers at Temple of the Sun, Northern Peru near Trujillo.*

*Elizabeth with the women of the community, Alpaca & Llama of Sacsayhuman, Peru.*

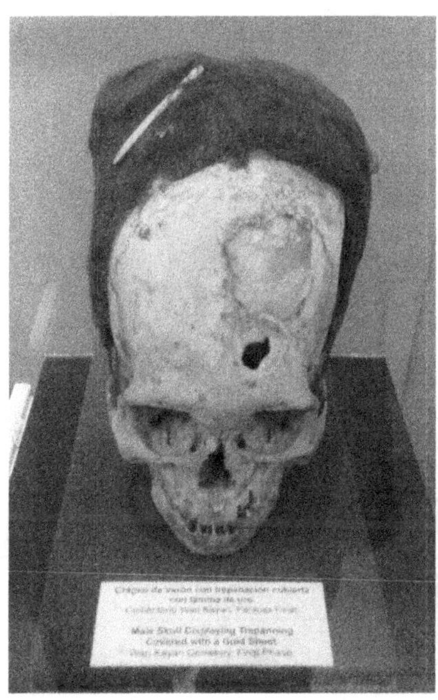

*Red Hair Paracus Skull from Paracus, Peru – (Remember, you can not gain volume by banding the skulls… clearly these are much larger and not human).*

*Below: Female Paracus Skull, Paracus Peru.*

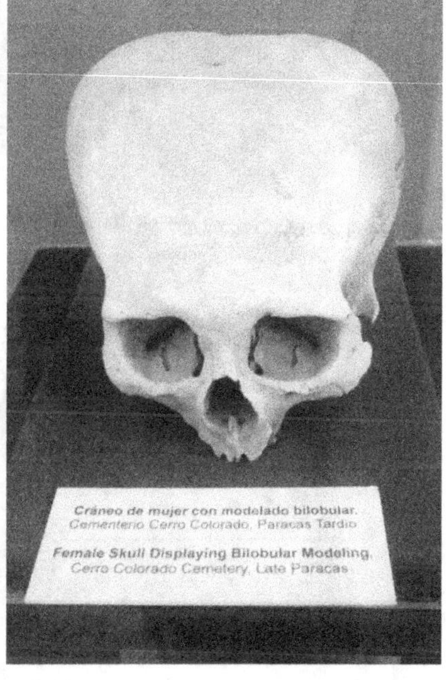

*Paracus Skull, Paracus, Peru.*

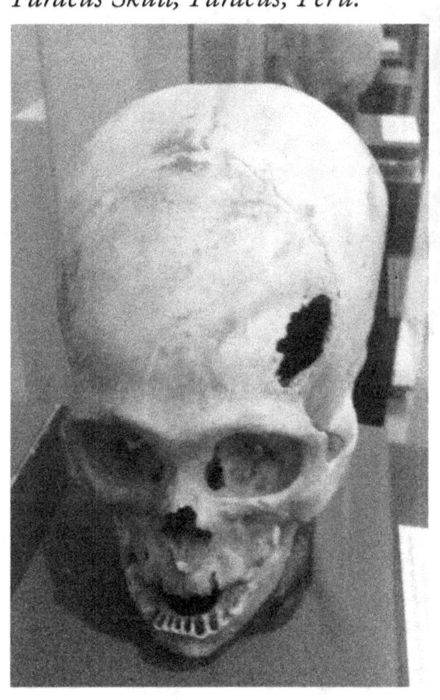

*Specimens in the archeological museum, Miraflores Peru*

*UFO Stone, side 1. Araypallpa, Peru*

*UFO Stone, side 2. Araypallpa, Peru*

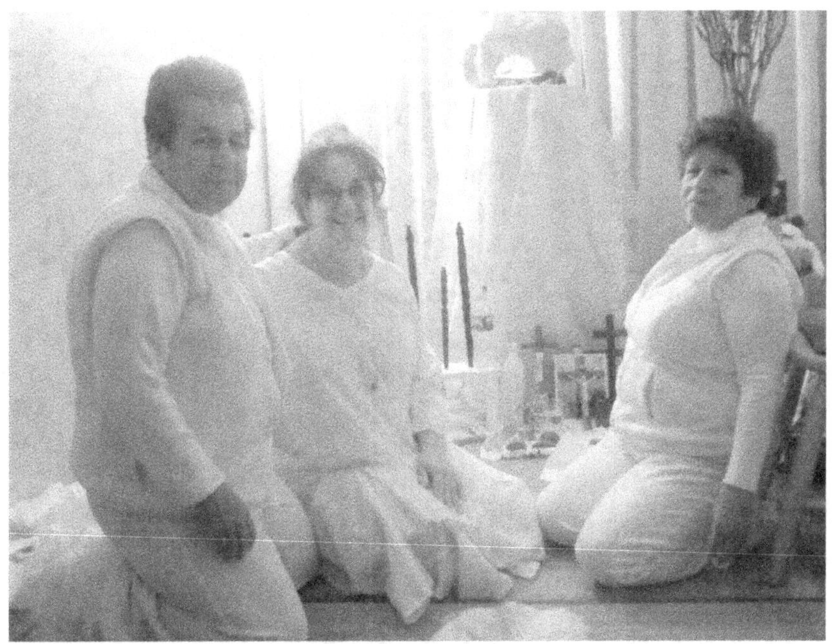

*Olinda, Elizabeth, Ysabel doing healings at White Light Bookstore, Cranston Rhode Island, USA*

*Mike Wright, Elizabeth (Welder), Elmore Thomson, South Street Station Power plant, Narragansett Electric, Providence, Rhode Island USA*

*Elizabeth, Sitting on the Turbine, Manchester Street Station Power Plant, Narragansett Electric, Providence, Rhode Island USA*

*Elizabeth welding Shed built by Al, 1992. Johnston, Rhode Island USA*

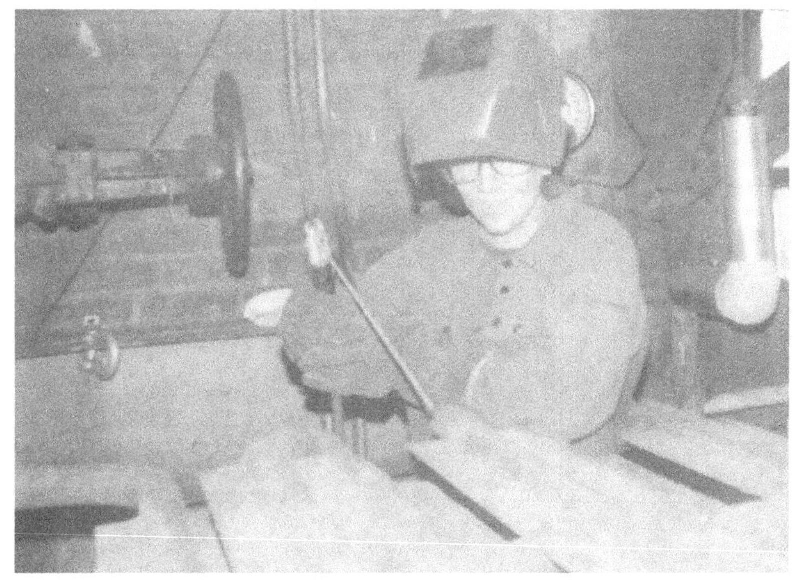

*Elizabeth welding on 5th fl. Economizer tubes,
Manchester Street Station Power Plant, Narragansett Electric,
Providence, Rhode Island USA*

*Elizabeth's Welder,
Miller Bobcat
8000watt welder
generator for Stick &
Tig welding, Johnston,
Rhode Island USA*

*When you want to get there fast "Vette-Stream". Al's 1964 Corvette stingray in front of our 1999 Airstream camper.*

*Elizabeth sitting in Al's '64 Vette*

*Al & Elizabeth, 1992 Corvette Convertible, Johnston, Rhode Island USA*

*Our American Bulldog "Bull"*

*Diesel with his favorite pal "Caddy"*

*Diesel sitting on Elizabeth*

*"Bull" sitting in my MESA (Portable Prayer Altar)*

*Tuma-guy—female deer with her babies has been coming to visit for the past 15 years with a tumor on her shoulder. She continued coming for many years after it burst it had a Beautiful "Star" shaped scar.*

*Dolores Cannon with Elizabeth (Elizabeth was the Only person in Rhode Island to be trained in QHHT Quantum Healing Hypnosis Therapy, directly by Dolores Cannon herself).*

*Elizabeth and (son) Marco*

*Elizabeth and Young Living Essential Oils
Tractor Trailer in Mona Utah*

*Left: Elizabeth with CDL license,
driving RSM Electric Bucket truck
on Mother's Day, Living Life,
Having Fun!*

*Elizabeth on scissor lift, helping
to paint RSM Electric (Local #99
Marco's Electric company)*

*Elizabeth teaching shamanism at the Providence Zen Center, Cumberland, Rhode Island, USA*

*Jesus statue in the Visitor's center at The Church of Jesus Christ of Latter-day Saints, Temple Square, Salt Lake City Utah, USA*

*St. Kateri Tekakwitha*

*My Jesus*

*Jose', our Yellow Napped Amazon Parrot,
lived to be 40 yrs old.*

*Marco & Elizabeth Summer 2023*

*Elizabeth & Al 1980*

*Marco and Al at our 25th wedding anniversary*

*Mary Young (Young Living Essential Oils) and Elizabeth 2017 Global Leadership Cruise.*

*Elizabeth & Mary Hardy, Global Leadership Cruise 2017*

*Manchester Street Station repowering project 1995*

*South Street Station, Narragansett Electric Power plant, Turbin Hall.*

*Elizabeth, Young Living Essential Oils Convention Salt Lake City, Utah USA*

*Our First Book "Ancient Wisdom" by Elizabeth Rainbow Dancer*

# Testimonials

QHHT Quantum Healing Hypnosis Therapy "My experience with QHHT was nothing short of astounding. The preliminary interview that is conducted just before the session began was handled with the utmost respect and professionalism. Elizabeth's knowledge and ability to bring a sense of ease and comfort creates a true sense of calm and assurance that everything discussed is approached without judgment and with the strictest of confidence. The session itself is a guided meditation in which you are brought to a very deep level of peace and meditation while remaining aware and in control. The experience is difficult to put into words, however it is a deeply personal journey that allows the sacred part of yourself to emerge. Once that level is reached, Elizabeth is able to work with your highest self and, with permission, ask the prearranged questions that you bring with you to the session. The answers to those questions are meant to enlighten and bring a deeper sense of clarity and insight into your life. Since each of us are unique, the QHHT experience will be different for everyone. The commonality that remains is that each of us has a life force, a soul, a connection to a higher level of consciousness which allows us the opportunity to access deeper levels of knowledge. With the wisdom and experience Elizabeth brings to each session, you can be sure you are well protected and in a place where you can allow yourself to truly relax, heal and allow your inner wisdom to come forward and help you in your life. Without question this experience was profound and enlightening for me, and I would highly recommend Elizabeth to anyone who wishes to try QHHT for themselves." ~ **Christin S.**

Elizabeth is such a gentle, compassionate soul who gives such genuine love towards her clients. Her work is done with passion and authenticity and she honors the centuries old tradition of shamanism. She is extremely knowledgeable in the practices of Shamanism and I feel in my heart that there is nothing that she is not capable of helping to heal in any individual.

I am blessed to have crossed paths with Elizabeth, even though it was for only a little while. She has a heart of gold and this is what allows her full spirit to come forth in all she does. Namaste, ~ **David L. (Cottonwood, AZ)**

Hi Elizabeth! Since our last meeting I've been walking around with a heartfelt gratitude for your healing. I was scared to drive to Michigan due to severe pain I couldn't get rid of, but I decided that if I have to be ill, being with all the Sisters/healers could only help. I benefited from your healing by being a participant in your demonstration. Thank you so very much. My love and gratitude. ~ **S.M. Allegan, MI**

I began my Usui Reiki training with Elizabeth in 2004. I found her online and when I called her for the first time, I felt nervous, not really knowing what to expect. I was impressed immediately by the way she made me feel completely at ease with her friendly and approachable manner. After speaking with her I felt excited to begin my Reiki training with someone with her skill set in the healing arts. When I met her in person I was so impressed with her exceptional professionalism, skill and knowledge, that I continued my studies with her and finished my Master/Teacher level of Reiki with her in 2006. I also received my Shamballa Multi- Dimensional Healing Level 1 certificate from Elizabeth in 2009. Over the last 6 years of working with Elizabeth, I have attended other various healing classes and seminars that she has hosted and taught. She always shows exceptional knowledge and understanding of the subject matter, and

I continue to learn from her in so many ways. She has devoted the last 13 years to her own training by studying with many Shamans and highly-skilled healers. She has traveled all over the world on her quest for healing knowledge and is one of the hardest working, most compassionate and responsible healers I know. Her dedication and commitment to teaching high-quality healing skills to each of her students is clearly evident in all of her classes and I am fortunate to have her in my life as a truly extraordinary teacher. ~ **Christin S.** Student (Chepachet, RI)

It is a pleasure to share this testimonial of my experience of the Shamanic Despacho and Fire Ceremony with Elizabeth. I was not familiar with the specifics and customs of a Shaman. I had never attended any of their ceremonies and when Elizabeth suggested a Despacho and Fire Ceremony for the specific intention I had at a time in my life when I was unclear of my direction and outcomes. She said the ceremonies would focus my intention and the energies would enhance my desired outcome. Having known Elizabeth for a short time on a personal level, I resonated with her suggestion. I was amazed with her knowledge and was joyous with her infectious enthusiasm for Shamanism. I learned much about the customs and enjoyed being exposed to the language and process of the fire ceremony. I highly recommend Elizabeth to anyone who is open to experience something new, open to high vibratory energies, and open to giving themselves permission to heal while Elizabeth holds and facilitates sacred space for your highest good. ~ **N.L. (Sedona, AZ)**

Hi Elizabeth. I want to thank you for removing the heavy energy and for the advice you gave me last week. I feel like my power has come back and I feel like myself again. I will give you a call next week. I would like to book another session with you. I am grateful to God and to you and feel blessed to have found you. May God bless you and your work. ~ **C.M. Rhode Island**

Hi Elizabeth, I appreciated the Ancient Wisdom class very much. I learned more than I expected to, most importantly, Prayer. Church attendance was mandatory for us until Confirmed and despite many years of Catholic Schooling I have never developed sufficient ability in prayer. I thought and spoke with devout intent for years, mostly during times I was instructed to, but could never feel. There was never the slightest sense of reciprocity. Meditation has always been difficult despite study and labors towards it as well, still I try. My wife repeats, "It's a practice, it takes practice…" Since you have related the two for me and we established a physical connection to Deity. Prayer is alive! Yesterday morning I prayed successfully for the first time! Thank You! ~ **J.M. RI**

Dear Elizabeth, Thank you for taking the time to do a telephone session with me — and to respond so quickly. I felt a need to check in with a higher power quickly and you were there to facilitate it. I was amazed at how much information I was provided, both some on-the-ground needed advice as well as techniques for spiritual and physical healing to keep me going. It was an interesting conversation to say the least! I hope to talk with you and your guides again soon. ~ **LT (Tampa, FL)**

Hi Elizabeth! It's the girl who you ever so graciously made time for last week before leaving for your weekend away. Thank you. I have taken your advice and have started practicing using the white light of the holy spirit. I have felt better about my life and its purpose in the last three days, then I ever have before. You are truly a gifted Spiritualist and I am grateful that I stumbled across your website in my time of need. Not that it was a coincidence by any means…as they say, "Coincidences are when God remains anonymous". I will continue to work on keeping my vibrations high and listening to my guides. I look forward to working with you again. There is no doubt that you are one of God's chosen light workers! Thank you for all your help, Blessed Be, ~ **T. (Cranston, RI)**

Elizabeth has been my healer for almost seven years now! But I actually have a problem with calling her my healer because she is so much more to me! I remember how crushed I was before the first time I saw her. She accepted me open hearted, warmly, like I am her best friend, like as if she knew me all her life. Her Spiritual treatment was immediately successful, I did not need to come again for that health problem and believe me, I was a mess! The magic of her work is not only in her healing performance but also in teaching. She has been teaching me how to think, react, and behave to stay healthy and happy.

I can tell her everything and anything, my deepest fears and secrets, and she will always find the most perfect words, solution, and healing method, so I can feel 100% better instantly. And she never ever judges, ever! Her heart is full of love and soul so clear, just like a fresh spring!

Elizabeth, thank you! Thank you from the bottom of my heart! ~ **JP (Worcester, MA)**

While being raised in a strict Irish catholic setting certainly gave me a religious foundation and ethical barometer in life, to which I'm grateful for, it left me seeking more. I had a passion for seeking the why's and questions to life, and a desire for self-empowerment and spiritual enlightenment. Over the past 10 years in an effort to embrace a greater appreciation for my life path, I would educate myself through workshops and seminars as to the different forms of spirituality and worship and the different paths to this enlightenment by exploring other spiritual paths; taking the concepts and ideas what I thought resonated and moving forward to the next. I had some excellent teachers but always felt after the class was completed it was time to keep going and went on with gratitude for their lessons.

When I met Elizabeth, I felt a connection to her that was magical. Her beauty lies deeply is in her presence and her message. Her passion for her medicine was incredible and contagious. Listening to her speak was beyond comforting and I felt as if I has finally arrived home. There was no doubt that I wanted to study with her, and I took great excitement and honor in being a student to her.

While she is empathetic and compassionate, she honored our growth path and process enough to challenge us by encouraging us all to trust in who and where we are so we can truly develop as spiritual beings. She did not want to hold us back even if it may have meant the possibility of a student surpassing the teacher. She is a true ambassador for Spirit and believes in our ability to reach our own earthly gifts and did all in her power to show us how we could achieve that goal. Her gentleness allowed for you to feel safe at times and moments of intense vulnerability, while her nudges allow for you to step outside of our self-created boundaries of comfort, so we can get to that next step without fear and discouragement.

Her knowledge is based upon her both textbook teachings and scholastic studies in conjunction with her wisdom gained through her fearlessness in her own journeys. She is honest yet considerate and a walker of her talk.

Elizabeth is without question the most dedicated, genuine, and sincere teacher I have had in all of my years of spiritual embarkment. I thank God every day for sending me to her so that I have been able to find this medicine and incorporate it into my daily life. Shamanism has changed my life and allowed be to heal and participate in my life in ways I'd never known possible.

Elizabeth and her classes are a true blessing, and without any reservation I suggest that if anyone is ready to be a student to the ancient wisdom and willing to comprehend the legitimate meaning of Shamanism, that you set sail on this journey with the most amazing teacher I know. ~ **Aho. C.R.B. (Bridgeport,CT)**

There are many whom can call themselves a 'Shaman'. There are many whom have studied with Shamans; and devote their being to this wondrous, splendid medicine. There are few whom can incorporate the teachings of so many 'wisdom' ones and energize it the way that Elizabeth does. Her enthusiasm and genuine love of this medicine; combines with her down to Earth generous nature. It allows her students to experience all of her wisdom and those handed down to her before. Also though it is a pleasure to learn from a down to Earth 'average' person, she is sweetly identifiable; familiar. Not 'Oh so Ethereal' and unattainable as many I have experienced. She makes the journey on your path to the Heaven accessible; brings it to your level of understanding and Spirituality raises you to it. What a wonderful thing! That, my dear is a true opportunity! Kate D. Apprenticing Mesa carrier ~ **(Gloucester, RI)**

Good day Elizabeth, How very good I feel when reading this (Ancient Wisdom by Elizabeth 'Rainbow Dancer' book), it is such a comfort for my being. Thanks, ~ **R.M. (Alberta, Canada)**

Elizabeth, Thank you very much for your healing work and channeling for me today at Dowsing conference. You are a wonderful human being. ~ **Peter V. (Lyndonville, VT)**

Hi Elizabeth! I am really enjoying your book! I have not finished it yet because I have been so-o busy, but I find it fascinating. I am very intrigued by all those experiences that you had!!! And I like how the book is so practical…. tells you what to do…how to do it…and why. I like it when people get right to the point and you really did that! ~ **Julie B. (Newport, RI)**

God bless you Elizabeth. I use something you've taught me at least once every day. ~ **Julie G. (Lincoln, RI)**

Hi Elizabeth, I just wanted to thank you for yesterday's class. I feel this calm that I have never felt before. It's as if a white noise in the back of my mind has quieted and been replaced with a comforting, peaceful silence. I feel like my senses have been piqued in every way.

I have begun my 21 days of drawing the Reiki symbol over my chakras and saying it three times. I feel more attuned to the universal flow today than I did yesterday. I cannot wait to reach day 21.

Your class was by far the best class I have attended. You break it down and explain things in detail while providing anecdotes to paint a colorful picture. I can't speak for everyone, but this helped me a lot. You are an amazing person and a wonderful teacher. I look forward to crossing paths with you again in the future. Whether it be, in life or in teachings.

Blessed Be, ~ **Stef C. (Boston, MA)**

Elizabeth 'Rainbow Dancer' has dedicated the last 14 years of her life toward learning the path of Spirituality and Shamanism. I believe the reason Elizabeth's book "Ancient Wisdom" contains so much insight in a variety of healing ways is due to the fact that she was born naturally gifted with internal wisdom and innately understood that she was not alone. In an unconscious way, I believe that the author always knew Mother Mary was guiding her. And 14 years ago, this unconscious knowledge simply became conscious!

I would consider this multifaceted book a must read because the author describe her journey, *share* methods of how to create, and includes her conversations with Mother Mary, Ascended Masters, and Angels in detail. Clearly, this author listens to her inner guidance and I, personally, think that is the mark of a brave person: being true to self.

Truly, this book "Ancient Wisdom" by Elizabeth Rainbow Dancer is delightful, easy read. ~ **J.L. (East Greenwich, RI) 2010**

*Look out for "Elizabeth ~ Rainbow Dancer ~ Book 2"*
*Coming soon!*